ALPHABETICAL AND ANALYTICAL

CATALOGUE

OF THE

LIBRARY

OF THE

UNIVERSITY OF VERMONT,

BURLINGTON.

BURLINGTON:
FREE PRESS OFFICE.
1854.

PREFACE.

In issuing a new edition of the Catalogue of the Library of the University of Vermont, it seems proper to offer a few words on some points touching the History and Character of the Library, and the plan on which the Catalogue is arranged.

1. The *original Library*, which had been made up by donations of benevolent individuals and friends of the University, was mostly destroyed by fire when the college edifice was burned in 1824.

2. The *present Library*, therefore, may be regarded as having had its beginning in the year 1836, when the sum of $10,000 was appropriated by the Corporation for the purchase of *a Library*. The Faculty of the University having been authorised to expend the money for that purpose, proceeded immediately to make up such a list of Books, in the different departments of learning, as, in their opinion, would be the best that could be had for the sum appropriated. Prof. Torrey was the Agent of the Faculty in effecting the purchases, and went to Europe the same year, for this purpose, with power to vary the list at his discretion.

The following Catalogue, although it contains many valuable books obtained by purchases and donations since, is mainly the fruit of those efforts. How far the character of the Library corresponds with what it was intended to be, the Catalogue itself will show. But it may not be improper to say, that in the judgment of many, whose opinions are entitled to weight, a better Library, on the whole, for the purposes of a College, is not to be found in the country, considering the number and cost of the books. And yet there is felt an urgent want of additions to all the departments, and it is earnestly hoped that a collection so well begun, and so good, so far as it goes, will not be suffered to remain much longer without a reasonable degree of growth and enlargement. The whole number of volumes contained in the Library, exclusive of loose Pamphlets, Maps, and Charts, is found by actual counting to amount to 8108.

3. The resources for the increase of the Library are at present confined to the following:

1. The fund of the "WHEELER LIBRARY;" yielding *forty-five dollars* annually, to be expended in the purchase of books in English Literature and History, $45,00

2. The "STRONG FUND;" yielding *thirty dollars* annually to be expended in the purchase of Periodicals, 30,00

3. STUDENTS' FEES; expended partly in keeping the books in repair—say, 150,00

4. Books are also received by donations to an annual amount of at least 100,00

4. In the first Catalogue of this Library which was prepared with great pains and published in 1836, the books were arranged and classified *by subjects;* but the impracticability of classifying in this way, without considerable repetition, works which comprise several distinct subjects, has led to a different arrangement in the present edition. The books, as will be seen, are now arranged by the names of the Authors in alphabetical order; and an *Index of Subjects* has been appended, to facilitate its use by the Students, whose wants were chiefly had in view in its preparation.

The haste with which it has been necessary to prepare the edition for the press, has been the occasion of several errors, most of which, it is hoped, will be found corrected in the list of "Errata" at the end. That such errors are so few is chiefly due to the care of MR. TUTOR BUCKHAM, under whose critical eye the proof-sheets passed. Our acknowledgements are due also to the PUBLISHER for the handsome manner in which the work has been got up.

P.

UNIVERSITY OF VERMONT,
March 7, 1854.

ALPHABETICAL CATALOGUE.

The Asterisk (*) prefixed to a Title denotes that the book cannot be taken from the Library without special leave from the President.

ABBT, THOS. Vermischte Werke. 3 vols. in 2. 12mo. Berlin. 1772.

ABDULLAH. Journal. 8vo. Singapura. 1838.

ABIPONES, of Paraguay. Account of, from the Latin of Dobrizhofer. 3 vols. 8vo. London. 1821.

ABORIGINES of America. Traits of. A Poem. 8vo. Cambridge. 1822.

ACCUM, FREDRICK. Practical Essay on the Analysis of Minerals. 12mo. Phila. 1809.

ACHILLES TATIUS ALEX. De Leucippes et Clitophontis Amoribus Libri octo. Ed. Jacobs. 2 vols. 8vo. Lipsiæ. 1821.

ACTS of the Apostles in Modern Greek. Malta. 1827.

ADAM, ALEXANDER. Roman Antiquities. Ed. by Wilson. 8vo. New York. 1814.

ADAM, ALEXANDER. The same. 8vo. New York. 1823.

ADAM, ALEXANDER. The same. 8vo. New York. 1826.

*ADAM, R. Ruins of the Palace of the Emperor Diocletian at Spalatro in Dalmatia. Fol. London. 1764.

ADAMS, GEORGE. Astronomical and Geographical Essays. 8vo. Phila. 1800.

ADAMS, GEORGE. Lectures on Natural and Experimental Philosophy. 4 vols. 8vo. Phila. 1806.

ADAMS, JOHN. Defence of the Constitution of Government of the United States of America. 3 vols. 8vo. London. 1787.

ADAMS, JOHN. Works, with a life of the Author by C. F. Adams. Vols. II–VIII. 8vo. Boston. 1850–1853.

ADAMS, JOHN QUINCY. Lectures on Rhetoric and Oratory. 2 vols. 8vo. Cambridge. 1810.

ADAMS, JOHN QUINCY. Letters on the Masonic Institution. 8vo. Boston. 1847.

ADAMS AND SMITH. Latin Tutor. 12mo. Newburyport. 1813.

ADANSON. Histoire Naturelle du Sénégal. 4to. Paris. 1757.

ADDISON, JOSEPH. Works, with notes by Hurd. 6 vols. 8vo. London. 1811.

ADVISER, or Vermont Evangelical Magazine. Vols. I–VI in 3 vols. 8vo. Middlebury. 1809–1814.

ÆLIANUS, CLAUDIUS. Varia Historia et Fragmenta. Ed. Kühn. 2 vols. 8vo. Lipsiæ. 1780.

ÆLIANUS, CLAUDIUS. De Natura Animalium Libri XVII. Ed. Schneider. 8vo. Lipsiæ. 1784.

ÆSCHINES SOCRATICUS. Dialogi Tres, Græce. Ed. Fischerus. 8vo. Lipsiæ. 1786.

ÆSCHYLUS. Tragœdiae et Fragmenta. Ed. Schütz. 5 vols. 8vo. Halis. 1809.

ÆSCHYLUS. Eumeniden, von K. O. Müller. 4to. Göttingen. 1833.

ÆSOPUS. Fabulæ. Ed. De Furia. 8vo. Lipsiæ. 1810.

ÆSOPUS. Eædem Græco-Latinæ. 12mo. Etonæ. 1807.

ÆSOPUS. Eædem Græco-Latinæ. 12mo. Bostoniae. 1812.

AFRICAN REPOSITORY. 2 vols. 8vo. Washington. 1826–1827.

AGNESI, DONNA M. G. Analytical Institutions. 2 vols. in one. 4to. London. 1801.

AGRICULTURE. Transactions of the New York State Agricultural Society. 11 vols. From 1841–1852. 8vo. Albany. 1842–1852.

AGRICULTURE of Massachusetts. Second Report on, by H. Coleman. 8vo. Boston. 1839.
Third Report. On Wheat and Silk. 8vo. Boston. 1840.
Fourth do. 8vo. Boston. 1841.

AGRICULTURAL TRACTS. See Pamphlets.

AGRICULTURIST, SOUTHERN. Vols. I–VI. Charleston, S. C. 1841–1846.

AGRICULTURE FRANÇAISE. Department de l' Isére. 8vo. Paris. 1843.
Department de la Haute Saronne. 8vo. Paris. 1843.
Department des Côtes du Nord. 8vo. Paris. 1844.
Department du Tarn. 8vo. Paris. 1845.

AGRICULTURE (de la), des Manufactures et du Commerce; Conseils Généraux. 4 vols. 4to. Paris. 1845–1846.

AIKIN, ARTHUR. Manual of Mineralogy. 12mo. Phila. 1815.

AINSWORTH, HENRY. Annotations on Genesis. Fol. London. 1639.

AINSWORTH. Dictionary, English and Latin. Ed. by G. Morell. 2 copies. 8vo. Phila. 1825.

AIRY, G. W. Mathematical Tracts on Physical Astronomy. 8vo. Cambridge, Eng. 1826.

AKBER, EMPEROR. Institutes of, transl. from the Persian by Francis Gladwin. 2 vols. 4to. London. 1800.

ALCIPHRON, RHETOR. Epistolæ. Ed. Wagner. 2 vols. 8vo. Lipsiæ. 1798.

ALDEN, TIMOTHY. Collection of American Epitaphs. 5 vols. 12mo. New York. 1814.

ALDRICH. Artis Logicæ Compendium. 18mo. Oxoniæ. 1696.

ALES (OR HALES) ALEXANDER. Super Tertium Sententiarum. Fol. Venetiis. 1475.

ALISON, ARCHIBALD. Essay on the Nature and Principles of Taste. 8vo. Boston. 1812.

ALISON, ARCHIBALD. History of Europe from 1798–1815. 4 vols. 8vo. New York. 1842.

ALLEN, ETHAN. Reason the only Oracle of Man. 8vo. Bennington, Vt. 1784.

ALLEN, ETHAN. Narrative of his Captivity, by himself. 12mo. Burlington. 1838.

ALLEN, IRA. Natural and Political History of the State of Vermont. 8vo. London. 1798.

ALLEN, IRA. Capture of the Olive Branch. 8vo. Burlington. 1802.

ALLSTON, WASHINGTON. Lectures on Art, and Poems. 12mo. New York. 1851.

AMBROSE, ISAAC. Complete Works. Fol. London. 1682.

AMERICA. History of, in Modern Greek. By G. Bentote. 12mo. Vienna. 1792.

AMERICA. Men and Manners in. 2 vols. 12mo. Phila. 1833.

AMERICA in 1655. By "N. N.," Gent. 32mo. London. 1655.

AMERICAN ACADEMY. Vol. I. Memoirs of the, to the end of the year 1783. 4to. Boston. 1785.
Vol. II. Part 1st. 4to. Boston. 1793.
Vol. II. Part 2d. 4to. Charleston. 1804.
Vol. III. Part 1st. 4to. s. l. et a.

American Academy. Vol. iv. Part 1st and 2d. 4to. Cambridge. 1818.
New Series Vol. i. 4to. Cambridge. 1833.

American Almanac, 1830 to 1839 inclusive, and 1843. 8vo. Boston.

American Annual Register for the year 1825–1826. 8vo. New York. 1827.

American Annual Register for the years 1827–1828–1829. 8vo. New York. 1835.

American Antiquarian Society. Proceedings of. 8vo. Worcester. 1820.

American Archives. Ed. by Peter Force. 4th Series. Vols. i–vi. 4to. Washington. 1837–1846.
5th Series. Vols. i, ii, and iii. 4to. Washington. 1848.

American Association. Proceedings of, at 2d meeting, 1849. 8vo. Boston. 1850.

American Board C. F. M. Annual Reports. Nos. 14, 17, 19, 22, 23, 40, and 41. 8vo. Boston. 1823–1849.

American Institute of Instruction. Lectures and Journal for the years 1840–1848 inclusive. 9 vols. 8vo. Boston. 1841–1848.

American Journal of Education. 2 vols. 8vo. Boston. 1826–1827.

American Journal of Science, from 1819–1853. 66 vols. with Index to the first fifty. 8vo. Hartford.

American Jurist. Vol. i. Nos. for Jan. and April, 1829. 8vo. Boston. 1829.

American Missionaries formerly connected with the Society of Inquiry at Andover. Memoirs of, and History of the Soc. 12mo. Boston. 1833.

American Preacher. 4 vols. 8vo. Elizabethtown. 1791, and New Haven. 1793.

American Quarterly Register, and Journal of Amer. Education Soc. 15 vols. (Two copies of x.) 8vo. Boston. 1827–1842.

American Quarterly Review. 22 vols. 8vo. Phila. 1827–1837.

American Quarterly Journal of Agriculture and Science. Vols. i and ii in one. 8vo. Albany. 1845.

American State Papers. 21 vols. viz:

Class i. Foreign Relations. 4 vols. Fol. Washington. 1832–1834.

Class ii. Indian Affairs. 2 vols. Fol. Washington. 1832–1834.

Class iii. Finance. 3 vols. Fol. Washington. 1832–1834.

Class iv. Commerce and Navigation. 2 vols. Fol. Washington. 1832–1834.

AMERICAN STATE PAPERS—Continued.

CLASS V. Military Affairs. 2 vols. Fol. Washington. 1832–1834.

CLASS VI. Naval Affairs. Fol. Washington. 1834.

CLASS VII. Post Office. Fol. Washington. 1834.

CLASS VIII. Public Lands. 3 vols. Fol. Washington. 1832–1834.

CLASS IX. Claims. Fol. Washington. 1834.

CLASS X. Miscellaneous. 2 vols. Fol. Washington. 1834.

AMES, FISHER. Works. 8vo. Boston. 1809.

ANALECTA VET. POETARUM GRÆCORUM. Ed. Brunck. 3 vols. 8vo. Argentorati. 1795.

ANATOMY, TREATISE ON. 12mo. Title page wanting.

ANDERSON, A. See Commerce.

ANDERSON, HENRY J. Mathematical Investigation of the Motion of Solids. 4to. Phila. 1828.

ANDERSON, WM. System of Surgical Anatomy. Vol. I. 4to. New York. 1832.

ANDRAL, G. Clinique Médicale. 5 vols. 8vo. Paris. 1834.

ANDREWS AND STODDARD. Grammar of the Latin Language. 8vo. Boston. 1837.

ANDRY, FELIX. Diseases of the Heart. 8vo. Boston. 1846.

ANECDOTA GRÆCA. Ed. De Villoison. 2 vols. 4to. Venetiis. 1821.

ANECDOTA GRÆCA. Ed. Im. Bekker. 3 vols. 8vo. Berolini. 1814.

ANNALES DES SCIENCES NATURELLES. IIIe Série. Botanique. 12vols. VII–XVIII. 8vo. Paris. 1847–1852.

ANNALES DES SCIENCES NATURELLES. IIIe Série. Zoologie. 12 vols. VII–XVIII. 8vo. Paris. 1847–1852.

ANNALES d' Industrie Nationale et Etrangère (1819). 4 vols. 8vo. Paris. 1819.

ANNALES d' Industrie Nationale et Etrangère (1820). 3 vols. and 3 Nos. 8vo. Paris. 1820.

ANNALES du Museum National d' Histoire Naturelle. 6 vols. 4to. Paris. 1802.

ANNALS of the Lyceum of Nat. Hist. of New York.

Vol. I. 2 Parts. 8vo. New York. 1824–1825.

Vol. II. 8vo. New York. 1828.

Vol. III. 8vo. New York. 1828–1836.

Vol. IV. Nos. 1, 2, 3, and 4. 8vo. New York. 1837.

ANNUAIRE du Bureau de Longitude pour l' an 1835. 24mo. Paris. 1834.

ANNUAIRE du Bureau de Longitude pour l' an 1836. 24mo. Paris. 1835.

ANNUAL of Scientific Discovery, or Year-book of Facts. 8vo. Boston. 1850.

ANSELMUS. Opera. Fol. Parisiis. 1721.

ANSON, GEORGE. Voyage round the World. With Plates. 4to. London. 1749.

ANSTICE, J. Selections from the Choric Poetry of the Greek Dramatists in English Verse. 8vo. London. 1832.

ANTAR. A Bedoueen Romance, Transl. by T. Hamilton. 4 vols. 8vo. London. 1820.

ANTHOLOGIA GRÆCA. See Jacobs.

ANTIQUITATES AMERICANÆ. Edidit Societas Regia Antiquariorum Septentrionalium. 4to. Hafniæ. 1837.

ANTONINUS, MARCUS AURELIUS. Meditations. By Graves. 8vo. Bath. 1792.

APOLLODORUS ATHENIENSIS. Bibliothecæ Libri tres et Fragmenta. Ed. Heyne. 8vo. Gottingæ. 1805.

APPOLLODORUS ATHENIENSIS. Observationes ad Bibliothecam. Heyne. 8vo. Gottingæ. 1803.

APOLLONIUS ALEXANDRINUS. De Constructione Orationis Libri IV. Ed. Bekker. 8vo. Berolini. 1817.

APOLLONIUS RHODIUS. Argonautica. Ed. Wellauer. 2 vols. 8vo. Lipsiæ. 1828.

APOLLONIUS RHODIUS. Argonauticorum Libri IV. Ed. Shaw. 8vo. Oxoniæ. 1779.

APOLLONIUS PERGÆUS. Conicorum Libri octo, Græc. et Lat. Fol. Oxoniæ. 1710.

APOLLONIUS PERGÆUS. Conicorum Libri IV, cum commentariis R. P. C. Richardi. Fol. Antverpiæ. 1655.

APOLLONIUS SOPHISTA. Lexicon Homericum. Ed. Bekker. 8vo. Berolini. 1833.

APOLLONIUS TYANENSIS. See Philostratorum quæ, &c.

APPIANUS, ALEXANDER. Historiarum Romanarum quæ supersunt. Ed. Schweighäuser. 3 vols. 8vo. Lipsiæ. 1785.

APPLETON, JESSE. Works. 2 vols. 8vo. Andover. 1837.

APULEIUS, LUCIUS MADAURENSIS, Platonicus Philosophus. Opera. Studiis Soc. Bipont. 8vo. Biponti. 1788.

APULEIUS, L. M. Opera. 32mo. Amstelodami. 1623.

ARABIC GRAMMAR. By J. Richardson. 4to. London. 1801.

ARABIC. Gospels in. 8vo. s. l. et a.

ARATUS. Cum Scholiis. Ed. Bekker. 8vo. Berolini. 1828.

Arbogast, F. A. De Calcul des Dérivations. 4to. Strasbourg. 1800.

Archæologia Americana. Transactions and Collections of the American Antiquarian Soc. Vol. iii. Part i. 8vo. Cambridge. 1850.

Aristænetus. Epistolæ, Græce. Ed. Pauw. 12mo. Traj. ad Rhenum. 1837.

Aristarchus, or the Principles of Composition. 8vo. London. 1832.

Aristophanes. Comediæ. Ed. Invernizius. 13 vols. 8vo. Lipsiæ. 1794.

Aristophanes. Comedies translated. 8vo. London. 1812.

Aristoteles. Opera, Græce. Ex recens. Bekker. 4 vols. 4to. Berolini 1831.

Aristoteles. De Arte Poetica. Ed. Hermann. 8vo. Lipsiæ. 1802.

Aristoteles. Meteorologica. Ed. Bekker. 8vo. Berolini. 1829.

Aristoteles. De Generatione Animalium Libri quinque. 8vo. Ber. 1829.

Aristoteles. Organon. Recens. Jul. Pacius. 12mo. Hanoviæ. 1611.

Aristotle. Metaphysics transl. by T. Taylor. 4to. London. 1801.

Aristotle. Treatise on Poetry transl. by T. Twining. 4to. Lon. 1789.

Aristotle. Rhetoric, Poetic, and Nichomachean Ethics transl. by T. Taylor. 2 vols. 8vo. London. 1818.

Arithmetica Universalis. 12mo. London. 1722.

Armenia. History of, by Chamich from B. C. 2247 to A. D. 1780. 2 vols. Transl. by Avdall. 8vo. Calcutta. 1827.

Arnim und Brentano. Des Knaben Wunderhorn. 3 vols. 8vo. Heidleberg. 1819.

Arrianus. Historia Indica. Ed. Schmieder. 8vo. Halis. 1798.

Arrianus. Expeditionis Alexandri Libri septem. Ed. Schmieder. Lipsiæ 1818.

*Art Union, and Apollo Association. Engravings published by, from 1840–1847 inclusive.

Ascham, Roger. Works, and life by Dr. Johnson. 12mo. London. 1815.

Ashmun, Jehudi. Life of, by R. R. Gurley. 8vo. New York. 1839.

Asiatic Dissertations. 2 vols. 8vo. London. 1792.

Astle, Thos. Origin and Progress of Writing. 4to. London. 1893.

Astronomie des Marins. 8vo. Avignon. 1766.

Athanasius, Archiepiscopus Alex. Opera omnia. 2 vols. Fol. Coloniae. 1686.

Athenæum. Vols. x and xi. Second Series Vols. ii, iv, and vii. 8vo. Boston. 1821–1825.

Athenæus. Deipnosophistarum Libri xv. Ed. Schweighäuser. 14 vols. 8vo. Argentorati. 1801.

ATHENIAN LETTERS. 2 vols. 8vo. Dublin. 1792.

ATLAS of Ancient and Modern History, by J. W. Tyson. 4to. Phila. 1845.

ATLAS, A new Universal. 4to. Brattleboro'. 1842.

ATWOOD, G. On Rectilinear Motion and the Rotation of Bodies. 8vo. Cambridge, Eng. 1784.

AUCHER, PASCHAL. Armenian and English Grammar. 8vo. Venice. 1819.

AUDUBON, J. J. Ornithological Biography. 4to. Phila. 1831.

AUGUSTINUS HIPPONENSIS EPISC. Opera omnia. 11 vols. in 7. Fol. Parisiis. 1637.

AUSONIUS, D. MAGNUS BURDIGALENSIS. Opera. Stud. Soc. Bipont. 8vo. Biponti. 1785.

AUSTIN, SAML. Economy of the Church of God. 8vo. Worcester. 1807.

AUSTIN, SAML. Dissertation on Christian Theology. 8vo. Worcester. 1820.

AUSTIN, WM. Letters from London, 1802–1803. 8vo. Boston. 1804.

AYEEN AKBERY. See Akber.

AYRE, JOSEPH. Practical Observations on the Treatment of Marasmus, &c. 18mo. Northampton. 1822.

BABER, MUHAMMED. Memoirs written by himself and transl. by Leyden. London. 1826.

BABRIUS. Fabularum Choliambicarum Libri III. Ed. Berger. 18mo. Monachii. 1816.

BACKUS, ISAAC. History of the Church of New England. 3 vols. 8vo. Boston. 1777–1796.

BACON, FRANCIS. Works. 4 vols. Fol. London. 1740.

BACON, ROGER. Opus Majus. Fol. Venetiis. 1750.

BAGAY, V. Nouvelles Tables Astronomiques et Hydrographiques. 4to. Paris. 1829.

BAGGESEN. Blandede Digte. 12mo. Kiobenhavn. 1807.

BAILEY, M. Universal English Dictionary. 8vo. London. 1731.

BAILEY, M. The Same. 8vo. London. 1776.

BAILLIE, E. M. Traité des Fièvres Intermittentes. 8vo. Paris. 1825.

BAILLIE, JOANNA. Metrical Legends. 8vo. London. 1821.

BAILLIE, JOANNA. Poems collected by. (Bound with above.) 8vo. London. 1823.

BAILLIE, M. Morbid Anatomy. 8vo. Albany. 1795.

BAILLY. Histoire de l' Astronomie Ancienne. 4to. Paris. 1781.

BAILLY. Histoire de l' Astronomie Moderne. 3 vols. 4to. Paris. 1785.

BAILLY. Traité de l' Astronomie Indienne et Orientale. 4to. Paris. 1787.

BAKER, SIR RICHARD. Chronicle of the Kings of England. Fol. Lond. 1674.

BAKEWELL, ROBT. Introduction to Geology. 8vo. London. 1815.

BALDVINUS, FRID. Epistolae prior et posterior ad Timotheum illustratae. 4to. Wittebergae. 1630.

BALDWIN, S. See Yale College.

BALGUY, THOS. Divine Benevolence Asserted. 8vo. London. 1803.

BALLOU, HOSEA. Candid Review of a Candid Reply. 12mo. Portsmouth. s. a.

BALLY, FRANÇOIS, PARISET. Histoire Médicale de la Fièvre Jaune en Espagne. 8vo. Paris. 1823.

BAMBA, N. Stoicheia. Graece. 2 Parts in one vol. 12mo. Venet. 1818.

BANCROFT, GEORGE. History of the United States. 4 vols. 8vo. Boston. 1837–1852.

BANDINI. See Vespucci.

BANK of the United States. Documentary History of, by Clark and Hall. 8vo. Washington. 1832.

BARBAULD, A. L. Works. 2 vols. 12mo. Boston. 1826.

BARBAULD, A. L. A Legacy for Young Ladies. 12mo. Boston. 1826.

*BARBAULT, M. Les plus beaux Monuments de Rome Ancienne. Fol. Rome. 1761.

*BARBAULT, M. Recueil de Divers Monumens Anciens. Fol. Rome. 1770.

BARCLAIUS, J. Argenis. 18mo. Amstelodami. 1659.

BARCLAY, JAMES. English Dictionary. 8vo. London. 1782.

BARCLAY, JOHN. Without Faith, without God. 12mo. London. 1836.

BARCLAY, ROBT. Apology for the True Christian Divinity. 8vo. Phila. 1805.

BARCLAY, ROBT. Life and Writings. 12mo. Phila. 1805.

BARCLAY, ROBT. General Assembly's Catechism and Faith. 12mo. New York. 1813.

BARDWELL, H. See Gordon Hall.

BARLOW, JOEL. Vision of Columbus. A Poem. 8vo. Hartford. 1787.

BARLOW, PETER. Theory of Numbers. 8vo. London. 1811.

BARLOW, PETER. New Mathematical and Philosophical Dictionary. 8vo. London. 1814.

BARLOW, PETER. Essay on the Strength of Timber. 8vo. London. 1826.

Barnwell, Wm. Physical Investigations and Deductions. 2 copies. 8vo. Phila. 1802.

Barrett. See Ximenes.

Barrow, Isaac. Geometrical Lectures. 8vo. London. 1735.

Barrow, Isaac. Mathematical Lectures. 12mo. London. 1734.

Barrow, John. Travels in China. 4to. London. 1806.

Barrow, John. Travels into the Interior of South Africa. 2 vols. 4to. London. 1806.

Barruel. See Jacobinism.

Barry, James. Works. 2 vols. 4to. London. 1809.

Barthelemy, J. J. Voyage du Jeune Anacharsis en Grèce. 7 vols. 8vo. Paris. 1822.

Barthelemy, J. J. Oeuvres Diverses. 2 vols. 8vo. Paris. 1823.

Bartholdt, F. W. Georg von Frundsberg, oder das Deutsche Kriegeshandwerk zur zeit der Reformation. 8vo. Hamburg. 1833.

Barton, W. P. C. Vegetable Materia Medica of the United States. 2 vols. 4to. Phila. 1817.

Bartram, Wm. Travels in North and South Carolina. 8vo. Dublin. 1793.

Bateman, Thos. Synopsis of Cutaneous Diseases. 8vo. Phila. 1818.

Bates, Wm. Works. Fol. London. 1723.

Batuta Ibn. Travels transl. from the Arabic by Samuel Lee. 4to. London. 1829.

Baudin, N. Voyages de Découvertes aux Terres Australes. 3 vols. 4to Paris. 1815.

Baumgarten, A. G. Acroasis Logica. 12mo. Halis. 1761.

Baumgarten-Crusius. De Homine Dei conscio. 4to. Jenae. 1813.

Baxter, Richard. Practical Works. 4 vols. Fol. London. 1707.

Baxter, Richard. Reliquiae Baxterianae, or Life and Times, by himself. Fol. London. 1696.

Bayle. Dictionaire Historique et Critique. 3 vols. Fol. Rotterdam. 1715.

Baylies. See Plymouth.

Bazin. Rapport sur une Version Chinoise des Fables d' Esope. (Pamphlet.)

Beasley, F. Search of Truth in the Science of the Human Mind. 8vo. Phila. 1822.

Beaufort, M. de. La Republique Romaine, ou Plan Général de l' Ancien Gouvernement de Rome. 2 vols. 4to. A la Haye. 1766.

Beaujour, Chev. Felix. Aperçu des Etats Unis depuis 1800 jusqu'en 1810. 8vo. Paris. 1814.

*Beaumont, Albanis. Travels through the Lepontine Alps from France to Italy, with Maps and Plates. Fol. London. 1806.

Beaumont and Fletcher. See Ben Jonson.

Beaumont, Joseph. Psyche, a Poem. 4to. Cambridge, Eng. 1702.

Bebelius, B. Ecclesiae Antediluvianae, Vera et Falsa. 4to. Argentorati. 1706.

Beccaria. See Voltaire.

Becke, David von der. Naturalium Rerum Principia. 12mo. Hamburgi. 1683.

Beckwith, George C. Peace Manual. 18mo. Boston. 1847.

Becquerel, M. Traité de Physique, dans ses Rapports avec la Chemie etc. 2 vols. 8vo. Paris. 1842.

Becquerel, M. Des Engrais Inorganiques en général et du Sel Marin en particulier. 8vo. Paris. 1848.

Beechy, F. W. and H. W. Proceedings of the Expedition to explore the Northern parts of Africa from Tripoli eastward. 4to. London. 1828.

Beechy, F. W. and H. W. Narrative of a Voyage to the Pacific and Beerings Straits. 8vo. Phila. 1832.

Behmen, Jacob. Works. 4 vols. 4to. London. 1764.

Behmen, Jacob. Memoirs of, by Okely. 12mo. Northampton. 1780.

Belknap, J. See New Hampshire.

Bell, Charles. Anatomy and Physiology of the Human Body. 2 vols. 8vo. New York. 1827.

Bell, John. Travels from St. Petersburgh to various parts in Asia. 8vo. Edinburgh. 1806.

Bell, John. Discourses on the Nature and Cure of Wounds. 2 vols. 8vo. Walpole, N. H. 1807.

Bellamy, Joseph. Millennium. 8vo. Elizabethtown. 1794.

Bellamy, Joseph. Works. 3 vols. 8vo. New York. 1811.

*Bellorius, J. P. Ichnographia Veteris Romae. Fol. Romae. 1764.

Beloe, Wm. Translation of Herodotus. 3 vols. 16mo. New York. 1836.

Belsham, Thos. Vindication of Certain Passages in a Discourse. 8vo. Boston. 1809.

Belzoni, G. Narrative of Operations and recent Discoveries in Egypt and Nubia. 2 vols. in one. 8vo. London. 1822.

Benedict, T. F. Observationes in Sophoclis Septem Tragoedias. 8vo. Lipsiae. 1820.

Benson. See Vocabularium.

Bentham, Jeremy. Introduction to Morals and Legislation. 8vo. London. 1823.

Bentham, Jeremy. Rationale of Judicial Evidence. 5 vols. 8vo. London. 1827.

Bentham, Jeremy. Rationale of Punishment. 8vo. London. 1830.

Bentley, John. Reply to Apeleutheros. 8vo. London. 1819.

Bentley, Richard. Dissertation on the Epistles of Phalaris, with an Answer to Boyle's Objections. 8vo. London. 1713.

Bentley, Richard. On Free Thinking. 8vo. Cambridge, Eng. 1743.

Bentley, Richard. Life by J. H. Monk. 2 vols. 8vo. London. 1833.

Bentote. See America.

Benyowsky, Count M. A. Memoirs and Travels. 2 vols. 4to. Lond. 1790.

Bergman, Torberni. Dissertation on Elective Attractions. 8vo. Lond. 1785.

Bergman, Torberni. Opuscula Physica et Chemica. 5 vols. 8vo. Lipsiae. 1788.

Berington, Joseph. Literary History of the Middle Ages. 4to. London. 1814.

Berington, Joseph. Lives of Abelard and Heloisa. 8vo. Phila. 1819.

Berkely, George. Works. 3 vols. 8vo. London. 1820.

Berkshire. History of the County of. 8vo. Pittsfield. 1829.

Bernardus. Opera omnia. Fol. Parisiis. 1640.

Berni, Francesco. Orlando Innamorato. 4to. Venezia. 1545.

Berni, Francesco. The same transl. by Rose. 12mo. Edinb. and Lond. 1823.

Bernoulli, Danielus. Hydrodynamica. 4to. Argentorati. 1738.

Bernoulli, Jacobus. Ars Conjectandi, et Tractatus de Seriebus Infinitis. 8vo. Basileae. 1713.

Bernoulli, Johannes. Opera omnia. 4 vols. 4to. Lausannae et Genevae. 1742.

Berthollet, C. L. Essay on Chemical Studies. 2 vols. 8vo. Lond. 1804.

Berthollet, C. L. and A. B. Elements of the Art of Dyeing, transl. by Ure. 2 vols. 8vo. London. 1824.

Beveredge, W. Private Thoughts. 12mo. Phila. 1796.

Beverly. Civil and Ecclesiastical History of, from 1630 to 1842. 8vo. Boston. 1843.

Bezout. Equations Algébriques. 4to. Paris. 1779.

Bible. The Holy. 4to. Brattleboro. 1816.

BIBLE. The Holy. 4to. Brattleboro. 1824.

BIBLE. La Sainte. Fol. Genève. 1638.

BIBLE. La Sainte, selon l' ed. de Paris de l' année 1805. 18mo. New York. 1815.

BIBLIA al Espagnol, de S. Miguel. 8vo. London. 1824.

BIBLIA HEBRAICA, Sebastiani Munsteri. Fol. Basileae. 1534.

BIBLIA HEBRAICA, Kennicotti. 2 vols. Fol. Oxford. 1776.

BIBLIA HEBRAICA, Ed. Boothroyd. 2 vols. 4to. Lond. et Edinb. s. a.

BIBLIA HEBRAICA, ab Van der Hooght. 2 vols. 8vo. Amstelodami. 1705.

BIBLIA HEBRAICA. The same. 2 vols. 8vo. Phila. 1814.

BIBLIA HEBRAICA. The same. Cum Novo Testamento. 8vo. Lond. 1822.

BIBLIA HEBRAICA, ex recens. Hahnii. 12mo. Lipsiae. 1834.

BIBLIA LATINA, Hieronymi. Vol. I. Fol. Venetiis. 1506.

BIBLIA LATINA. Vol. II. Fol. Coloniae. 1475.

BIBLIA LATINA. Vulgatae Editionis cum Interpretatione Germanica. 2 vols. Fol. Augsburg. 1748.

BIBLICAL REPOSITORY. Vol. III, IV, V, VI, VII, IX, XI, XII, 2d series. Vols. I, II, III, 3d series. 8vo.

BIBLIOTHECA AMERICANA. See also Catalogues. O. Rich. 8vo. Paris. 1831.

BIBLIOTHEQUE ITALIQUE, ou Histoire Litteraire de l'Italie. Vols. XIII–XVIII. 18mo. Geneva. 1732.

BIBLIOTHEQUE UNIVERSELLE et Historique. 24 vols. 32mo. Amsterdam. 1687–1693.

BICHAT, XAVIER. Physiological Researches upon Life and Death, transl. by Watkins. 8vo. Phila. 1809.

BICHAT, XAVIER. Treatise on the Membranes in general. Transl. by Coffin. 2 copies. 8vo. Boston. 1813.

BICHAT, XAVIER. Pathological Anatomy. 8vo. Phila. 1827.

BIELBY, Bishop of London. Evidences of Christian Revelation. 12mo. New Bedford. 1802.

BIERDEMANN, A. Anfangsgründe der Arithmetik. 12mo. Leipsig. 1833.

BIGELOW, JACOB. Elements of Technology. 2d ed. 8vo. Boston. 1831.

BIGLAND, J. History of England. 2 vols. 8vo. Boston and New York. 1814.

BIGNON, M. Histoire de France, depuis 1799 jusqu'à 1807. 6 vols. 8vo. Paris. 1829–1830.

BINGHAM, JOSEPH. Origines Ecclesiasticae. 10 vols. 8vo. Londini. 1710.

Biographia Brittanica, or the Lives of the most Eminent Persons of Great Britain and Ireland by Andrew, Kippis, and others. 5 vols. Fol. London. 1788–1793.

Biographical Dictionary, American. By W. Allen. 8vo. Boston. 1832.

Biot, J. B. Traité de Physique. 4 vols. 8vo. Paris. 1816.

Bishop, Thos. Eight Sermons. 8vo. London. 1726.

Blackall, John. On the Dropsy. 8vo. Phila. 1820.

Blackstone, Sir Wm. Commentaries on the Laws of England, with Notes by Edward Christian. 4 vols. 8vo. Portland. 1807.

Blackstone, Sir Wm. The same, with additional Notes by J. F. Archbold. 8vo. Phila. 1825.

Blackwall. See Homer.

Blainville. Travels through Holland, Germany, Switzerland, and other parts of Europe. 3 vols. 4to. London. 1743.

Blair, Hugh. Sermons. 2 vols. 8vo. London. 1792.

Blair, Hugh. Lectures on Rhetoric and Belles Letters. 2 vols. Phila. 1799.

Blair, Hugh. The same. 8vo. Boston. 1802.

Blair, Hugh. Life and Writings, by John Hill. 8vo. Phila. 1808.

Blake, J. L. Conversations on Natural Philosophy. 12mo. Boston. 1838.

Bland, Robt. Collections from Greek Anthology, by Merivale. 8vo. London. 1833.

Blondeau. Chrestomathie pour un cours Elementaire du Droit Privé des Romains. 8vo. Paris. 1830.

Bloomfield, S. T. Greek Testament, with English Notes. 2 vols. 8vo. London. 1836.

Bluemenbach, J. F. Decas prima Collectionis suae Craniorum diversarum gentium. 4to. Gottingae. 1820.

Bluemenbach, J. F. Manual of the Elements of Natural History. 8vo. London. 1825.

Bluemenbach, J. F. Ueber den Bildungstrieb. 12mo. Göttengen. 1791.

Bluemner, H. Ueber die Idee des Schiksals in den Tragödien des Aeschylus. 8vo. Leipsig. 1814.

Blume, D. F. Iter Italicum. 3 vols. 12mo. Halis. 1830.

Blunt. See Nautical Almanac.

Boaden, James. See Kemble and Siddons.

Bocaccio, G. Il Decamerone. 4to. Vinegia. 1546.

Bockshammer. Freedom of the Human Will. By Kaufman. 12mo. And. 1835.

BODE, J. E. Allgemeine Beschreibung und Nachweisung der Gestirne. Fol. Berlin. 1801.

*BODE, J. E. Uranographia, viginti tabulis incisa. Fol. Berolini. 1801.

BOECKH, AUGUST. Philolaos des Pythagoreers Lehren. 8vo. Berlin. 1819.

BOECKH, AUGUST. Die Staatshaushaltung der Athener. 2 vols. 8vo. Berlin. 1817.

*Tafeln der Inschriften dafür. 4to.

BOETHIUS, A. M. S. Consolationes Philosophiae. 18mo. Lugduni. 1656.

BOETTICHER, GUIL. Lexicon Taciteum. 8vo. Berolini. 1830.

BOGUE AND BENNET. History of Dissenters. 4 vols. 8vo. London. 1808.

BOILEAU DESPREAUX. Oeuvres, avec des Eclaircissements Historiques par lui meme. 2 vols. Fol. Amsterdam. 1729.

BOILEAU DESPREAUX. Oeuvres completes précédés des Oeuvres de Malherbe, et suivies des Oeuvres poétiques de J. B. Rousseau. 8vo. Paris. 1825.

BOLINGBROKE, LORD. Works, with a Life. 4 vols. 8vo. Phila. 1841.

*BONAPARTE, CHARLES LUCIEN. American Ornithology, or Natural History of Birds in the U. S. A. not given by Wilson, with colored plates. 4 vols. Fol. Phila. 1825.

BOPP, FRANZ. Vergleichende Grammatik des Sanskrit, Zend, Griechischen, Lateinischen, Lithauischen, Gothischen, und Deutschen. 2 vols. 4to. Berlin. 1833.

BORN, IGNATIUS A. Testacea Musei Caesarei Vindobonensis. Fol. Vindobonae. 1780.

BOS, LAMBERTUS. Ellipses Graecae. Ed. Schäffer. 8vo. Lipsiae. 1808.

BOSCHIUS, H. Parerga Horatiana. 8vo. Halis Sax. 1818.

BOSCOVICH, R. J. De Lentibus et Telescopis Dioptricis Dissertatio. 4to. 4to. Romae. 1755.

BOSCOVICH, R. J. Philosophiae Naturalis Theoria. 4to. Viennae. 1759.

BOSCOVICH, R. J. Opera Pertinentia at Opticam et Astronomiam. 5 vols. 4to. Basileae. 1785.

BOSSUET. Exposition de la Doctrine de l'Eglise Catholique. 8vo. Paris. 1822.

BOSSUT, JOHN. History of Mathematics transl. from the French. 8vo. London. 1803.

BOSSUT, M. L'ABBE. Traité d'Hydrodynamique. 2 vols. 8vo. Paris. 1786–1787.

BOSTON RECORDER. Vols. I, II, III, and IV. Fol. Boston. 1816–1819.

BOSTON, THOS. Fourfold State. 12mo. Phila. 1814.

BOSWELL, JAMES. Life of Saml. Johnson. 5 vols. 8vo. London. 1831.

Bosworth, James. Anglo-Saxon Grammar. 8vo. London. 1823.

Bosworth, James. Dictionary of the Anglo-Saxon Language. 8vo. Lond 1838.

Botta, Charles. American War of Independence. 3 vols. dupl. of Vol. i. 8vo. Phila. 1820.

Botta, Charles. Storia d'Italia continuata da quella del Guicciardini dal 1530 al 1789. 10 vols. 8vo. Paris. 1832.

Botta, Charles. Storia d'Italia dal 1789 al 1814. 4 vols. 8vo. Paris. 1832.

Böttiger, C. A. Sabina, oder Morgenszenen im Putzzimmer einer Reichen Römerin. 2 vols. 8vo. Leipsig. 1806.

Boucharlat, J. L. Elémens de Calcul Differentiel et Integral. 8vo. Paris. 1830.

Bouchette, J. Geographical Description of Lower Canada. 8vo. London. 1815.

Boudinot, E. Star in the West. 8vo. Trenton. 1816.

Bougainville, Lewis de. Voyage round the World. 4to. London. 1772.

Boulay Paty. Cours de Droit Commercial Maritime. 4 vols. 8vo. Paris. 1834.

Boullenois, Fred. de. Vers à Soie. 8vo. Paris. 1842.

Bourdaloue. Oeuvres. 3 vols. 8vo. Paris. 1834.

Bourdon. Application de l'Algèbre à la Géométrie. 8vo. Paris. 1831.

Bourdon. Algèbre. 8vo. Paris. 1834.

Bourdon. Arithmétique. 8vo. Paris. 1835.

Bourne, Vincent. Miscellaneous Poems, Original and Translated. 4to. London. 1762.

Bouterwek, F. Aesthetik. 2 vols. 8vo. Göttingen. 1824.

Bouterwek, F. Ideen zur Metaphysik des Schönen. 12mo. Leipsig. 1807.

Bouvard, M. A. Tables Astronomiques. 4to. Paris. 1821.

Bowden, John. Apostolic Origin of Episcopacy. 3 vols. 8vo. New York. 1808.

Bowditch, Nathaniel. Practical Navigator. 8vo. (Title page wanting.)

Bower, Archibald. See Popes.

Bowles, W. L. Controversy on Pope. 12mo. London. 1819.

Boyer. French Dictionary. 8vo. Boston. 1836.

Boyer. Nouveau Dictionaire Français-Anglais. 8vo. Paris. 1831.

Boyle, Charles. Examination of Dr. Bentley's Dissertation on the Epistles of Phalaris and the Fables of Æsop. 8vo. London. 1699.

BOYLE, ROBT. Philosophical Works. Comprising Physics, Statics, Pneumatics, Natural History, Chemistry, and Medicine. 3 vols. 4to. London. 1738.

BRACCIOLINI, FRANCESCO. Lo Scherno degli Dei. 8vo. Milano. 1804.

BRADBURY, THOS. Duty and Doctrine of Baptism. 12mo. New York. 1810.

BRADFORD, A. See Massachusetts.

BRAGGE, FRANCIS. Miracles of our Savior. 2 vols. 8vo. London. 1710.

BRAHE, TYCHO. Astronomiae Instauratae Mechanica. Fol. Noribergae. 1611.

BRAND, JOHN. Observations on Popular Antiquities. 8vo. London. 1810.

BRANDE, W. T. Dissertation on the Progress of Chemical Philosophy. 8vo. s. l. et a.

BRANTÔME. Oeuvres. 8 vols. 8vo. Paris. 1787.

BREWSTER, SIR DAVID. Treatise on new Philosophical Instruments. 8vo. Edinburgh. 1813.

BRIDGES, MATTHEW. The Roman Empire under Constantine the Great. 8vo. London. 1828.

BRIEGLIB, J. A. De Momentis Moralibus Religionum Graecarum et Romanarum. 4to. Gottingae. s. a.

BRIGHAM, WM. Compacts, Charter and Laws of New Plymouth. 8vo Boston. 1836.

BRISSON. Une Thèorie des Ombres et de la Perspective, extraite des papiers de Monge. 4to. See Monge.

BRITISH ESSAYISTS. Collected by Chalmers. Including Tatler, Spectator, Guardian, Rambler, Advertiser, World, Connoisseur, Idler, Mirror, Lounger, Observer, and Looker-on, with Index. 45 vols. 18mo. Lond. 1808.

BRITISH POETS. Works, with Prefaces, Biographical and Critical. By Anderson. 13 vols. 8vo. London. 1795.

Vol. 1. Chaucer, Surrey, Wyat, Sackville, and a complete Glossary.
2. Spenser, Shakspeare, Davies, Hall.
3. Drayton, Carew, Suckling.
4. Donne, Daniel, Browne, P. Fletcher, G. Fletcher, B. Jonson, Drummond, Crashaw, Davenant.
5. Milton, Cowley, Waller, Butler, Denham.
6. Dryden, Rochester, Roscommon, Otway, Pomfret, Dorset, Stepney, Philips, Walsh, Smith, Duke, King, Sprat, Halifax.
7. Parnell, Garth, Rowe, Addison, Hughes, Sheffield, Prior, Congreve, Blackmore, Fenton, Granville, Yalden.
8. Pope, Gay, Tickell, Somerville, Pattison, Hammond, Savage, Hill, Broome, Pitt, Blair.

BRITISH POETS—Continued.

9. Swift, Thomson, Watts, Hamilton, Mallett, Akenside, Harte.

10. Young, Gray, B. West, Lyttleton, Moore, Boyse, Thompson, Cawthorne, Churchill, Falconer, Lloyd, Cunningham, Green, Cooper, Goldsmith, P. Whitehead, Brown, Grainger, Smollet, Armstrong.

11. Wilkie, Dodsley, Shaw, Smart, Langhorne, Bruce, Chatterton, Graeme, Glover, Lovibond, Penrose, Mickle, Jago, Scott, Johnson, W. Whitehead, Jenyns, Logan, Warton, Cotton, Blacklock.

12. Pope's Iliad and Odyssey, West's Pindar; Dryden's Virgil, Persius, and Juvenal; Pitt's Æneid, Rowe's Lucan, Homer's Hymn to Ceres, Pye's Olympic Odes.

13. Cook's Hesiod; Fawkes' Theocritus, Anacreon, Sappho, Bion, Moschus, Musaeus, and Apollonius Rhodius; The Rape of Helen of Coluthus Lycopolites by Mr. C.; Creech's Lucretius, and Grainger's Tibullus.

BRITISH STATE PAPERS, viz:

Domesday Book. 2 vols. Fol. London. 1783.

Additamenta. Fol. London. 1816.

Parliamentary Writs. 2 vols. bound in 4. Fol. London. 1827–1834.

Foedera. 6 vols. Fol. London. 1816–1830.

Inquisitionum retornatarum Abbreviatio. 3 vols. Fol. London. 1811–1816.

Inquisitionum in Offic. Rot. Canc. Hiberniae. 2 vols. Fol. Dublin. 1826–1829.

Calend. Rotulorum, etc. Canc. Hiberniae Hen. II–Hen. VII. Fol. Dublin. 1818.

Rotuli Literarum Clausarum. Vol. I. Fol. London. 1833.

Rotuli Scotiae. Edv. I–Hen. VIII. 2 vols. Fol. London. 1814–1819.

Rotuli Hundredorum. Temp. Hen. III–Edv. I. 2 vols. Fol. London. 1812–1818.

Nonarum Inquisitiones in curia Scaccarii. Fol. London. 1807.

Liber Foedorum in curia Scaccarii. Fol. London. 1807.

Rotulorum Originalium in curia Scaccarii Abbreviatio. 2 vols. Fol. London. 1805–1810.

Rotuli Literarum Patentium. Vol. I. Part I. Fol. London. 1835.

Rotuli Chartarum. Fol. London. 1837.

Registrum Magni Sigilli Regum Scotorum. Fol. London. 1814.

Calendar of the Proceeding in Chancery during the Reign of Elizabeth. 3 vols. Fol. London. 1827–1832.

BRITISH STATE PAPERS—Continued.

Ducatus Lancastriae, Calendar to Pleadings from the Reign of Hen. VII to the end of the Reign of Eliz., also Calendarium Inquis. post mortem, &c. Edv. I–Carol. I. 3 vols. Fol. London. 1823–1834.

MSS. in the Harleian Collection. 4 vols. Fol. London. 1808–1812.

Catalogue of the Lansdowe MSS. in the British Museum. Fol. Lond. 1819.

Placita de Quo Warranto. Fol. London. 1818.

Placitorum Abbreviatio. Ric. I–Edv. II. Fol. London. 1811.

Calendarium Inquisitionum post mortem. Hen. III–Ric. II. 4 vols. Fol. London. 1806–1828.

Valor Ecclesiasticus, Hen. VIII Institutus. 6 vols. Fol. London. 1810–1834.

Ancient Laws and Institutes of England. Also Monumenta Eccles. Angl. Fol. London. 1840.

Ancient Laws and Institutes of Wales. Fol. London. 1841.

Record Commission. Report to the King on the Public Records. Fol. London. 1837.

Record of Caernarvon. Fol. London. 1838.

Acts of the Parliament of Scotland, Vols. II–XI, from 1424–1707. 10 vols. Fol. London. 1814–1824.

Statutes of the Realm. 9 vols. in 10. From 1235 to 1713, with the Original Charters of Liberties in Vol. I. Fol. London. 1810–1828.

Alphabetical Index from Magna Charta to the end of Anne's Reign. Fol. London. 1824.

Chronological Index for the same. Fol. London. 1828.

General Introduction to Domesday Book, with Indexes by Sir H. Ellis. 2 vols. 8vo. London. 1833.

Original Authority of the King's Council by Sir F. Palgrave. 8vo. London. 1834.

Papers and Documents relating to the evidence of certain witnesses in relation to the Record Commission. 8vo. London. 1837.

Excerptae Rotulis Finium in Turri Londinensi. 2 vols. 8vo. London. 1836.

Rotuli Curiae Regis. 2 vols. 8vo. London. 1835.

Rotuli Normanniae in Turri Londinensi. 8vo. 1835.

Rotulus Cancellarii. 8vo. London. 1833.

Rotuli de Oblatis et Finibus in Turri Londinensi asservati. 8vo. London. 1835.

Fines. 8vo. London. 1835.

Calendar and Inventories of his Majesty's Exchequer. Ed. by Palgrave. 3 vols. 8vo. London. 1836.

Rotuli selecti ex Archivis. 8vo. London. 1834.

BRITISH STATE PAPERS—Continued.

Documents and Records illustrative of the History of Scotland. Vol. I. 8vo. London. 1837.

Proceedings and Ordinances of the Privy Council of England. 7 vols. 8vo. London. 1834–1837.

Rotulus Magnus Pipae. 8vo. London. 1833.

BROCCHI, G. Conchiologia Fossile Subappenina. 2 vols. 4to. Milano. 1814.

BRODIE, D. C. Diseases of the Joints. 8vo. Phila. 1821.

BROGNIART, A. Histoire Naturelle des Crustacés Fossiles. 4to. Paris. 1822.

BROGNIART, A. Tableau des Terrains qui composent l'Ecorce du Globe. 8vo. Paris. 1829.

BRONSON. See Pamphlets.

BROSSE, CHARLES DE. Histoire de la Republique Romaine. See Saluste.

BROUSSAIS, F. J. V. Histoire des Phlegmasies. 3 vols. 8vo. Paris. 1822.

BROUSSAIS, F. J. V. Treatise on Physiology applied to Pathology. 8vo. Phila. 1832.

BROWN, D. Contrast between Christianity and Calvinism. 12mo. Fredonia. 1824.

BROWN, JOHN. Dictionary of the Holy Bible. 4to. Boston. 1824.

BROWN, JOHN. Right Understanding of the Oracles of God. 12mo. Albany. 1783.

BROWN, J. W. See Da Vinci.

BROWNE, S. Defence of the Religion of Nature and Revelation. 8vo. London. 1732.

BROWNE, THOS. Works. Fol. London. 1686.

BROWNSON, O. A. The Laboring Classes. 8vo. Boston. 1840.

BROWNSON, O. A. Quarterly Review. See Pamphlet Case 34.

BRUCE, JAMES. Travels to the Source of the Nile. 7 vols. 8vo. Edin. 1813.

Atlas to the above. 4to. Edinburgh. 1813.

BRUCKERUS, JACOBUS. Historia Critica Philosophiae. 6 vols. 4to. Lipsiae. 1767.

BRUNET, J. C. Manuel du Libraire. 4 vols. 8vo. Paris. 1820.

BRUNET, J. C. Nouvelles Recherches bibliographiques pour supplement. 3 vols. 8vo. Paris. 1834.

BRUNO, GIORDANO. Opere. 2 vols. 8vo. Lipsia. 1830.

BRUNO, GIORDANO. Scripta quae Latine confecit. 8vo. Stuttgardiae. s. a.

BRYANT, JACOB. Analysis of Ancient Mythology. 6 vols. 8vo. London. 1807.

BRYANT, JACOB. Observations on the Poems of Rowley. 8vo. London. 1834.

BUCH, LEOPOLD VON. Reise durch Norwegen und Lapland. 2 vols. 12mo. Berlin. 1810.

BUCHAN, EARL OF. See Fletcher.

BUCHANAN, CHARLES. Christian Researches in Asia. 8vo. New York. 1812.

BUCHANAN, G. Opera omnia, Historica, Chronologica, Juridica, Politica, Satirica, et Poetica. 2 vols. Fol. Edinburgh. 1715.

BUCHANAN, JAMES. Regular English Syntax. 18mo. Phila. 1792.

BUCKLAND, WM. Reliquiae Diluvianae. 4to. London. 1824.

BUFFIER. Cours de Séances sur des Principes nouveaux et simples. Fol. Paris. 1732.

BUHLE, J. G. Geschichte der Künste und Wissenschaften. 8 vols. in 7. 8vo. Berlin. 1800–1805.

BULL, GEORGE. Primitive Christianity, in Sermons. 3 vols. 8vo. Oxford. 1816.

BULWER AND FORBES on the Water Treatment. 12mo. New York. 1849.

BULWER, E. L. L'Etudiant, Contes Nouvelles et Esquisses Litteraires. 2 vols. 8vo. Paris. 1835.

BULWER, H. L. France, Social, Literary, and Political. 2 vols. 8vo. New York. 1824.

BUNYAN, JOHN. Works. 2 vols. Fol. London. 1768.

BUNYAN, JOHN. Pilgrim's Progress. 12mo. Phila. 1811.

BURCKHARDT, J. L. Travels in Syria and the Holy Land. 4to. London. 1822.

BURCKHARDT, J. L. Travels in Nubia. 4to. London. 1822.

BURCKHARDT, J, L. Travels in Arabia. 2 vols. 8vo. London. 1829.

BURCKHARDT, J. L. Reisen in Syrien, Palaestina, und der Gegend des Berges Sinai. 2 vols. 8vo. Weimar. 1823.

BURCKHARDT, J. L. Notes on the Bedouins and the Wahabis. 2 vols. 8vo. London. 1831.

BURCKHARDT, M. Tables Astronomiques. 4to. Paris. 1812.

BURDER, SAMUEL. Oriental Customs. 8vo. Phila. 1804.

BURGERDICUS, F. Institutiones Metaphysicae. 18mo. Lugduni. 1740.

BURGESSE, ANTHONY. Original Sin. Fol. London. 1658.

BURGH, J. Political Disquisitions. 8vo. Phila. 1775.

BURKE, EDMUND. Works, with a Memoir. 3 vols. 8vo. New York. 1836.

BURKITT, WM. Expository Notes on the New Testament. Fol. Phila. 1796.

Burlamaqui, J. J. Principles of Natural Law. 2 vols. 12mo. London. 1776.

Burnap, G. W. Lectures on the Doctrines of Christianity. 12mo. Boston. 1828.

Burnap, G. W. Popular Objections to Unitarian Christianity answered. 12mo. Boston. 1848.

Burnap, U. C. The Youth's Etherial Director. (Astronomical.) 12mo. Middlebury. 1822.

Burnes, Alexander. Travels into Bokhara, and a Voyage on the Indus. 3 vols. 8vo. London. 1834.

Burnes, John. Dissertation on Inflammation. 2 vols. in one. 8vo. Albany. 1812.

Burnet, Gilbert. History of the Reformation of the Church of England. 6 vols. 8vo. London. 1820.

Burnet, Gilbert. The same. 2d Part. Fol. London. 1681.

Burnet, Gilbert. The same. Vol. iii. Fol. London. 1715.

Burnet, Gilbert. History of his own time. 6 vols. 8vo. Oxford. 1823.

Burnet, Thos. The Sacred Theory of the Earth. 2 vols. 8vo. London. 1759.

Burns, Robert. Works and Life. By Allan Cunningham. 8 vols. 18mo. London. 1834.

Burr, Col. Aaron. Reports of Trials of, for Treason, by Robinson. 2 vols. 8vo. Phila. 1808.

Burton, Asa. Principles of Ethics, Metaphysics, and Theology. 8vo. Portland. 1824.

Burton, Robt. Anatomy of Melancholy. 2 vols. 8vo. London. 1813.

Burton, Thos. Cromwellian Diary. 4 vols. 8vo. London. 1828.

Butler, Charles. Philological and Biographical Works. 5 vols. s. l. et a.

Butler, J. D. See Pamphlets, Antiquarian.

Butler, Joseph. Fifteen Sermons preached at the Rolls Chapel. 8vo. London. 1749.

Butler, Joseph. Analogy of Religion. 8vo. Boston. 1809.

Butler, Joseph. Works. 2 vols. 8vo. London. 1817. and Cambridge, E. 1827.

Butler, Samuel. Hudibras with Notes by Grey. 2 vols. 8vo. London. 1764.

Butler, Samuel. Poetical Remains, with Notes by Thyer. 8vo. London. 1827.

BUTTMANN, PHILIP. Lexilogus, oder Beiträge zur Griechischen Worterklärung, hauptsächlich für Homer und Hesiod. 2 vols. 8vo. Berlin. 1825.

BUTTMANN, PHILIP. Griechische Sprachlehre. 2 vols. 8vo. Berlin. 1830.

BUXTORFIUS, J. Epitome Grammaticae Hebraicae. 12mo. Lugd. Batav. 1672.

BUXTORFIUS, J. Lexicon Hebraicum et Chaldaicum. 12mo. Basileae. 1676.

BYRON, LORD. Works, with a Sketch of his Life, by Lake. 8vo. Phila. 1836.

BYZANTINE HISTORIANS. See Corpus, &c.

CABANIS, P. J. G. Essay on the Certainty of Medicine. 8vo. Phila. 1828.

CADELL, W. A. Journey in Carniola, Italy, and France. 2 vols. 8vo. Edinburgh. 1820.

CÆDMON. Metrical Paraphrase of Parts of the Holy Scriptures in Anglo-Saxon, with an English translation, Notes and Verbal Index, by Thorpe. 8vo. London. 1832.

CÆSAR, JULIUS. Quae extant, in usum Delphini. 8vo. London. 1794.

CÆSAR, JULIUS. Commentarii. Ed. Oudendorpius. 2 vols. 8vo. Stuttgardiae. 1822.

CAILLE, RENE. Travels through Central Africa and Timbuctoo. 2 vols. 8vo. London. 1830.

CALDWELL, C. See Greene.

CALEPINUS, AMBROSIUS. Dictionarium Octolingue. Fol. Coloniae. 1609.

CALIFORNIA. Reports on Cases before the Supreme Court, by Bennett. Wilson's Edition. Vol. I. 8vo. San Francisco. 1853.

CALLET, FRANÇOIS. Logarithmes. 8vo. Paris. 1795.

CALMET. Dictionary of the Holy Bible. 4 vols. 4to. Charlestown. 1812.

Sacred Geography to accompany, by Wells. 4to. Charlestown. 1817.

CALVIN, JOHN. Commentarii in Epistolas Pauli. 4to. Genevae. 1557.

CALVIN, JOHN. Commentarii in Novum Testamentum. Ed. Tholuck. 8vo. Berolini. 1833.

CALVIN, JOHN. Institutio Christianae Religionis. Ed. Tholuck. 2 vols. 8vo. Berolini. 1834.

CAMBDEN, WM. Brittania, transl. into English by Gibson. Fol. London. 1695.

Cambridge Mathematics. Algebra and Geometry. 8vo. Cambridge. 1825.

Cambridge Mathematics. Trigonometry and Topography. 8vo. Cambridge. 1825.

Cambridge Physics. Electricity and Magnetism. 8vo. Cambridge. 1826.

Cambridge Physics. Optics. 8vo. Cambridge. 1826.

Cambridge Physics. Astronomy. 8vo. Cambridge. 1827.

Cambridge (Eng.) Classical Examinations. 8vo. Cambridge, Eng. 1830.

Campanella, Thos. De Sensu rerum et Magia. 4to. Francofurti. 1620.

Campbell, Colin. History of the Balearic Islands. 8vo. London. 1716.

Campbell, Duncan. Life and Adventures. 12mo. London. 1720.

Campbell, George. Philosophy of Rhetoric. 2 copies. 8vo. Boston. 1823.

Campbell, George. On Miracles, with Sermons and Tracts. 8vo. London. 1834.

Campbell, George. The four Gospels, with Notes. 2 vols. 8vo. Andover. 1837.

Campbell, Thos. Specimens of British Poets, and an Essay on English Poetry. 7 vols. 12mo. London. 1819.

Campbell, Thos. Poetical Works. 18mo. London. 1836.

Camus. Treatise on the Teeth of Wheels, Pinions, &c. 8vo. London. 1806.

*Candolle, A. P. De. Memoire sur la Famille des Mélastomacées, avec dix planches. 4to. Paris. 1828.

Candolle, A. P. De. Prodromus Systematis Naturalis Regni vegetabilis. 4 vols. 8vo. Parisiis. 1824.

Candolle, A. P. De. Organographie vegetale. 2 vols. 8vo. Paris. 1827.

Candolle, A. P. De. Physiologie vegetale. 3 vols. 8vo. Paris. 1832.

Candolle and Sprengel. Elements of the Physiology of Plants. 4 vols. 8vo. Paris. 1824.

Canning, George. Political Life from 1822–1827, by Stapleton. 3 vols. 8vo. London. 1831.

Cantemir, Demetrius. Growth and Decay of the Ottoman Empire. Fol. London. 1766.

Capefigue. Histoire De Philippe Auguste. 4 vols. 8vo. Paris. 1829.

Caradoc. See Wales.

Carey, M. Miscellaneous Essays. 8vo. Phila. 1830.

Carlyle, J. D. Specimens of Arabian Poetry. 4to. Cambridge, Eng. 1796.

Carlyle, J. D. Poems suggested by scenes in the East. Bound with the above. 4to. London. 1805.

Carmina Quadrigesimalia. 8vo. Oxoniae. 1723.

Carnot, L. N. M. Géométrie de Position. 4to. Paris. 1803.

Carnot, L. N. M. De la Défense des Places fortes. 4to. Paris. 1811.

Carnot, L. N. M. Principes de L'Equilibre et du Mouvement. 8vo. Paris. 1803.

Carnot, L. N. M. Réflexions sur la Metaphysique du Calcul Infinitesimal. 8vo. Paris. 1813.

Carpenter, Wm. B. Use and Abuse of Alcoholic Liquors. 18mo. Boston 1851.

Carter, N. H. Letters from Europe. 2 vols. 8vo. New York. 1829.

Cartwright, John. Appeal on the Subject of the English Constitution. 8vo. London. 1799.

Cartwright, John. English Constitution produced and illustrated. 8vo. London. 1823.

Cartwright, John. England's Ægis. 12mo. London. 1804.

Cartwright, John. Life and Correspondence. Edited by his Niece. 2 vols. 8vo. London. 1826.

Carver, J. Travels through the Interior Parts of North America. 8vo. London. 1781.

Carus, C. G. Traité Elementaire d'Anatomie comparée. Trad. par Jourdain. 2 vols. 8vo. Bruxelles. 1838.
*Atlas de 31 Planches.

Carus, F. A. Psychologie der Hebraer. 8vo. Leipsig. 1809.

Caryl, Joseph. Exposition on the Book of Job. 2 vols. Fol. Lond. 1676.

Casaubon, Isaac. De Satirica Graecorum Poësi et Romanorum Satira Libri duo. Ed. Rambach. 8vo. Halis. 1774.

Casiodore. La Vie. 18mo. Paris. 1685.

Casti, G. B. Gli Animali Parlanti, Poema Epico. 3 vols. 8vo. Paris. 1802.

Catalogues of Books, viz:

Of the U. S. Library. 4to. Washington. 1815.

Of the Mercantile Library Association, New York. 8vo. New York. 1837.

Of the Library of Andover Theological Seminary. 8vo. Andover. 1838.

Of the Library of Congress at Washington. 8vo. Washington. 1840.

Of Books relating to America. 8vo. London. 1832.

Of the Library of Harvard University. 3 vols. 8vo. Cambridge. 1830.

Of the Law Library of do. 8vo. Cambridge. 1846.

Of Maps and Charts of do. 8vo. Cambridge. 1831.

Of Boston Athenæum Library. 8vo. Boston. 1827.

Catalogues of Books—Continued.

Coleman's, of rare and curious Books. 8vo. New York. 1825.

Of Books on the Masonic Institution. Boston. 1832.

Of Books in the Theological Library of the town of Boston and in the Library of the late Rev. J. S. Buckminster. 8vo. Boston. 1812.

Bibliotheca Theologica. 8vo. Stüttgart. 1833.

Strakers's, of British and Foreign Theology. 8vo. London. 1835.

O. Rich's, Bibliotheca Americana Nova. Vol. II. 8vo. London. 1846.

H. G. Bohn's, of Books. Vol. I. 8vo. London. 1847.

John Bohn's, of English Books. 8vo. London. 1820.

John Bohn's, of Books in French, Spanish, &c. 8vo. London. 1833.

John Bohn's, of Books in Natural History. 8vo. London. 1835.

Vogel. Lexicon Literaturae Academico-Juridicae. 2 vols. 8vo. Lipsiae. 1835.

T. E. Friedrich. Bibliotheca Historico-Geographica. 8vo. Berolini. 1825.

C. G. G. Theile. Thesaurus Literaturae Theologico-Academicae. 8vo. Lipsiae. 1841.

Of the Library of John Fleming. 8vo. Montreal. 1833.

Of the University Institute Society of the U. V. M. 8vo. Burlington. 1851.

Bibliotheca Dissertationum et Minorum Librorum. J. A. G. Weigelius. 8vo. Lipsiae. 1837.

The same. Pars secunda. Lipsiae. 1839.

The same. Partes tertia et quarta. Lipsiae. 1840.

Catalogues of the principal Booksellers and Publishers in this Country, Great Britain, France, and Germany.

Catechisme, ou Abrégé de la Doctrine Chrétienne (Catholique). 18mo. Baltimore. 1809.

*Catesby, Mark. Natural History of Carolina, Florida, and the Bahama Islands. 2 vols. Fol. London. 1731.

Caussinus, N. De Eloquentia Sacra et Humana Libri XVI. 4to. Lugduni. 1643.

Caussinus, N. De Sapientia Ægyptorum. 18mo. s. l. et a.

Cavallo, T. Theory and Practice of Electricity. 2 vols. 8vo. London. 1786.

Caylus, Comte de. Recueil d'Antiquités. 7 vols. 4to. Paris. 1771–1777.

Cecil, Richard. Works. 4 vols. 8vo. London. 1811.

Celestial Comforter, a Collection of Scriptural Promises. 18mo. Phila. 1814.

CELLA, PAOLO DELLA. Narrative of an Expedition from Tripoli to the Western frontier of Egypt. 8vo. London. 1822.

CELLARIUS, CHRISTOPHER. Notitia Orbis Antiqui. 2 vols. 4to. Lipsiae. 1773.

CELLIER, N. H. Cours de Redaction Notarialle. 8vo. Paris. 1840.

CELLINI, BENVENUTO. Vita, da Carpani. 3 vols. 8vo. Milano. 1806.

CELLINI, BENVENUTO. Memoirs of, by himself, transl. by Roscoe. 2 vols. 8vo. Milano. 1823.

CELSUS, A. C. De Medicina, cum Notis. 2 vols. 8vo. Argentorati. 1806.

CENSUS OF THE U. S. A. Report of the 5th Census, 1830. Fol. Washington. 1832.

CENSUS OF THE U. S. A. Statistical View of the Population of the U. S. A. 1790–1830. Fol. Washington. 1835.

CENSUS OF THE U. S. A. Report of the 6th Census, 1840. Fol. Washington. 1841.

CENSUS OF THE U. S. A. Statistics of the above. Fol. Washington. 1841.

CENSUS OF THE U. S. A. Compendium of the Returns of the above. 2 copies. Fol. Washington. 1841.

CENSUS OF PENSIONS for Military Services under the 6th Census. Fol. Washington. 1841.

CENTENNIAL CELEBRATION at Danvers, Mass. 8vo. Boston. 1852.

CEREMONIAL du Sacre des Rois de France. Paris. 1775.

CERVANTES. Don Quixote de la Mancha. 4 vols. 18mo. Burdeos. 1804.

CHALKHILL, JOHN. Thealma and Clearchus. 18mo. Chiswick. 1820.

CHALMERS, THOS. On Political Economy. 8vo. New York. 1832.

CHAMBAUD, LEWIS. Exercises in French Speech. 12mo. London. 1795.

CHAMBERS, E. Cyclopædia. 2 vols. Fol. London. 1751.

CHAMBERS, E. Supplement to the above. Fol. London. 1753.

CHAMBERS, SIR WM. Treatise on the Decorative part of Civil Arohitecture. Fol. London. 1791.

CHAMBERS, SIR WM. Dissertation on Oriental Gardening. 4to. London. 1772.

CHAMICH, FATHER MICHAEL. See Armenia.

CHAMPLAIN, SIEUR DE. Voyages, ou Journal et Découvertes de la N. France. 2 vols. 8vo. Paris. 1830.

CHAMPOLLION LE JEUNE. Système Hyèroglyphique des anciens Egyptiens. 8vo. Paris. 1828.

Planches et Explication a celà. 8vo. Paris. 1829.

CHAMPOLLION LE JEUNE. Lettres écrites d'Egypte et de Nubie en 1828–1829. 8vo. Paris. 1833.

CHANCELLERIE DE L'ANGLETERRE. Lettres sur la cour de, par Roger Collard. Paris. 1830.

CHANDLER, R. Travels in Asia Minor and Greece. 2 vols. 4to. London. 1817.

CHANNING, WM. ELLERY. Discourses, Reviews, and Miscellanies. 8vo. Boston. 1830.

CHANNING, WM. ELLERY. Works. 6 vols. 12mo. Boston. 1847.

CHANNING, WM. ELLERY. Memoir of, with Extracts from his Correspondence and MSS. 3 vols. 12mo. Boston. 1848.

CHAPLIN, EBENEZER. Sacraments. 12mo. Worcester. 1802.

CHAPMAN, GEORGE. Hymns of Homer. 12mo. Chiswick. 1818.

CHARACTERE der vornehmsten Dichter aller Nationen nebst Kritischen und Historischen Abhandlungen über Gegenstände der Schönen Künste und Wissenschaften von Einer Gesellschaft von Gelehrten. 8 vols 8vo. Leipsig. 1792.

CHARAS, MOYSE. Pharmacopée. 2 vols. Lyons. 1753.

CHARDIN, CHEVALIER. Voyage en Perse et autres lieux en Orient. 10 vols. 8vo. Paris. 1811.

*Atlas of Plates to the above. Fol. Paris. 1811.

CHARDON DE LA ROCHETTE, S. Mélanges de Critique et de Philologie. 3 vols. 8vo. Paris. 1812.

CHARDON, Z. Du Dol et de la Fraude. 3 vols. 8vo. Paris. 1838.

CHARNOCK, J. History of Marine Architecture. 3 vols. 4to. London. 1800.

*CHARNOCKE, STEPHEN. Discourses on the Existence and Attributes of God. Fol. London. 1682.

CHART of Narragansett Bay, surveyed in 1832 by Capt. Wadsworth.

CHART of George's Shoal and Bank, by Lieut. Wilkes. 1832.

CHASTELLUX, MARQUIS DE. Travels in North America, in 1780–1782. 8vo. New York. 1827.

CHATEAUBRIAND. Oeuvres complétes. 4 vols. 8vo. Paris. 1834.

CHATEAUBRIAND. The Martyrs, or the Triumph of the Christian Religion.. 3 vols. 12mo. New York. 1812.

CHATTERTON, THOS. Works and Life, by Gregory. 3 vols. 8vo. London. 1803.

CHAUCER, GEOFFREY. Life, by William Godwin. 4 vols. 8vo. Lond. 1804.

CHAUCER, GEOFFREY. Canterbury Tales, by Tyrwhitt. 5 vols. 12mo. London. 1822.

CHAUNCY, CHARLES. Twelve Sermons. 8vo. Boston. 1765.

CHAUNCY, CHARLES. A compleat view of Episcopacy. 12mo. Boston. 1771.

CHEVALIER, CHARLES. Sur l'usage des Chambres obscures et des Chambres claires. 8vo. Paris. 1833.

CHEYNE, DR. GEORGE. Essay on Health and Long Life. 8vo. Lond. 1745.

CHIABRERA, GABRIELLA. Opere. 3 vols. 8vo. Milano. 1807.

CHILI. Geographical, Natural, and Civil History of, from the Italian of Molina. 2 vols. 8vo. Middletown, Ct. 1848.

CHILLINGWORTH, W. Works. 3 vols. 8vo. London. 1820.

CHINESE REPOSITORY. Vols. III and IV. 1834–1836. 8vo. Canton, China.

CHIPMAN, NATHANIEL. Principles of Government. 8vo. Burlington. 1833.

CHIPMAN, NATHANIEL. Life and Writings, by Daniel Chipman. 8vo. Boston. 1846.

CHIPMAN, NATHANIEL. The same. 12mo. Rutland. 1793.

CHIPMAN, NATHANIEL. Reports and Dissertations. 12mo. Rutland. 1793.

CHLADNI, F. F. Traité d'Acoustique. 8vo. Paris. 1809.

CHORON. Méthodes d'Harmonie de Albrechtsberger, traduit. 2 vols. 8vo. Paris. 1830.

CHRISTIAN, M. Traité de Mecanique Industrielle. 3 vols. 4to. Paris. 1822.
Planches a celà. 4to.

CHRYSOSTOMUS, JOHANNES. Opera, Graece. 8 vols. Fol. Etoniae. 1613.

CHUBB, THOS. Collection of Tracts on various subjects. 4to. London. 1730.

CHURCHMAN, JOHN. Magnetic Atlas. 4to. New York. 1800.

CIBBER, COLLEY. Life, by himself, with notices of his Theatrical Contemporaries and the Stage for forty years. 8vo. London. 1822.

CICERO, M. TULLIUS. Dialogi tres de Oratore. Ed. Smith. 8vo. Walpole. 1804.

CICERO, M. TULLIUS. Orationes quaedam Selectae. Ed. Campbell. 8vo. Novi Eboraci. 1804.

CICERO, M. TULLIUS. Orationes quaedam Selectae et de Senectute et de Amicitia. 8vo. Phila. 1815.

CICERO, M. TULLIUS. De Natura Deorum, Libri tres. Ed. Creuzer. 8vo. Lipsiae. 1818.

CICERO, M. TULLIUS. Orationes quaedam Selectae. Ed. Smart. 2 copies. 8vo. Phila. 1826.

Cicero, M. Tullius. Selectae quaedam Epistolae. Ed. Hurlburt. 8vo. Phila. 1836.

Cicero, M. Tullius. De Officiis, Libri tres. Ed. Beierus. 2 vols. 8vo. Lipsiae. 1840.

Cicero, M. Tullius. Opera quae supersunt omnia. Ed. Schütz. 28 vols. 12mo. Lipsiae. 1814–1821.

Cicero, M. Tullius. Letters, transl. by Wm. Melmoth. 3 vols. 8vo. London. 1753.

Cicero, M. Tullius. Cato and Laelius, transl. by Wm. Melmoth. 2 vols. 8vo. London. 1785.

Cicero, M. Tullius. Select Orations, transl. by Duncan. 8vo. London. 1796.

Ciocci, Raffaele. Narrative of barbarities practiced at Rome in the 19th century. 12mo. Phila. 1845.

Clairaut. Théorie de la Figure de la Terre. 8vo. Paris. 1808.

Claius, Johannes. Graecorum Poematum libri tres. 4to. Wittebergae. 1570.

Clare, John. Poems descriptive of Rural Life and Scenery. 18mo. London. 1820.

Clarendon, Eeward, Earl of. History of the Rebellion and Civil Wars in England. 6 vols. 8vo. Oxford. 1731.

Clarendon, Edward, Earl of. Life, by himself, and a Continuation of his History of the Rebellion. 3 vols. 8vo. Oxford. 1827.

Clarendon, Edward, Earl of. Collection of several Tracts. 12mo. Lond. 1727.

Clarendon, Henry Hyde, Earl of. Correspondence, and Diary from 1687–1790. 2 vols. 4to. London. 1828.

Clark, Rev. John. Remarks on his Character, and a Narrative by W. Jay. 8vo. Boston. 1821.

Clarke, E. D. Life and Remains, by Otter. 8vo. New York. 1827.

Clarke, E. D. Travels in Europe, Asia, and Africa. 3 vols. 12mo. New York. 1815.

Clarke, Samuel. Discourse on the Being and Attributes of God. 8vo. London. 1732.

Clarkson, Thos. Portraiture of Quakerism. 3 vols. 8vo. New York. 1806.

Claudianus, C. Quae extant. Ed. Gessner. 8vo. Lipsiae. 1759.

Claudius, Matthias. Werke. 4 vols. 12mo. Hamburg. 1829.

Clavigero. See Mexico.

Clay, Henry. Obituary Addresses on. 8vo. Washington. 1852.

Clemens, Alexandrinus. Opera, Graece et Latine. Fol. Paris. 1641.

Cleveland, C. D. First Lessons in Latin. 12mo. Boston. 1831.

Cleveland, John. Works. 18mo. London. 1687.

Cloquet, Jules. Anatomie de l'homme. 6 vols, Fol. Paris. 1831.

Coast Survey. Sketches accompanying Annual Report of the Supt. 1851. 4to.

Cobbett, Wm. Le Tuteur Anglais. 8vo. Phila. 1805.

Cobbett, Wm. French Grammar. 8vo. London. 1835.

Cobden, Edward. Poems. 12mo. London. 1748.

Cochrane, J. D. Narrative of a Pedestrian Journey in Russia and Tartary. 2 vols. 8vo. London. 1825.

Cockerell, C. R., and others. Antiquities of Greece, supplementary to Stewart. Fol. London. 1830.

Coddington, Henry. Elementary Treatise on Optics. 8vo. Cambridge. Eng. 1825.

Code d'Instruction Criminelle Expliquée. J. A. Rogion. 12mo. Paris. 1839.

Code Pénal, Expliquée par des Motifs, par des Examples, et par la Jurisprudence. J. A. Rogion. 12mo. Paris. 1840.

Codes, Les Six. 12mo. Paris. 1829.

Cogan, T. Philosophical Treatise on the Passions. 8vo. Boston. 1821.

Coleman, Lyman. Antiquities of the Christian Church. 8vo. Andover. 1841.

Coleridge, S. T. The Friend. 8vo. Burlington. 1831.

Coleridge, S. T. Biographia Litteraria. 8vo. New York. 1834.

Coleridge, S. T. Statesman's Manual. 12mo. Burlington. 1832.

Coleridge, S. T. Letters, Conversations, and Recollections. 2 vols. 12mo. London. 1836.

Coleridge, S. T. Poetical Works. 3 vols. 18mo. London. 1835.

Collectio Epistolarum Graecarum. Ed. Orellius. 8vo. Lipsiae. 1815.

Collier, J. Payne. Poetical Decameron, or his Conversations on English Poets and Poetry, of the reigns of Elizabeth and James I. 2 vols. 12mo. Edinburgh. 1820.

Collingwood, Lord. Selections from his Public and Private Correspondence, with Memoirs of his Life, by G. L. N. Collingwood. 8vo. New York. 1829.

Collinson. See Thuanus.

COLMAN, B. Moses a Witness, with a Discourse by Judah Monis. 12mo. Boston. 1722.

COLUMBIA. Notes on, by a U. S. Officer. 8vo. Phila. 1827.

COLUMBIAN PREACHER. Vol. I. 8vo. Cattskill. 1808.

COLUMBUS, CHRISTOPHER. Memorials of. 8vo. London. 1823.

COLUMBUS, CHRISTOPHER. Personal Narrative of his first Voyage. 8vo. Boston. 1827.

COMBE, ANDREW. Observations on Mental Derangement. 8vo. Boston. 1834.

COMBE, ANDREW. Physiology of Digestion. 18mo. Boston. 1834.

COMBE, GEORGE. A System of Phrenology. 8vo. Boston. 1837.

COMBE, GEORGE. The Constitution of Man. 12mo. Boston. 1836.

COMBE, GEORGE. Lectures on Moral Philosophy. 12mo. Boston. 1836.

COMBE, GEORGE. Testimonials in behalf of, as a Candidate for the Chair of Logic in the University of Edinburgh. 8vo. Edinburgh. 1836.

COMINES, PHILIPPE DE. Memoirs, par Godefroy. 4 vols. 12mo. Bruxelles. 1706.

COMMERCE, Origin of. By Anderson. 2 vols. Fol. London. 1764.

COMMERCIUM EPISTOLICUM de varia re Mathematica. 8vo. Londini. 1725.

COMMON PRAYER, The Book of. 12mo. New York. 1813.

COMPTES Rendus des Séances de l'Académie des Sciences. Vols. XVIII–XXVII. Paris. 1844–1848.

COMSTOCK, CYRUS. Essays on the Duty of Parents and Children. 12mo. Hartford. 1810.

*CONCHYLIOLOGIE, qui traite des Coquillages de Mer, de Rivière et de Terre. 4to. Paris. 1757.

CONDER, JOSIAH. Protestant Nonconformity. 2 vols. 8vo. London. 1818.

CONDORCET. Moyens d'apprendre de compter. 12mo. Paris. 1799.

CONFERENCES on the Idolatry of the Romish Church. 12mo. London. 1679.

CONFUCIUS. Works, in Chinese. s. l. et a.

CONGRESSIONAL DOCUMENTS, viz:

- Report of the Sec. of the Treasury for 1813. Fol. Washington. 1814.
- Statement of unsettled Accounts from the Sec. of the Treasury for 1813. Fol. Washington. 1813.
- Report of the Sec. of the Treasury for 1814. Fol. Washington. 1814.
- Annual Report of do. for 1814. Fol. Washington. 1814.
- Reports, &c., of the 13th Congress, 3d Session. Fol. Washington. 1815.

CONGRESSIONAL DOCUMENTS—Continued.

Letter of the Sec. of the Navy in relation to Contracts for 1815. Fol. Washington. 1816.

Annual Report of the Sec. of the Treasury, for 1816. Fol. Washington. 1816.

Treasurer's Accounts for 1816. Fol. Washington. 1816.

Report of the Comptroller of the Treasury. Fol. Washington. 1817.

Congressional Globe. Vol. XXI, Parts 1 and 2. 4to. 2 vols. Washington. 1850.

Congressional Globe. Appendix Vol. XXII. Parts 1 and 2. 2 vols. 4to. Washington. 1850.

Congressional Globe. Vol. XXIII. 4to. Washington. 1851.

Congressional Globe. Vol. XXIV. Parts 1, 2, 3. 3 vols. 4to. Washington. 1852.

Congressional Globe. Appendix Vol. XXV. 4to. Washington. 1852.

Congressional Globe. Vol. XXVI. 4to. Washington. 1853.

Annual Report of the Superintendent of the Coast Survey for 1851. 8vo. Washington. 1852.

Maps accompanying the above. 2 copies. 4to.

Patent Office Report for 1848. 2 copies. 8vo. Washington. 1849.

The same for 1849. Part 1st, Arts and Manufactures. Part 2d, Agriculture. 8vo. Washington. 1850.

The same for 1850. Part 1st, Arts and Manufactures. Part 2d, Agriculture. 8vo. Washington. 1851.

The same for 1852–1853. Part 1st, Arts and Manufactures. Part 2d, Agriculture. 8vo. Washington. 1853.

Plates to Magnetic and Meteorological Observations made at Girard College, Phila., and reported to the Senate of the U. S. Dec. 1844. 8vo. Washington. 1845.

Annual Message and Accompanying Docs., 32d Congress, 1st Session. 8vo. Washington. 1852.

Abstract of the 7th Census of 1850. 2 vols. 8vo. Washington. 1853.

Register of the Naval Officers of the U. S., 1852. 12mo. Washington. 1852.

JOURNALS OF CONGRESS. 1774–1778. 13 vols. 8vo.

Secret Journals of Congress. 1775–1778. 4 vols. 8vo.

(One vol. Domestic Affairs.)

(Three vols. Foreign Relations.)

Journal, Acts, and Proceedings of the Convention of 1787. 8vo.

Journal of the 5th Congress, 3d Session. 1798–1799. 8vo.

Congressional Documents—Continued.

Journals of the Senate.

Of the 14th Congress, 1st Session. 8vo.

Of the 15th Congress, 1st Session. 8vo.

Of the 16th Congress, 1st and 2d Sessions. 2 vols. 8vo.

Of the 17th Congress, 1st and 2d Sessions. 2 vols. 8vo.

Of the 18th Congress, 1st Session. 8vo.

From the 19th Congress, 1st Session, to the 32d Congress, 1st Session, inclusive. 29 vols. 8vo.

Journals of the House of Representatives.

Of the 14th Congress, 1st and 2d Sessions. 2 vols. 8vo.

Of the 15th Congress, 1st Session. 8vo.

From the 16th Congress, 1st Session, to the 32d Congress, 1st Session, inclusive. 35 vols. 8vo.

State Papers. From the 14th Congress, 2d Session, to the 21st Congress, 1st Session, inclusive. 115 vols. 8vo. (Wanting, Vol. x of the Series, for the 16th Congress, 2d Session, and Vols. i, iv, vi, vii, x, xi, xii, and xiii of the Series, for the 17th Congress, 1st Session.)

Executive Documents. From the 21st Congress, 2d Session, to the 32d Congress, 1st Session, inclusive. 157 vols. 8vo.

Executive Papers. Of the 17th Congress, 1st Session. Vols. i, iv, v, vi, and vii. 8vo.

Commercial Relations. 18th Congress, 1st Session. 1 vol. 8vo.

Senate Papers. For the 17th Congress, 1st and 2d Sessions. 4 vols. 8vo.

Senate Documents. From the 18th Congress, 1st Session, to the 32d Congress, 1st Session, inclusive. 172 vols. 8vo. (Wanting Vol. ii for the 32d Congress, special Session, and Vol. xiv for the 32d Congress, 1st Session.)

Senate Reports.

Of the 30th Congress, 1st and 2d Sessions. 2 vols. 8vo.

Of the 31st Congress, 1st and 2d Sessions. 2 vols. 8vo.

Of the 32d Congress, 1st Session. 2 vols. 8vo.

Senate Miscellaneous. From the 30th Congress, 1st Session, to the 32d Congress, 1st Session, inclusive. 7 vols. 8vo.

House Miscellaneous. From the 30th Congress, 1st Session, to the 32d Congress, 1st Session, inclusive. 5 vols. 8vo.

Index to House Documents from 1831 to 1839.

Reports of Committees. From the 17th Congress, 1st Session, to the 32d Congress, 1st Session. 84 vols. 8vo. None for the 25th Congress, 1st Session, and for the 27th Congress.

CONGRESSIONAL DOCUMENTS—Continued.

ACTS of the 14th Congress, 1st Session, and of the 15th Congress, 1st and 2d Sessions. 3 vols. 8vo.

DUPLICATES.

State Papers. 15th Congress, 1st Session. 11 vols., with a triplicate of the 2d of the above series read before the House.

Reports of Committees, on the Georgia Controversy. 19th Congress, 2d Session. 8vo.

Executive Docs. of 22d Congress. 2d Session. 3 vols. 8vo.

House Journals of 22d and 23d Congresses. 4 vols. 8vo.

Senate Journals of the 22d Congress, 2d Session. 8vo.

CONNECTICUT COLONY. Acts and Laws. 1710–1753. Fol. New London. 1753.

CONNECTICUT EVANGELICAL MAGAZINE. July 1800–June 1803. 3 vols. 8vo. Hartford.

CONNECTICUT. Civil and Ecclesiastical History of, from 1630 to 1764, with an Appendix containing the original Patent of New England. By Trumbull. 2 vols. 8vo. Hartford. 1818.

CONNECTICUT. Letters from the English Kings and Queens to the Governors thereof, with answers thereto and other Antiquities. By Hinman. 8vo. Hartford. 1836.

CONON. Narrationes Ptolemaei Historiae. Ed. Teucherus. 12mo. Lipsiae. s. a.

CONSTANCE. Histoire du Concile de, par L'Enfant. 2 vols. 4to. Amsterdam. 1727.

CONSTITUTION of the Reformed Dutch Church in the United States. 12mo. New York. 1793.

CONYBEARE AND PHILIPS. Outlines of the Geology of England and Wales. 8vo. London. 1822.

CONYBEARE, J. J. Illustrations of Anglo-Saxon Poetry. 8vo. Lond. 1826.

COOKE, CAPT. JAMES. Voyages by Byron, Wallis, Carteret, and Cooke. 3 vols. 4to. London. 1773.

COOKE, CAPT. JAMES. Voyage toward the South Pole and round the World. 2 vols. 4to. London. 1779.

COOKE, CAPT. JAMES. Voyage to the Pacific. 3 vols. 4to. London. 1785.

COOKE, CAPT. JAMES. Life, by Andrew Kippis. 4to. London. 1788.
Atlas of Plates to Voyages. Fol. London. 1788.

COOKE, REV. P. The Divine Law of Beneficence. 12mo. New York. s. a.

COOKE, REV. P. The same, and Scripture Plan of Benevolence. 12mo. New York. s. a.

Cooper, Sir Astley. Series of Lectures on Modern Surgery. 8vo. Boston. 1823.

Cooper, Sir Astley. Lectures on the Principles and Practice of Surgery. 3 vols. 8vo. Boston. 1825.

Cooper, Charles P. Reports of some Cases in Chancery in the years 1837–1838. 4 vols. 8vo. London. 1838–1841.

Cooper, Saml. Dictionary of Practical Surgery. 8vo. London. 1813.

Coos County. Historical Sketches of, by Grant Powers. 12mo. Haverhill. 1841.

Coote, Charles. History of Modern Europe. 8vo. Phila. 1811.

Copernicus, N. Astronomia Instaurata. 4to. Amstelodami. 1617.

Corneille, P. Oeuvres complètes, suivies des Oeuvres Choisies de Th. Corneille. 2 vols. 8vo. Paris. 1834.

Cornelius, Elias. Memoir of. By B. B. Edwards. 12mo. Boston. 1834.

Cornelius Nepos. De Vita Excellentium Imperatorum. Ed. Bremi. Zurich. 1827.

Corpus Juris Civilis. 2 vols. 4to. Lugduni. 1662.

Corpus Scriptorum Historiae Byzantinae. Editio consilio B. G. Niebuhrii Instituta. 23 vols. 8vo. Bonnae. 1828.

Agathias, Historiarum Libri v. Ed. Niebuhr. 8vo. Bonnae. 1828.

Cantacuzenus, Hist. Libri iv. Ed. Schopenus. 3 vols. 8vo. Bonnae. 1828.

Constantinus Porphyrog. Rec. Reiskius. 2 vols. 8vo. Bonnae. 1829.

Chronicon Paschale. Ed. Dindorfius. 2 vols. 8vo. Bonnae. 1832.

Dexippus, Eunapius, Petrus Patricius, Priscus, etc. Ed. Bekker et Niebuhr. 8vo. Bonnae. 1829.

Ducas, Hist. Byzantina. Ed. Bekker. 8vo. Bonnae. 1834.

Georgius Pachymeres. Recogn. Bekker. 2 vols. 8vo. Bonnae. 1835.

Joannes Cinnamus, Nicephorus Bryennius. Rec. Meineke. 8vo. Bonnae. 1836.

Joannes Malalas. Ex recens. Dindorfii. 8vo. Bonnae. 1831.

Georgius Syncellus. Ex recens. Dindorfii. 2 vols. 8vo. Bonnae. 1829.

Leo Diaconus. Ed. C. B. Hasius. 8vo. Bonnae. 1828.

Nicephorus Gregoras, cura Schopeni. 3 vols. 8vo. Bonnae. 1829.

Nicetas Choniata. Ed. Bekker. 8vo. Bonnae. 1835.

Procopius. Ex recens. Dindorfii. 2 vols. 8vo. Bonnae. 1833.

Theophylactus Simocatta, Genesius. Recogn. Bekker. 8vo. Bonnae. 1834.

Corregio. Memorie Istoriche. 3 vols. 8vo. Parma. 1817–1821.

COTES, ROGER. Lectures on Hydrostatics and Pneumatics. 8vo. London. 1775.

COULOMB, C. A. Thèorie des Machines simples. 4to. Paris. 1821.

COURS DE REDACTION. Oeuvres de Platon. 8 vols. 8vo. Paris. 1822.

COUSIN, VICTOR. Rapport sur l'état de l'Instruction Publique. 8vo. Paris. 1833.

COUSTOS, JOHN. Sufferings of, at the Inquisition of Lisbon. By Gavin. 12mo. Hartford. 1820.

COWLEY, ABRAHAM. Poems. 4to. London. 1656.

COWPER, WM. Poems. (Incomplete.) 18mo. New York. 1814.

COXE, J. R. Philadelphia Medical Dictionary. 8vo. Phila. 1817.

COXE, TENCH. View of the United States. 1787–1794. 8vo. Phila. 1794.

COXE, WM. Memoirs of the Kings of Spain of the House of Bourbon from Philip v to Charles III. 3 vols. 4to. London. 1813.

COXE, WM. History of the House of Austria from 1218–1792. 5 vols. 8vo. London. 1820.

CRABB, GEORGE. History of English Law. 8vo. Burlington. 1831.

CRAMER, J. A. Geographical and Historical Description of Ancient Greece. 3 vols. 8vo. Oxford. 1828.

CRANMER, THOS. Remains. 4 vols. 8vo. Oxford. 1832.

CRANZ. See Greenland.

CREMER, BERN. SEBASTIANUS. Prodromus Typicus. 4to. Amstelod. 1727.

CRENIUS, THOS. Fascis exercitationum Philologico-Historicarum. 3 vols. 16mo. Lugduni in Batavis. 1697.

CREUZER, F. Dionysius, sive Commentationes Academicae de rerum Bacchicarum Orphicarumque Originibus et Caussis. 4to. Heidelbergae. 1808.

CREUZER, F. Abbildungen zu Symbolik und Mythologie, mit Tafeln. 4to. Leipsig. 1819.

CREUZER, F. Mythologische Schriften Schellings, &c. 8vo. Heidelberg. 1817.

CREUZER, F. Symbolik und Mythologie der Alten Völker, besonders der Griechen. 6 vols. 8vo. Leipsig. 1819.

CREUZER, G. F. Die Historische Künst der Griechen. 8vo. Leipsig. 1803.

CRISIS. A Weekly Journal. Jan. 1775 to Oct. 1776. Fol. London.

CROLY, GEORGE. The Apocalypse of St. John, being a new Interpretation. 12mo. Phila. 1827.

Crombie Alexander, Gymnasium, sive Symbola Critica. 2 vols. 8vo. London. 1830.

Cromwell, Oliver. Life and Times, by Thos. Cromwell. 8vo. London. 1822.

Cudworth, Ralph. Intellectual System of the Universe. 4 vols. 8vo. London. 1820.

Cudworth, Ralph. Eternal and Immutable Morality. 8vo. Andover. 1838.

Cullen, Wm. First Lines of the Practice of Physic. 3 vols. 12mo. Worcester. 1790.

Cullen, Wm. Synopsis Nosologiae Methodicae. Ed. altera, redacta. 18mo. Londini. 1816.

Cullum, George W. Register of the Officers and Graduates of the U. S. Military Academy. 12mo. New York. 1850.

Cumberland, Richard. Memoirs written by himself. 4to. London. 1806.

Cumberland, Richard. Anecdotes of Eminent Painters in Spain. 2 vols. 8vo. London. 1787.

Cumberland, Richard. Calvary, a Poem. 8vo. Morristown. 1815.

Curtis, J. H. Physiology and Diseases of the Ear. 8vo. London. 1826.

Curtius, Rufus Q. Historia Alexandri Magni. 8vo. Lugduni. 1658.

Curtius, Rufus Q. De rebus gestis Alexandri Magni. 8vo. Argentorati. 1801.

Cutter, Calvin. Anatomy and Physiolygy. 12mo. Boston. 1846.

*Cuvier, Baron G. Recherches sur les Ossemens Fossiles. 7 vols. 4to. Paris. 1825.

*Cuvier, Baron G. Histoire Naturelle des Poissons. 12 vols. avec planches. 4to. Paris. 1828–1837.

Cuvier, Baron G. Histoire du Progrès des Sciences Naturelles. 4 vols. 8vo. Paris. 1817.

Cuvier, Baron G. Règne Animal. 4 vols. 8vo. Paris. 1817.

Cuvier, Baron G. The same transl. by McMurtrie. 4 vols. 8vo. New York. 1831.

Cyprianus, Cæcilius. Opera. Fol. Paris. 1666.

Cyprian. Genuine Works. Fol. London. 1717.

Da Costa, E. M. Elements of Conchology. 8vo. London. 1776.

DAGLEY, R. Death's Doings. 2 vols. 8vo. Boston. 1828.

DALE, A. VAN. De Oraculis Veterum Ethnicorum. 4to. Amstelod. 1700.

D'ALEMBERT. Traité de Dynamique. 8vo. Paris. 1796.

D'ALEMBERT. Oeuvres. 5 vols. 8vo. Paris. 1821.

DALRYMPLE, SIR JOHN. Memoirs of Great Britain and Ireland, from the Dissolution of the last Parliament of Charles II, to the Battle off La Hogue. 2 vols. 4to. London and Edinburgh. 1771–1773.

DALZELL, ANDREAS. Analecta Graeca Minora. 8vo. London. 1808.

DAMOISEAU, BARON DE. Tables de la Lune, formées par la seule Théorie de l'Attraction. Fol. Paris. 1828.

DANA, FREEMAN AND SAMUEL. See Geology.

DANA, JAMES. Sermons to Young People. 8vo. New Haven. 1806.

DANA, JAMES D. System of Mineralogy. 2d Ed. 8vo. New York and London. 1844.

DANA, RICHARD H. Poems and Prose Writings. 18mo. Boston. 1823.

DANIELL, J. F. Meteorological Essays and Observations. 8vo. Lond. 1827.

DANTE, ALIGHIERI. Opere. 5 vols. 4to. Venezia. 1758.

DANTE, ALIGHIERI. Inferno. Transl. by J. C. Wright. 8vo. Lond. 1833.

D'ANVILLE. Compendium of Ancient Geography. 2 vols. 8vo. New York. 1814.

D'ARGENS, MARQUIS. Timée de Locres, en Grec et en François. 12mo. Berlin. 1763.

DARIUS ET HIDARNE. Les Familles. 2 vols. in one. 18mo. Lyons. 1770.

DARU, P. Histoire de la Republique de Venise. 7 vols. 8vo. Paris. 1819.

D'ARVIEUX, CHEVALIER. Memoires. 6 vols. 18mo. Paris. 1735.

DARWIN, DR. ERASMUS. Phytologia. 8vo. Dublin. 1800.

DARWIN, DR. ERASMUS. Zoönomia. 2 vols. 8vo. Dublin. 1800.

DARWIN, DR. ERASMUS. The same. 2 vols. 8vo. Boston. 1809.

DAUB UND CREUZER. Studien. 6 vols. 8vo. Frankfort. 1806.

D'AUBIGNE, J. H. MERLE. History of the Reformation in Germany, France, and Switzerland. 8vo. Phila. 1843.

D'AUVIGNY. Les Vies des Hommes illustres de la France. Vols. VII and VIII. 18mo. Amsterdam. 1743.

DAVANZATI. See Tacito.

DAVENPORT, JOHN. Dictionary, English, Italian, and French. Vols. II and III in one. 8vo. London. 1828.

DAVIES, EDWARD. Celtic Researches on the Origin, Traditions, and Language of the Ancient Britons. 8vo. London. 1804.

DAVILA, D. M. Catalogue systematique et raisonné des Curiosités de la Nature et de l'Art. 3 vols. 8vo. Paris. 1767.

*DA VINCI, LEONARDO. Trattato della Pittura. 8vo. Milano. 1804.

DA VINCI, LEONARDO. Life, with a Critical Account of his Works. By J. W. Brown. 8vo. London. 1828.

DAVIS, JACOB S. Evolution of Powers. Bound with Gill's Mathematical Miscellany. Cincinnati. 1839.

DAVIS, JOHN. New England's Memorial, by Morton. 8vo. Boston. 1826.

DAVY, SIR HUMPHREY. Elements of Chemical Philosophy. Part I. Vol. I. 8vo. London. 1812.

DAWESIUS, RICARDUS. Miscellania Critica. Ed. T. Kidd. 8vo. Londini. 1827.

DAWSON, JOAN. Lexicon Novi Testamenti Alphabeticum. 8vo. Londini. 1797.

DAY, JEREMIAH. Navigation and Surveying. 8vo. New Haven. 1817.

DEAN, AMOS. Principles of Medical Jurisprudence. 8vo. Albany. 1815.

DEAN, AMOS. Lectures on Phrenology. 12mo. Albany. 1834.

DE BOYNE, CHARLE. Du Cheval en France. 8vo. Paris. 1843.

DE CALLIERES. De la Manière de négocier avec les Souverains. 2 vols. 12mo. London. 1750.

DE FOE, DANIEL. Novels. 12 vols. 18mo. Edinburgh. 1810.

DE FOE, DANIEL. Memoirs of Life and Times, with a Review of his Writings, by Walter Wilson. 3 vols. 8vo. London. 1830.

DE GENLIS, LA COMTESSE. Memoires sur le dix-huitieme siècle et la Revolution Française. 8 vols. 8vo. Paris. 1835.

DEGERANDO, LE BARON. Self-Education. 8vo. Boston. 1830.

DE GUIGNES. Histoire générale des Huns, des Turcs, et des Mogols. 5 vols. 4to. Paris. 1756–1758.

DE GUIGNES. Voyage à Peking, Manille, et l'Ile de France. 3 vols. 8vo. Paris. 1808.

*Atlas to the above. Fol. Paris. 1808.

DE KAY. Sketches of Turkey. 8vo. New York. 1833.

DELAFOND, O. Traité sur la Maladie de Poitrine du gros Betail. 8vo. Paris. 1844.

DE LAMBRE, J. B. J. Méthodes analytiques pour la détermination d'un arc du Méridien. 4to. Paris. 1799.

DE LAMBRE, J. B. J. Tables Astronomiques. 4to. Paris. 1806.

De Lambre, J. B. J. Histoire de l'Astronomie Moderne. 2 vols. 4to. Paris. 1812.

De Lambre, J. B. J. Histoire de l'Astronomie Ancienne. 2 vols. 4to. Paris. 1817.

De Lambre, J. B. J. Histoire de l'Astronomie du Moyen age. 4to. Paris. 1819.

De Lambre, J. B. J. Histoire de l'Astronomie du 18me Siècle. 4to. Paris. 1827.

De Lambre, J. B. J. Astronomie Théoretique et Practique. 3 vols. 4to. Paris. 1814.

Delano, Amasa. Voyages and Travels. 8vo. Boston. 1817.

Delille, J. Oeuvres, avec des Notes. 8vo. Paris. 1835.

De Lolme, J. L. On the Constitution of England. 8vo. London. 1822.

De Luc, J. A. Recherches sur les Modifications de l'Atmosphère. 4 vols. 8vo. Paris. 1784.

De Luc, J. A. Idées sur la Météorologie. 2 vols. 8vo. London. 1786.

De Moivre, A. Doctrine of Chances, or the Method of calculating probabilities in play. 4to. London. 1756.

De Montgon, Abbe. Memoires. 8 vols. 18mo. Lausanne. 1750–1753.

Demosthenes. Vide Oratores Graeci.

Demosthenes. Apparatus Critici, Wolfius et Taylor. 3 vols. 8vo. Lipsiae. 1774.

De Mountfort, Denys. Conchyliologie Systematique. 2 vols. 8vo. Paris. 1808.

Denham and Clapperton. Narrative of Travels and Discoveries in Northern and Central Africa. 2 vols. 8vo. London. 1828.

Denham and Clapperton. The same. 1 vol. Boston. 1826.

Denman, T. Midwifery. 8vo. Brattleboro. 1807.

Denon, Vincent. Voyage dans la Basse et la Haute Egypte. 2 vols. 8vo. Paris. 1829.

Atlas de Planches à cela. Fol. Paris. 1829.

Dens, Peter. Synopsis of Moral Theology of, by Berg. 8vo. Phila. 1842.

De Retz, Cardinal. Memoires. 4 vols. 12mo. Geneva. 1777.

Derham, W. Physico-Theology. 8vo. London. 1754.

Desault, Xavier. On Fractures, Luxations, and other Diseases of the Bones. 8vo. Phila. 1805.

Des Campes, J. B. La vie des Peintres Flamands, Allemands, et Hollandais. 4 vols. 8vo. Paris. 1753–1764.

Des Campes, J. B. Voyage pittoresque de la Flandre et du Brabant. 8vo. Paris. 1769.

Des Cartes, R. Principia Philosophiae. 4to. Amstelodami. 1677.

Des Cartes, R. Oeuvres par Cousin. 11 vols. 8vo. Paris. 1824.

Deshayes, M. G. P. Description des Coquilles charactéristiques des Terrains. 8vo. Paris. 1831.

Desmahis. Oeuvres divers. 12mo. Genève. 1762.

*Desmarest, A. G. Considérations générales sur la classe des Crustacés. 8vo. Paris. 1825.

De Tocqueville, Alexis. Democracy in America. 2 vols. 8vo. New York. 1841.

De Vega, Lope Felix. Life and Writings, by Lord Holland. 8vo. London. 1806.

Deveze. Sermons. 12mo. Autrecht. 1690.

Dewees, Wm. Treatise on Diseases of Females. 8vo. Phila. 1828.

Diaz, Burnall. True History of tho Conquest of Mexico. Transl. from the Spanish by Keatinge. 4to. London. 1800.

Dibdin, Thos. F. Reminiscences of, and of Theatres Royal, &c. 2 vols. in one. 8vo. New York. 1828.

Dibdin, T. F. Biographical, Antiquarian, and Picturesque Tour in France and Germany. 3 vols. 8vo. London. 1829.

*Dichiarazione dei Desegni del Reale Palazzo di Caserta di Carlo Re di Napoli. Fol. Napoli. 1756.

Dickinson, Baxter. Prize Letters to Students. 12mo. New York. 1831.

Dickinson, R. Elements of Geography. 8vo. Boston. 1843.

Dictionaire Universel, Contenant tous les Mots Francais. Par A. Furetiere. 3 vols. Fol. Rotterdam. 1690.

Dictionarium Hebraicum. Fol. Bisileae. 1557.

Dictionary, English. Fol. s. l. et a.

Dictionary, English-German, and German-English. 2 vols. in one. 8vo. Phila. 1835.

Dictys Cretensis et Dares Phrygius. De Bello Trojano, cum Interpretatione Annae Daceriae. 8vo. Amstelodami. 1702.

Diez, Philippus. Sermones Quadrigesimales. (Incomplete.) s. l. et a.

Digby, Sir Kenelm. Nature of Bodies and Man's Soul. 4to. Lond. 1645.

Dillwyn, L. W. Descriptive Catalogues of recent Shells. 2 vols. 8vo. London. 1817.

DIO CASSIUS COCCEIANUS. Historiarum Romanarum quae supersunt. Ed. Sturz. 8 vols. 8vo. Lipsiae. 1824.

DIO CHRYSOSTOMUS. Orationes. Ed. Reiske. 2 vols. 8vo. Lipsiae. 1798.

DIODORUS SICULUS. Bibliothecae Historicae Libri qui supersunt. Ed. Eyringius. 11 vols. 8vo. Biponti. 1793.

DIOGENES LAERTIUS. De Vitis Philosophorum. 8vo. Lipsiae. 1759.

DIONYSIUS HALICARNASSENSIS. Opera omnia, Graece et Latine. Ed. Reiské. 6 vols. 8vo. Lipsiae. 1774.

DIOPHANTES ALEXANDRINUS. Arithmeticorum libri sex, et de Numeris Multangulis liber unus. Graece et Latine. 4to. Paris. 1621.

DIOSCORIDES, P. De Materia Medica. Ed. C. Sprengel. 2 vols. 8vo. Lipsiae. 1829.

DISNEY. See Sykes.

DISPENSATORY, Edinburgh New. 8vo. Phila. 1796.

DISPENSATORY, Eclectic and General. 8vo. Phila. 1827.

DOBRIZHOFFER. See Abipones.

DOCTRINE of Baptism and the Lord's Supper. 12mo. Phila. 1811.

DODDRIDGE, PHILIP. Works. 10 vols. 8vo. Leeds. 1802.

DODDRIDGE, PHILIP. Family Expositor, Abridged. 2 vols. 8vo. Hartford. 1807.

DODDRIDGE, PHILIP. Correspondence and Diary. 5 vols. 8vo. Lond. 1829.

DODDRIDGE, PHILIP. Rise and Progress of Religion in the Soul. 12mo. Brookfield. 1810.

DODDRIDGE, PHILIP. The same. 18mo. New York. 1812.

DODWELL, E. Classical Tour through Greece. 2 vols. 4to. London. 1819.

DODSLEY, J. Collection of Poems. 6 vols. 12mo. London. 1775.

DODSLEY, J. See Old Plays.

DOMAT. Les Lois Civiles, le Droit Publique, et Legum Delectus. 2 vols. in one. Fol. Paris. 1756.

DRACO STRATONICENSIS. De Metris Poeticis. Ed. G. Hermann. 8vo. Lipsiae. 1812.

DRAKE, E. C. Universal Collection of Authentic and Entertaining Voyages and Travels, from the Earliest Accounts. Fol. London. 1768.

DRELINCOURT, C. Abrégé des Controversés. 12mo. Rotterdam. 1736.

DRUMMOND. See Herculanensia.

DRYDEN, JOHN. Prose Works, Critical and Miscellaneous, by Malone. 4 vols. 8vo. London. 1800.

DRYDEN, JOHN. Poetical Works, with Notes by the Wartons. 4 vols. 8vo. London. 1811.

DUANE. Hand Book for Infantry. 8vo. Phila. 1813.

DU BOS. Réflexions Critiques sur la Poésie et sur la Peinture. 3 vols. 18mo. Paris. 1750.

DUBUAT. Principes d'Hydraulique et de Pyrodynamique. 3 vols. 8vo. Paris. 1816.

DUCAS, THEODORE. Travels, by Mills. 2 vols. 8vo. London. 1822.

DU FIEF, M. G. Nature displayed in teaching Man Language. 2 vols. in one. 12mo. Phila. 1804.

DU FIEF, M. G. Universal and Pronouncing Dictionary of the French and English Languages. 3 vols. 12mo. Phila. 1810.

DU FRESNOY, ABBE L. Chronological Tables of Universal History. 2 vols. 8vo. London. 1762.

DU HALDE, J. B. Description Géographique et Historique de l'Empire de Chine et de la Tarterie Chinoise. 4 vols. 4to. Hague. 1736.

DU HAMEL DU MONCEAU. La Physique des Arbres. 2 vols. 4to. Paris. 1755.

DU HAMEL DU MONCEAU. Traité des Arbres et Arbustes. 2 vols. 4to. Paris. 1755.

DU HAMEL DU MONCEAU. Elémens de l'Architecture Navale. 4to. Paris. 1758.

DU HAMEL DU MONCEAU. Des Semis et Plantations des Arbres. 4to. Paris. 1760.

DUMAS, M. L'ABBE. Méthodes pour resoudre les Equations. 8vo. Riom. 1815.

DUMAS, M. J. Memoires de Chimie. 8vo. Paris. 1843.

DUMESNIL, G. Synonymes Latins. 8vo. Paris. 1813.

DUMONT, BARON. Military History of Prince Eugene and the Duke of Marlborough. Fol. London. 1736.

DUMONT, E. See Mirabeau.

DU MOULIN. De la Vocation des Pasteurs. 12mo. Sedan. 1618.

DUNCAN. Translation of Caesar. 2 vols. 16mo. New York. 1833.

DUNLAP, W. History of the American Theatre. 8vo. New York. 1832.

DUNLOP, JOHN. History of Roman Literature. 2 vols. 8vo. Phila. 1827.

DUNN, H. Guatimala. 8vo. New York. 1828.

DUPERRON, A. Oupnek 'hat, sive Theologia et Philosophia Indica. 2 vols. 4to. Argentorati. 1801–1802.

DUPIN, CHARLES. Voyages dans la Grand Bretagne entrepris relativement aux services publics de la Guerre, de la Marine, et des Ponts et Chaussées. 3 vols. 4to. Paris. 1820.

*Planches aux Voyages. Fol.

DU PONT, S. F. Report on the National Defences. Washington. 1852. (See Pamphlets.)

DUPPA. See Michael Angelo.

DUVIVIER, C. P. G. Grammaire des Grammaires. 2 vols. 8vo. Paris. 1819.

DWIGHT, DR. TIMOTHY. Travels in New England and New York. 4 vols. 8vo. New Haven. 1821.

DWIGHT, DR. TIMOTHY. Theology explained and defended in a series of Sermons. 4 vols. 8vo. New Haven. 1836.

DYCE, ALEXANDER. Remarks on Collier's and Knight's Editions of Shakspeare. 8vo. London. 1845.

DYMOND, JONATHAN. Inquiry into the Accordance of Wars with the Principles of Christianity. 8vo. Boston. 1842.

EATON, AMOS. Manual of Botany for the Northern and Middle States. 12mo. Albany. 1818.

EATON, AMOS. Botanical Dictionary. 12mo. New Haven. 1819.

EATON, AMOS. Index to the Geology of the Northern States. 12mo. Troy. 1820.

EATON, AMOS. Chemical Instructor. 12mo. Albany. 1822.

EATON, AMOS. Zoological Text-Book. 12mo. Albany. 1826.

EATON, GEN. WM. Life. 8vo. Brookfield. 1813.

ECKERMANN, N. G. C. Observationes Criticae in obscuriores quosdam Horatii et Sophoclis locos. 4to. Berolini. 1813.

ECKHEL, M. L'ABBE. Choix des pierres gravés. Fol. Vienne. 1788.

EDINBURGH ENCYCLOPÆDIA. By David Brewster. 18 vols. 4to. Phila. 1832.

EDINBURGH REVIEW. See Reviews.

EDMONSTONE, SIR A. Journey to the Oases of Upper Egypt. 8vo. London. 1822.

EDWARDS, BELA B. See Cornelius.

EDWARDS, B. B., AND PARK. Selections from German Literature. 8vo. Andover. 1839.

Edwards, Bryan. History of the British Colonies in the West Indies. 3 vols. 8vo. London. 1801.

Edwards, Bryan. See St. Domingo.

Edwards, Jonathan. Inquiry into the Freedom of the Will. 8vo. Wilmington. 1790.

Edwards, Jonathan. The same. 12mo. Andover. 1840.

Edwards, Jonathan. On Liberty and Necessity. 8vo. Worcester. 1797.

Edwards, Jonathan. Thoughts on a Revival in New England. 8vo. Worcester. 1808.

Edwards, Jonathan. Original Sin. 8vo. Worcester. s. a.

Edwards, Jonathan. On Religious Affections. 8vo. Phila. 1821.

Edwards, Jonathan. Works. 10 vols. 8vo. New York. 1830.

Edwards, Jonathan. Miscellaneous Observations on Theological Subjects. 12mo. London. 1793.

Edwards, Jonathan. Life. 12mo. Northampton. 1804.

Edwards, Peter. Candid Reasons for renouncing Anti-Pædobaptism. 12mo. Wilmington. 1806.

Egede, Hans. Description of Greenland, with Historical Introduction and a Life of the Author. 8vo. London. 1818.

Eichhorn, J. G. Allgemeine Geschichte der Cultur und Litteratur des neueren Europa. 2 vols. 8vo. Göttingen. 1796.

Elemens de Chymie, pour servir aux cours publics de l'Académie de Dijon. 4 vols. 12mo. Dijon. 1777.

Elgin, Earl of. Memorandum on his Pursuits in Greece. 8vo. London. 1815.

Ellesmere, Earl of. Guide to Northern Archaeology. 8vo. Lond. 1848.

Ellis, George. Specimens of the Early English Poets, with Sketch of the rise and progress of the English Poetry and Language. 3 vols. 12mo. London. 1811.

Ellis, George. Specimens of Early English Romances, with an Introduction. 2 vols. 12mo. London. 1811.

Ellis, Henry. Journal of the Proceedings of the late Embassy to China. 8vo. Phila. 1818.

Ellis, Henry. Original Letters illustrative of English History. 3 vols. 8vo. London. 1825.

Ellis, Henry. The same, second series. 4 vols. 8vo. London. 1827.

Ellis, J. Historical Account of Coffee. 4to. London. 1774.

*Ellis, J. Natural History of Zoophytes, arranged by Dr. Solander. 4to. London. 1786.

Ellis, Sir Henry. Account of Cædmon's Metrical Paraphrase. 4to. London. 1833.

Elmes, James. Dictionary of the Fine Arts. 8vo. London. 1826.

Eloquence of the United States. By E. B. Williston. 5 vols. 8vo. Middletown. 1827.

Elton, C. A. Specimens of the Classic Poets. 3 vols. 8vo. London. 1814.

Ely, Ezra Stiles. Ecclesiastical Proceedings of a Church in Philadelphia. 12mo. Phila. 1814.

Emerson, J. Letters from the Ægean. 8vo. New York. 1829.

Empedocles Agrigentinus, Carmina Reliquiae, Graece. Ed. Sturz. 8vo. Lipsiae. 1805.

Encyclopædia of Religious Knowledge. 8vo. Brattleborough. 1836.

Encyclopædia Metropolitana. Nos. 18, 19, 20, and 21, on Heat, Light, and Chemistry. 4to. London.

Enfield, Wm. History of Philosophy from the Earliest Periods to the beginning of the present Century. 2 vols. 4to. London. 1791.

Enfield, Wm. Institutes of Natural Philosophy. 4to. London. 1799.

England and America. Social and Political State of. 8vo. New York. 1834.

Ennius, Q. Animalium Librorum xviii Fragmenta. 8vo. Lipsiae. 1825.

Entick. New Latin-English Dictionary. Ed. Crakelt. Baltimore. 1832.

Epictetus. Dissertationum Libri iv. Graece et Latine. Ed. Schweighäuser. 5 vols. 8vo. Lipsiae. 1799.

Epicurus. Physica et Meteorologica, Graece. Ed. Schneider. 8vo. Lipsiae. 1813.

Epicurus. Fragmenta Librorum ii et xi de Natura, Graece et Latine. Ed. Orellius. 8vo. Lipsiae. 1818,

Epistolae Obscurorum Virorum. 18mo. s. l. 1556.

Ersch, J. S. Literatur der Philosophie, Philologie, und Pädegogik. 8vo. Leipsig. 1822.

Eschemayer, C. A. Die Hegel'sche Religions-Philosophie, verglichen mit dem Christlichen Princip. 8vo. Tübingen. 1834.

Espy, James P. Reports on Meteorology. (2d and 3d.) 4to. s. l. et a.

Essais de Morale. 8 vols. 12mo. Paris. 1682.

Etymologicon Magnum. Ed. Sylburgius. 4to. Lipsiae. 1816.

Etymologicum Gudianum Graecae Linguae. Ed. Sturzius. 4to. Lipsiae. 1818.

Etymologicon, Orionis Thebani. Ed. Wolfius. 4to. Lipsiae. 1820.

ETYMOLOGICON MAGNUM. An English Work. Cambridge, Eng. s. a.

EUCLIDE. Oeuvres, en Grec, en Latin, et en Français. 3 vols. 4to. Paris. 1813–1818.

EUGENIE, JEUNE. Report on the case of, by Mason. 8vo. Boston. 1832.

EULER, LEONARD. Mechanica. 2 vols. 4to. Petropoli. 1736.

EULER, LEONARD. Tentamen Novae Theoriae Musicae. 4to. Petropoli. 1739.

EULER. Methodus inveniendi Lineas Curvas. 4to. Genevae. 1744.

EULER. Opuscula. 2 copies. 4to. Berolini. 1746.

EULER. Opuscula et Conjectura physica circa propogationem Soni et Luminis, una cum aliis Dissertationibus Analyticis. 4to. Bero. 1746–1750.

EULER. Introductio in Analysin Infinitorum. 2 vols. in one. 4to. Lausannae. 1748.

EULER. Scientia Navalis. 2 vols. 4to. Petropoli. 1749.

EULER. Institutiones Calculi Differentialis, et ejus usus in Analysi finitorum ac doctrina Serierum. 4to. Petropoli. 1755.

EULER. Dioptricae. 3 vols. 4to. Petropoli. 1769–1771.

EULER. Construction des Vaisseaux. 8vo. Paris. 1776.

EULER. Elémens d'Algèbre. 2 vols. 8vo. Paris. 1807.

EURIPIDES. Tragoediae et Fragmenta, Graece. Ed. Matthias. 9 vols. 8vo. Lipsiae. 1813.

EURIPIDES. Iphigenia in Aulide. Ed. Hermann. 8vo. Lipsiae. 1831.

EURIPIDES. Hecuba. Ed. Hermann. 8vo. Lipsiae. 1831.

EURIPIDES. Translation of, by Potter. 3 vols. 16mo. New York. 1836.

EUSEBIUS, PAMPHILUS. Evangelica Praeparatio et Demonstratio, Graece. Fol. Paris. 1544–1545.

EUSEBIUS, PAMPHILUS. Historia Ecclesiastica. Coloniae Allob. 1612.

EUTROPIUS. Breviarium Historiae Romanae, cum Metaphrasi Graeca Paeanii. Ed. Havercampus. 8vo. Lugduni Batav. 1729.

EVELYN, JOHN. Sylva, or a Discourse on Forest Trees. 4to. York. 1786.

EVELYN, JOHN. Memoirs. Diary from 1641–1706. 5 vols. 8vo. London. 1827.

EVENEMENS MILITAIRES. 2 vols. 8vo. Hamburgh. 1769.

EVERETT, A. H, Europe. 8vo. Boston. 1822.

EVERETT, A. H. New Ideas on Population. 8vo. Boston. 1823.

EVERETT, A. H. America. 8vo. Phila. 1827.

EWELL, THOS. Elements or Principles of Modern Chemistry. 8vo. New York. 1806,

EWING, ALEXANDER. Practical Astronomy. 8vo. Edinburgh. 1797.

EXCERPTA quaedam e Scriptoribus Latinis probatioribus. 8vo. Bostoniae. 1810.

EXHORTATION to the Inhabitants of the South Parish of Glasgow. 12mo. Glasgow. 1751.

EXLEY, THOS. Principles of Natural Philosophy. 8vo. London. 1829.

EXPOSITION des Produits de l'Industrie Française. (1844.) Vol. III. 8vo. Paris. 1844.

FABER, B. Thesaurus Eruditionis Scholasticae. 2 vols. Fol. Francofurti. 1749.

FABER, GEORGE S. View of the Prophecies. 2 copies. 8vo. Boston. 1809.

FABLIAUX, ou Contes du XIIme et du XIIIme Siècle, par Le Grande D'Aussy. 4 vols. 12mo. Paris. 1779–1781.

FABRICIUS, J. A. Bibliotheca Latina. Ed. Ernesti. 3 vols. 8vo. Lipsiae. 1773.

FAGNANI, PROSPER. Commentarii in Secundum Librum Decretalium. Fol. Coloniae. 1681.

FAGNANI, PROSPER. Jus Canonicum. Fol. Coloniae. 1681.

FAGNANI, PROSPER. Commentarii in Quartum Librum Decretalium. Fol. Coloniae. 1682.

FAIRFAX. See Tasso.

FALCONER, WILLIAM. The Shipwreck. 18mo, New York. 1800.

FARADAY, MICHAEL. Chemical Manipulations. 8vo. London. 1830.

FARADAY, MICHAEL. Experimental Researches in Electricity. 2 vols. 8vo. London. 1839.

FARMER, JOHN. Genealogical Register of the First Settlers of New England. 8vo. Lancaster. 1829.

FARMER'S ENCYCLOPÆDIA. 8vo. Phila. 1844.

FARRAR, TIMOTHY. Report of the Case of the Trustees of Dartmouth College. 8vo. Portsmouth. 1819.

FAWCETT, JOSEPH. Sermons. 2 vols. 8vo. London. 1801.

FEDER, J. G. Ueber Raum und Caussalität. 12mo. Göttingen. 1787.

FEDERALIST. On the New Constitution. 8vo. Hallowell. 1831.

FELIBIEN. Entretiens sur les Vies et sur les Ouvrages des plus excellens Peintres anciens et modernes, avec la Vie des Architects. 6 vols. 18mo. Trevoux. 1725.

FELLTHAM, OWEN. Resolves; Divine, Moral, and Political. 8vo. London. 1820.

FELT, JOSEPH B. Massachusetts Currency. 8vo. Boston. 1839.

FENELON. Oeuvres, précédés d'Etudes sur sa vie par M. Aimé-Martin. 3 vols. 8vo. Paris. 1835.

FENN, JOSEPH. Elements of Numerical Arithmetic. 4to. Dublin. s. a.

FENN, JOSEPH. System of Algebra. 4to. Dublin, s. a.

FERGUSON'S Astronomy explained on Newton's Principles, with notes by Brewster. 2 vols. 8vo. Edinburgh. 1811.

*Plates to the above by Brewster. 4to. Edinburgh. 1811.

FERGUSON, ADAM. Institutes of Moral Philosophy. 12mo. Edinburgh. 1785.

FESSENDEN, THOMAS. Science of Sanctity. 8vo. Brattleboro. 1804.

FICHTE, J. G. Ueber die Bestimmung des Gelehrten. 12mo. Jena. 1794.

FICHTE, J. G. Ueber das Wesen des Gelehrten. 12mo. Berlin. 1806.

FICHTE, J. G. Leben und Litterarischer Briefwechsel. 2 vols. 12mo. Sulzbach. 1830.

FIELDING, HENRY. Works, with Introductory Essay by Murphy. 10 vols. 8vo. London. 1821.

FILICAIA, VINCENZODA. Poesie Toscane. 2 vols. 18mo. Firenze. 1827.

FIORILLO, J. D. Geschichte der Zeichnender Künste. 4 vols. 8vo. Hanover. 1815.

FISK, NATHAN. 22 Sermons. 8vo. Worcester. 1794.

FITZ-OSBORNE, THOS. Letters, by Melmoth. 8vo. London. 1773.

FLAVEL, JOHN. The Whole Works of. 2 vols. Fol. London. 1740.

FLAXMAN, J. Lectures on Sculpture. 8vo. London. 1839.

FLEMING, ROBERT. Fulfilling of the Scripture. 12mo. Boston. 1743.

FLEMING, ROBERT. Epistolary Discourse, as Assistance to the Christian's Faith. 18mo. London. 1692.

FLETCHER OE SALTOUN, and the Poet THOMPSON. Essays on the Lives and Writings of, by David Stuart, Earl of Buchan. 8vo. London. 1792.

FLETCHER, WILLIAM. Twenty Sermons. 8vo. Dublin. 1772.

FLINDERS, MATTHEW. Voyage to Terra Australis. 2 vols. 4to. London. 1814.

*Atlas to the above. Fol.

FLINT, ABEL. System of Geometry, Trigonometry, and Surveying. 8vo. Hartford. 1813.

FLINT, TIMOTHY. History and Geography of the Mississippi Valley. 2 vols. in one. 8vo. Cincinnati. 1832.

FLÖGEL, C. F. Geschichte der Romischen Litteratur. 4 vols. 8vo. Leipzig. 1784.

FLORUS, L. A. Epitome Rerum Romanarum. 2 vols. in one. 8vo. Amstelodami. 1702.

FLORUS, L. A. Idem, ill. Anna T. Fabri filia. 8vo. Londini. 1714.

FLORUS, L. A. Idem, et Lucii Ampelii Liber memorialis. 8vo. Argentorati. 1810.

FLOWER, B. French Constitution. 8vo. London. 1792.

FONTENELLE. Oeuvres. 8 vols. 8vo. 1790–1792.

FOOTE, W. H. Historical and Biographical Account of North Carolina. 8vo. New York. 1846.

FORCELLINUS, AEGIDIUS. Totius Latinitatis Lexicon. 4 vols. Fol. Schneebergae. 1831–1835.

FORD, JOHN. Dramatic Works. Ed. by Henry Weber. 2 vols. 8vo. Edinburgh. 1811.

FORDYCE, GEORGE. Five Dissertations on Fever. 8vo. Boston. 1815.

FORDYCE, J. Addresses to Young Men. 12mo. Boston. s. a.

FORNMANNA SÖGUR. 8vo. Kaupmannahofn. 1828.

FORSKAEL, PETRUS. Descriptiones Animalium, Avium, Insectorum, et Vermium quae in Itinere Orientali observavit. 4to. Hanniae. 1775.

FORSKAEL PETRUS. Flora Aegyptiaco-Arabica. 4to. Hanniae. 1775.

FORSTER, THOS. Researches about Atmospheric Phenomena. 8vo. London. 1813.

FORSYTH, JOSEPH. Remarks on Antiquities, Arts, and Letters, made during an Excursion into Italy. 8vo. Boston. 1818.

FORTEGUERRI, NICCOLO. Il Ricciardetto. 3 vols. 18mo. Venezia. 1789.

FOSTER, JOHN. Essay on Accent and Quantity. 8vo. London. 1820.

FOSTER, M. Report of the Trial of the Rebels of 1746. 8vo. Lond. 1776.

FOX, JOHN. Book of Martyrs. Fol. London. 1732.

FRANCESON, C. T. Essai sur Homère. 12mo. Berlin. 1818.

FRANCIA, DR. Reign of, in Paraguay. 8vo. London. 1827.

FRANCOEUR, L. B. Goniometrie. 8vo. Paris. 1820.

FRANCOEUR, L. B. Astronomie Practique. 8vo. Paris. 1830.

FRANKIUS, JOHANNES. Tenebrae Lucidae. 4to. Lipsiae. 1710.

FRANKLIN, BENJAMIN. Works and Life, by J. Sparks. 5 vols. 8vo. Boston. 1837.

FRANKLIN, JOHN. Narrative of a Journey to the Shores of the Polar Sea. 4to. London. 1823.

FRANKLIN, JOHN. Narrative of Second Voyage to the Shores of the Polar Sea. 4to. London. 1828.

FRASER, J. B. Tour through the Himmalaya Mountains. 4to. Lond. 1820.

FREEMASONRY, by a Master Mason. 8vo. New York.. 1828.

FREEMASONRY. Letters on. 8vo. Boston. 1849.

FRIES, JACOB. Logik. 8vo. Heidelberg. 1811.

FRIES, JACOB. Die Mathematische Natur-Philosophie. 8vo. Heidelberg. 1822.

FRIES, JACOB. Metaphysik. 8vo. Heidelberg. 1824.

FRIES, JACOB. Kritik der Vernunft. 3 vols. 8vo. Heidelberg. 1828.

FRIES, JACOB. System der Philosophie. 12mo. Leipzig. 1804.

FRISBIE, PROF. Miscellaneous Writings, and Life by Norton. 8vo. Boston. 1823.

FRÖMMICHEN, C. H. Philosophia Academica. 4to. Gottingae. 1770.

FRONTINUS, SEXTIUS JULIUS. Opera. Stud. Soc. Bipont. 8vo. Biponti. 1788.

FUELLEBORN, G. G. Beiträge zur Geschichte der Philosophie. 10 vols. in 9. 8vo. Jena. 1799.

FULLER, ANDREW. Works. 8 vols. 8vo. Phila. 1820.

FULLER, ANDREW. Defence of a Treatise on the Gospel of Christ. 12mo. Phila. 1810.

FULLER, THOS. Church History of Great Britain from the birth of Jesus Christ to the year 1648. 4to. London. 1655.

FULLER, THOS. History of the Worthies of England. 2 vols. 4to. London. 1811.

FULLER, THOS. Introduction to Prudence. 18mo. London. 1815.

FUNCCIUS, JOHN NIC. De Pueritia Latinae Linguae. 4to. Marburgi. 1720.

FUNCCIUS, JOHN NIC. De Origine et Pueritia Latinae Linguae Libri duo. 4to. Marburgi. 1735.

FUNCCIUS, JOHN NIC. De imminente Latinae Linguae Senectute. 4to. Marburgi. 1736.

FURLONG, LAWRENCE. American Coast Pilot. 8vo. Newburyport. 1804.

FUSELI, HENRY. Life and Writings, by John Knowles. 3 vols. 8vo. Lond. 1831.

GABLER, G. A. System der Theoretischen Philosophie. 8vo. Erlangen. 1827.

GAIUS ET JUSTINIANUS. Institutiones Juris Romani. 4to. Berolini. 1829.

GALE, THEOPHILUS. Court of the Gentiles. 4 vols. 4to. Oxford. 1669.

GALENUS. Adhortatio ad Artes. Ed. Willet. 8vo. Lugduni. 1812.

GALILEO GALILEI. Mathematical Discourses. 4to. London. 1730.

GALILEO GALILEI. Opere. 13 vols. 8vo. Milano. 1808–1811.

GALLEY. Dissertations against Greek Accents. Bound with J. Foster.

GALLUP, J. A. Sketches of Epidemic Diseases in Vermont. 2 copies. 8vo. Boston. 1815.

GARDINER, COL. JAMES. Life, by Dr. Doddridge. 12mo. Phila. 1795.

GARDINER, JOHN. Inquiry into the Cause and Cure of the Gout. 12mo. Phila. 1793.

GASSENDUS PETRUS. Opera omnia. 6 vols. Fol. Lugduni. 1658.

GASSENDUS, PETRUS. Institutio Astronomica. 12mo. London. 1653.

GAUSS, C. F. Recherches Arithmétiques. 4to. Paris. 1807.

GAUSS, C. F. Theoria Motus Corporum Celestium in Sectionibus conicis Solem ambientium. 4to. Hambergae. 1809.

GAUSS, C. F. Determinatio Attractionis. 4to. Gottingae. 1818.

GEDDES, ALEXANDER. Memoirs of Life and Writings, by J. N. Good. 8vo. London. 1803.

GELL, W. Geography and Antiquities of Ithaca. 4to. London. 1807.

GELL, W. The Itinerary of Greece. 4to. London. 1810.

*GELL, W. Pompeiana. 2 vols. 8vo. London. 1835.

GELLERT, C. F. Schriften. 10 vols. Vols. I and III wanting. 12mo. Reuttlingen. 1786.

GELLIUS, AULIUS. Noctes Atticae. Ed. Lion. 8vo. Gottingae. 1825.

GENESIS of the World. Divine History of. 4to. London. 1670.

GENLIS, MADAME DE. Le Siége de la Rochelle, ou le Malheur et la Conscience. 2 vols. 12mo. Paris. 1823.

GEOLOGICAL REPORT on the elevated Country between the Missouri and Red Rivers. By Featherstonhaugh. 8vo. Washington. 1835.

GEOLOGICAL SURVEY of Wisconsin, Iowa, and Minnesota. Fol. Phila. 1852.

Illustrations of the above. Fol. Phila. 1852.

GEOLOGICAL SURVEY of the District adjoining the Eric Canal. Part I. 8vo. Albany. 1824.

Geological Survey of New York. Reports to the Assembly for years 1837–1841 inclusive. 5 vols. 8vo.

Plates to the above. 4to.

Geology. Lectures on, by Dr. J. Van Rensalaer. 8vo. New York. 1825.

Geology.

Of South Carolina. Report by M. Tuomey. 4to. Columbia. 1848.

Of Connecticut. Report by J. G. Percival. 8vo. New Haven. 1832.

Of Massachusetts. Report by Edward Hitchcock. 8vo. Amherst. 1835.

Of Massachusetts. Economical, Reëxamination by Hitchcock. 8vo. Boston. 1838.

Of Massachusetts. Final Report, by Hitchcock. 2 vols. 4to. Northampton. 1841.

*Plates illustrative of the Geology and Scenery of Massachusetts. 4to.

Of Maine. First Report, by C. F. Jackson. 8vo. Augusta. 1837.

Of do. Second Report, do. 8vo. Augusta. 1838.

Of do. Third Report, do. 2 copies. 8vo. Augusta. 1839.

Of Aroostook County, by E. Holmes. 8vo. Augusta. 1839.

Atlas of Plates for Geol. of Maine. 4to.

Of Maine and Massachusetts Lands. Second Annual Report by C. F. Jackson. 8vo. Augusta. 1838.

Maps and Charts accompanying the above.

Of Green Bay and Wisconsin Territory, by G.W. Featherstonhaugh. 8vo. Washington. 1836.

Of Michigan. Second Annual Report of the State Geologist, D. Houghton. 8vo. Detroit. 1839.

Of New Jersey. Final Report of H. D. Rogers. 8vo. Phila. 1840.

Of Vermont. First Annual Report by C. B. Adams. 8vo. Burlington. 1845.

Second do. 8vo. Burlington. 1846.

Third do. 8vo. Burlington. 1847.

Geology and Mineralogy of Boston and Vicinity, by F. and S. L. Dana. 8vo. Boston. 1818.

Georgia Historical Society. Collections. 3 vols. 8vo. Savannah. 1840–1848.

Gera, Dr. F. de Conegliano. La Fabrication du Fromage. 8vo. Paris. 1843.

Gerard, G. Institutes of Biblical Criticism. 8vo. Boston. 1823.

GERVAISE, D. Lettres d'un Théologien. 5 vols. 12mo. Paris. 1724.

GESANGBUCH der Ev. Reformirten Gemeinen in den V. S. von America. 12mo. Germantaun. 1813.

GIBBON, EDWARD. Decline and Fall of the Roman Empire. 12 vols. 8vo. London. 1821.

GIBBONS, THOS. Juvenilia. (Poems.) 12mo. London. 1750.

GIBBS, JOSIAH. A Manual Hebrew and English Lexicon. 8vo. Andover. 1828.

GIBSON, EDMUND. Codex Juris Ecclesiastici Anglicani. 2 vols. Fol. Oxford. 1761.

GIBSON, ROBERT. A Treatise of Practical Surveying. 8vo. New York. 1803.

GIFFORD, WILLIAM. Baviad and Maeviad. 18mo. London. 1800.

GILBERTUS, GULIELMUS. Tractatus de Magnete. Sedini. 1628.

GIL BLAS. Aventuras. 4 vols. 32mo. Paris. 1826.

GILL, C. Mathematical Miscellany. Vols. I and II, bound in one. 8vo. New York. 1836–1839.

GILLIES, JOHN. History of Ancient Greece, its Colonies and Conquests till the Division of the Macedonian Empire in the East, including the History of Literature, Philosophy, and the Fine Arts. 4 vols. 8vo. New York. 1814. (Vol. III wanting.)

*GILPIN, W. On the Highlands of Scotland. 8vo. London. 1792.

*GILPIN, W. Observations on the River Wye. 8vo. London. 1800.

*GILPIN, W. Essay on Prints. 8vo. London. 1802.

*GILPIN, W. Observations on the Coast of Hampshire, Sussex, and Kent. 8vo. London. 1804.

*GILPIN, W. Two Essays on Landscape Drawing. 8vo. London. 1804.

*GILPIN, W. Three Essays on Picturesque Beauty. 8vo. London. 1808.

*GILPIN, W. Observations on the Western Parts of England. 8vo. Lond. 1808.

*GILPIN, W. Observations on Cumberland and Westmoreland. 2 vols. 8vo. London. 1808.

*GILPIN, W. Forest Scenery. 2 vols. 8vo. London. 1808.

*GILPIN, W. Observations on the Counties of Essex, Suffolk, Norfolk, and South Wales. 8vo. London. 1809.

GIRARD, STEPHEN. Arguments and Judgment on the Will of. 8vo. Phila. 1844.

Gisborne, Thos. Christian Survey of the Christian Religion. 12mo. New York. 1807.

Glanville, Joseph. Scepsis Scientifica. 4to. London. 1665.

Gnomici Poetae Graeci. Ed. Brunck. 12mo. Argentorati. 1784.

Goddard, Thomas H. General History of the Banks in Europe. 8vo. New York. 1831.

Godman, J. D. American Natural History. 3 vols. 8vo. Phila. 1826.

Godwin, Wm. Enquiry concerning Political Justice. 8vo. London. 1796.

Godwin, Wm. Essays on Education, Manners, and Literature. 8vo. Lond. 1797.

Goethe. Memoirs, written by himself. 8vo. New York. 1824.

Goethe. Faust, a Dramatic Poem, transl. by Hayward. 8vo. London. 1834.

Goethe. Werke. 55 vols. 12mo. Stuttgart und Tübingen. 1827–1834.

Goethe. Inhalts-und Namen-Verzeichnisse über Goetheschen Werke. 12mo. Stuttgart und Tübingen. 1835.

Goethe, Wilhelm Meister's Apprenticeship, transl. by Carlyle. 3 vols. 18mo. Boston. 1828.

Goguet. De l'Origine des Lois, des Artes, et des Sciences. 3 vols. 4to. Paris. 1758.

Goldoni, Carlo. Commedie Scelte. 4 vols. 8vo. Milano. 1821.

Goldsmith, Rev. J. Geographical View of the World. 12mo. New York. 1826.

Good, John M. Book of Nature. 2 vols. 8vo. Boston. 1826.

Goodrich, C. A. Elements of Greek Grammar. 8vo. Hartford. 1828.

Gordon, P. Geographical Grammar. 8vo. London. 1741.

Gorham, John. Elements of Chemical Science. 2 vols. 8vo. Boston. 1819.

Goring and Pritchard. Microscopic Illustrations. 8vo. London. 1830.

Görres, J. Altteutsche Volks und Meisterlieder. 8vo. Frankf. a. M. 1817.

Gozzi, Gasparo. Opere Scelte. 5 vols. 8vo. Milano. 1821.

Graham, James. The Sabbath, a Poem. 18mo. New York. 1805.

Graham, James D. Observations on Magnetic Dip. 4to. Phila. 1846.

Graham, Wm. S. Remains, with a Memoir by Prof. Allen. 12mo. Phila. 1849.

Grant, Robert. History of the East India Company. 8vo. London. 1813.

Grattan, Henry. Speeches. 4 vols. 8vo. London. 1822.

Gravina Vincenzo. Della Ragion Poetica Libri due, et della Tragedia Libro uno. 4to. Venezia. 1731.

GRAY, ALONZO. Elements of Chemistry. 12mo. New York. 1841.

GRAY, J. Priesthoods of Jesus Christ and Melchisedeck. 12mo. Phila. 1810.

GREECE, MODERN. History of, with Geography, Antiquities, and present Condition. 8vo. Boston. 1827.

GREEN, RICHARD W. The Scholar's Companion. 12mo. Phila. 1836.

GREENE, GEN. NATHANIEL. Life, by Caldwell. 8vo. Phila. 1819.

GREENEWAY, R. Annals of Tacitus. Fol. London. 1612.

GREENHOW, ROBERT. Memoir, Historical and Political, of the North-west Coast of North America. 8vo. Washington. 1840.

GREENHOW, ROBERT. History of Oregon, California, and other North-west Territories. 8vo. Boston. 1844.

GREENLAND. History of, and of the Mission carried on there for thirty years by the Unitas-Fratrum. By David Crantz. 2 vols. 8vo. London. 1767.

GREEN MOUNTAIN GEM, 1843. 4to. Bradford, Vt.

GREEN MOUNTAIN GEM, 1846–1849. 8vo. Bradford, Vt.

GREEN MOUNTAIN REPOSITORY for the year 1832. Ed. by Z. Thompson. 12mo. Burlington.

GREENOUGH, G. B. Critical Examination of the first Principles of Geology. Fol. London. 1819.

GREGOIRE, H. Enquiry into the Intellectual and Moral Faculties of Negroes. 8vo. Brooklyn. 1810.

GREGOIRE, H. Histoire des Sectes Religieuses. 2 vols. 8vo. Paris. 1810.

GREGORIUS CORINTHUS, et alii Grammatici. Libri de Dialectis Linguae Graecae. Ed. Schäffer. 8vo. Lipsiae. 1811.

GREGORIUS NAZIANZENUS. Omnia quae reperiuntur. Fol. s. l. 1550.

GREGORY, GEORGE. Elements of the Theory and Practice of Physic, with Notes by Peixotto. 8vo. New York. 1830.

GREGORY, OLINTHUS. Mechanics. 2 vols. 8vo. London. 1826.

Plates to the above. 8vo. London. 1826.

GRELLMANN, H. M. G. Dissertation on Gypsies. Transl. from the German by Raper. 4to. London. 1787.

GRESSET. Oeuvres. 2 vols. 8vo. Paris. 1811.

GRESWELL, W. P. Annals of Parisian Typography. 8vo. London. 1818.

GREY, RICHARD. Memoria Technica. 12mo. Dublin. 1796.

GRIMKE, T. S. Character and Objects of all Science and Literature. 12mo. New Haven. 1831.

Grimm et Diderot. Correspondance litteraire, philosophique, et critique, depuis 1753 jusqu'à 1790. 15 vols. 8vo. Paris. 1829–1831.

Grimm et Diderot. Correspondance inedite, et Recueil de Lettres, Poesies, Morceaux, et Fragmens retranchés par la Censure Imperiale. 8vo. Paris. 1829.

Grosvenor, Benjamin. The Mourner. 18mo. Andover. 1838.

Grotius, Hugo. Opera omnia Theologica. 3 vols. Fol. Amstelodami. 1679.

Grotius, Hugo. De Jure Belli ac Pacis. 8vo. Amstelodami. 1679.

Gualtierus, Nicolaus. Index Testarum Conchyliorum. Fol. Florentiae. 1742.

Guerard, A. Essai sur l'Histoire du Droit privé des Romains. 8vo. Paris. 1841.

Guicciardini. Historie of the Warres of Italie, reduced into English by Geffray Fenton. Fol. London. 1718.

Guicciardini. Storia d'Italia, dal 1490 al 1534. 6 vols. 8vo. Paris. 1832.

Guilford, Baron; Francis North; Sir Dudley North; and Dr. J. North; Lives, by R. North. 3 vols. 8vo. London. 1826.

Guion, Lady. Life, and Lives of Fénelon, Molino, and Ste. Teresa. 8vo. New York. 1821.

Guischard, C. Memoires Militaires sur les Grecs et les Romains. 2 vols. 8vo. Lyons. 1760.

Gummere, John. Surveying. 8vo. Phila. 1814.

Gurney, Jos. J. On the Sabbath, with notes by M. Stuart. 12mo. Andover. 1833.

Guthrie, Wm. Christian's great Interest. 12mo. Andover. 1815.

Gutzlaff, Chas. Sketch of Chinese History, Ancient and Modern. 8vo. London. 1834.

Gwilt, J. On the Equilibrium of Arches. 8vo. London. 1826.

Hackett, H. B. Chaldee Grammar by Winer. 8vo. Andover. 1845.

Hackett, H. B. Commentary on the Acts of the Apostles. 8vo. Boston. 1852.

Hackett, H. B. Plutarch de Sera Numinis Vindicta, with notes. 12mo. Andover. 1844.

Hackett, H. B. Exercises on Hebrew Grammar. 12mo. Andover. 1847.

HAIGH, JAMES. The Dyer's Assistant. 12mo. Phila. 1810.

HAKLUYT, RICHARD. Collection of the Early Voyages, Travels, and Discoveries of the English Nation. 5 vols. 4to. London. 1809.

HALES, STEPHEN. Statistical Tables of Vegetables. 8vo. London. 1731.

HALFDANASAGA BRONUFOSTRA. (Incomplete.) 8vo.

HALL, GORDON. Memoirs by Bardwell. 12mo. New York. 1841.

HALL, JOSEPH. Memoirs of Life and Writings, by Jones. 8vo. London. 1826.

HALL, JOSEPH. Satires. 12mo. Chiswick. 1824.

HALL, M. Principles of Diagnosis. 8vo. New York. 1835.

HALLAM, HENRY. The Middle Ages. 4 vols. 8vo. Phila. 1821.

HALLAM, HENRY. Constitutional History of England from Henry VII to George II, inclusive. 3 vols. 8vo. London. 1829.

HALLEY, EDMUND. Astronomical Tables. 4to. London. 1752.

HALYBURTON, THOS. Principles of Modern Deists. 8vo. Albany. 1812.

HAMANN. Schriften, von Roth. 7 vols. 12mo. Berlin. 1821.

HAMILTON, FRANCIS. An Account of the Kingdom of Nepal. 4to. Edinburgh. 1819.

HAMILTON, WM. History of Medicine, Surgery, and Anatomy. 2 vols. 8vo. 1831.

HAMMOND, HENRY. Works. Fol. London. 1684.

HAMPDEN, JOHN. Some Memorials of, by Lord Nugent. 2 vols. in one. 8vo. London. 1832.

HANCOCK, THOS. On Peace. 12mo. Boston. 1843.

HARBOR MAPS.

Of Oyster Bay, Long Island. 1847.

Of Holmes' Hole and Tarpaulin Cove. 1847.

Of New London, Conn., by Lieut. Blake. 1848.

HARLAN, RICHARD. Fauna Americana; being a description of the Mammiferous Animals of North America. 8vo. Phila. 1825.

HARLEIAN MISCELLANY. 12 vols. 8vo. London. 1808–1814.

HARLES, T. C. Introductio in Historiam Linguae Graecae. 2 vols. 8vo. Altenburgi. 1792.

Supplementum. 2 vols. in one. 8vo. Genae. 1804.

HARLES, T. C. Brevior Notitia Litteraturae Romanae. 8vo. Lipsiae. 1789.

Supplementa. 3 vols. 8vo. Lipsiae. 1799.

HARMON, D. W. Journal of Voyages and Travels in the Interior of North America. 8vo. Andover. 1820.

HARMONY of the Gospels in Greek, by Wm. Newcomb. 4to. Andover. 1814.

HARRINGTON, JAMES. Works. Fol. London. 1737.

HARRIS, JAMES. Miscellanies. 4 vols. 8vo. London. 1783.

HARRIS, JOHN. Voyages and Travels. 2 vols. Fol. London. 1744.

HARRIS, T. M. Discourses on Free Masonry. 8vo. Charlestown. 1801.

HARRIS, T. M. Journal of a Tour into the Territory North-west of the Alleghany Mountains. 8vo. Boston. 1805.

HART, NATHANIEL C. Documents relative to the House of Refuge. 8vo. New York. 1832.

HARTLY, DAVID. Observations on Man. 3 vols. 8vo. London. 1801.

HARTSHORNE, C. H. Ancient Metrical Tales. 12mo. London. 1829.

HARTUNG, J. A. Lehre von den Partikeln der Griechischen Sprache. 2 vols. 8vo. Erlangen. 1832.

HARVARD UNIVERSITY.

Annnal Report of the President to the Overseers for 1825. 8vo. Cambridge. 1827.

History of, by B. Pierce. 8vo. Cambridge. 1833.

History of, by Josiah Quincy. 8vo. Cambridge. 1840.

HASKEL, DANIEL. Gazeteer of the U. S., and Maps.

HASKINS, R. W. History and Progress of Phrenology. 12mo. Buffalo. 1839.

HASLEWOOD, JOSEPH. Ancient Critical Essays upon English Poets and Poesy, edited by. 2 vols. 4to. London. 1811–1815. Containing:

I. The Arte of English Poesie, by George Puttenham. Lond. 1589.

II. Certayne Notes of Instruction concerning the making of Verse or Ryme in English, by George Gascoigne. London. 1575.

III. A Discourse of English Poetrie, by William Webbe. Lond. 1586.

IV. A Treatise of the Airt of Scottis Poesie, by King James. Edinb. 1584.

V. An Apologie of Poetrie, by Sir John Harrington. s. l. 1591.

VI. A comparative Discourse of our English Poets with the Greeke, Latine, and Italian Poets, by Francis Meres. London. 1598.

VII. Observations in the Art of English Poesie, by Thomas Campion. London. 1602.

VIII. A Defence of Rhyme, (against the above "Observations,") by Sa: D. London. 1603.

IX. Hypercritica, or a Rule of Judgment for writing, or reading our History's, by Edmund Bolton. Oxford. 1722.

HASLEWOOD, JOSEPH—Continued.

X. Three proper, and wittie familiar Letters, (between Edmund Spenser and Gabriel Harvey). London. 1580.

XI. Two other very commendable Letters of the same mens writing. London. 1580.

HAUY, M. L'ABBE. Traité de Cristallographie. 2 vols. 8vo. Paris. 1822.

HAWEIS, REV. T. History of the Church of Christ. 2 vols. 8vo. Baltimore. 1807.

HAWKS, F. L. Contributions to the Ecclesiastical History of the U. S. A. 2 vols. in one. 8vo. New York. 1836.

HAY, BISHOP. The pious Christian instructed. 12mo. Phila. 1800.

HAYDEN, HORACE H. Geological Essays. 8vo. Baltimore. 1820.

HAZEN, EDWARD. Panorama of Professions and Trades. 4to. Phila. 1826.

HAZLITT, WM. Lectures on the English Comic Writers. 8vo. Phila. 1819.

HEAD, CAPT. F. B. Journey to the Pampas and the Andes. 8vo. Boston. 1827.

HEARNE, SAML. Journey to the Northern Ocean in the years 1769–1772. 4to. London. 1795.

HEARNE, THOMAS. Works. See Langtoft and Robert of Gloucester.

HEBER, REGINALD. Narrative of a Journey through the upper Provinces of India. 3 vols. 8vo. London. 1828.

HEBER, REGINALD. Life and Writings, by his Widow. Vol. I. 8vo. New York. 1830.

HEBREW GRAMMAR. By I. Lyons and R. Grey. 8vo. Boston. 1763.

HEEREBORD, A. Meletemata Philosophica. 4to. Neomagi. 1665.

HEEREN, A. H. L. Geschichte des Studiums der Griechischen und Romischen Litteratur. 2 vols. 8vo. Göttingen. 1801.

HEEREN, A. H. L. Ideen Ueber die Politik den Verkehr und den Handel der Vornehmsten Völker der Alten Welt. 5 vols. 8vo. Göttingen. 1824.

HEEREN, A. H. L. Commentatio de Fontibus Geographicorum Ptolemaei. 4to. Gottingae. 1827.

HEEREN, A. H. L. De iisdem et auctoritate Vitarum parallelarum Plutarchi. 8vo. Gottingae. 1827.

HEEREN, A. H. L. Manual of the History of the Political System of Europe and its Colonies. 2 vols. 8vo. Oxford. 1834.

HEGEL, G. W. F. Werke. 13 vols. 8vo. Berlin. 1832–1836.

HEGEWISCH, D. H. Einleitung in die Historische Chronologie. 8vo. Altona. 1811.

HEINE, H. Romantische Schule. 12mo. Hamburg. 1836.

HELLANICUS LESBIUS. Fragmenta. Ed. Sturz. 8vo. Lipsiae. 1826.

HENNICKE, J. F. Commentatio de Geographica Africae Herodotea. 4to. Gottingae. s. a.

HENRY VII. Histoire de, par Marsolier. 18mo. Paris. 1700.

HENRY, ROBERT. History of Great Britain. 12 vols. 8vo. London. 1805–1806.

HENRY, T. CHARLTON. Letters to an anxious Inquirer. 8vo. Charleston. 1827.

HENRY, WILLIAM. An Epitome of Chemistry. 8vo. New York. 1808.

HENRY, WILLIAM. Elements of Chemistry. (Title page wanting.)

HEPHAESTION ALEXAND. Enchiridion. Ed. Gaisford. 8vo. Oxoniae. 1810.

HERACLIDES PONTICUS. Fragmenta de rebus publicis. Ed. Köler. 8vo. Halae. 1804.

HERACLIDES PONTICUS. Allegoriae Homericae. Ed. Heyne. 12mo. Gottingae. 1782.

HERACLITUS, et Anonymus. De incredibilibus libellis, Graece. Ed. Teucherus. 12mo. Lemgoriae. 1796.

HERBART, JOHANN FRIEDRICH. Psychologie als Wissenschaft, neugegründet auf Erfahrung, Metaphysik, und Mathematik. 2 vols. 8vo. Königsberg. 1825.

HERBART, J. F. Lehrbuch zur Einleitung in die Philosophie. 8vo. Königsberg. 1834.

HERBELOT, M. Bibliothèque Orientale, ou Dictionnaire Universel de l'Orient. 6 vols. 8vo. Paris. 1781–1783.

HERCULANENSIA, or Archaeological and Philological Dissertations, by Drummond. 4to. London. 1810.

HERDER, J. G. Philosophy of the History of Man. 2 vols. 8vo. London. 1803.

HERDER, J. G. The Spirit of Hebrew Poetry, transl. by James Marsh. 2 vols. 12mo. Burlington. 1833.

HERICART DE THURY. Description des Catacombes de Paris. 8vo. Paris. 1815.

HERMANN, GODFREY. Elementa Doctrinae Metricae. 8vo. Lipsiae. 1816.

HERMANN, GODFREY. Epitome ejusdem. 8vo. Lipsiae. 1818.

HERODES ATTICUS. Quae supersunt. Ed. Heyne. 8vo. Lipsiae. 1801.

HERODIANUS. Historiarum Libri VIII. Ed. Bekker. 8vo. Berolini. 1826.

HERODOTEAE COMMENTATIONES. Creuzer. 8vo. Lipsiae. 1819.

HERODOTEUM LEXICON. Ed. Schweighäuser. 2 vols. Londini. 1824.

HERODOTUS. Musae, sive Historiarum Libri IX. Ed. Schweighäuser. 12 vols. 8vo. Argent. et Parisiis. 1816.

HERODOTUS. Historiarum Libri IX. 2 vols. in one. 18mo. 2 copies. Lipsiae. 1839.

HERODOTUS. Geographical System of. Ed. G. J. Rennell. 2 vols. 8vo. London. 1830.

HERMELUS, a Poem in Modern Greek. 12mo. s. l. et a.

HERSCHEL, J. F. W. Preliminary Discourse on the Study of Natural Philosophy. 12mo. London. 1833.

HERSCHEL, J. F. W. Treatise on Astronomy. 12mo. Phila. 1835.

HERVEY, JAMES. Character of, by John Ryland. 8vo. London. 1791.

HESYCHIUS MILESIUS. Opuscula duo quae supersunt. Ed. Orellius. 8vo. Lipsiae. 1820.

HEVELIUS, J. Selenographia, sive Lunae Descriptio. Fol. Gedani. 1647.

HEYDENREICH, K. H. Natur und Gott nach Spinoza. Ersten Band. 12mo. Leipzig. 1789.

HEYDENREICH, K. H. Mann und Weib. 12mo. Leipzig. 1789.

HEYNE, C. G. Opuscula Academica. 6 vols. 8vo. Gottingae. 1785.

HEYNE, C. G. Vorlesungen über die Archäologie der Künst des Alterthums. 8vo. Braunschweig. 1822.

HEZEL, W. F. Greichenlandes aelteste Geschichte und Sprache. 12mo. Leipzig. 1797.

HIEROCLES. Comment. in Aurea Carmina, de Providentia et Fato. Graece et Latine. Ed. Needhamus. 8vo. Cantabrigiae. 1709.

HIERONYMUS SANCTUS. Opera omnia. 12 vols. in 2. Fol. Francofurti. 1684.

HILDEBURTUS. Opera. Fol. Paris. 1708.

HILLHOUSE, JAMES A. Hadad, a Dramatic Poem. 8vo. New York. 1825.

HILLHOUSE, JAMES A. Complete Works. 2 vols. in one. 12mo. Boston. 1839.

HIMERIUS SOPHISTA. Eclogae et Declamationes. Ed. Wernsdorf. 8vo. Gottingae. 1790.

HINDMARSH, JAMES. Dictionary of Correspondences. 12mo. Lond. 1794.

HINDOOSTAN. History of, from the earliest time. Transl. from the Persian, with a Dissertation on the Religion and Theology of the Brahmins, by Alexander Dow. 2 vols. 4to. London. 1768.

HIRSCHE, MEYER. Tables of Integral Formulae, transl. from the German. 8vo. London. 1823.

Hirt, A. Geschichte der Baukunst bei den Alten. 3 vols. 4to. Berlin. 1821.

Tafeln zur Geschichte. Fol.

Histoire Générale de la Compagnie de Jésus. 4 vols. 12mo. s. l. 1761.

Historiae Augustae Scriptores sex, viz :

Aelius Spartianus. Vulc. Gallicanus.
Julius Capitolinus. Trebellius Pollio.
Aelius Lampridius. Flavius Vopiscus.
2 vols. 8vo. Biponti. 1787.

Historical Collections. Ed. by Farmer and Moore. Vols. ii and iii. 8vo. Concord. 1823–1824.

Historicorum Graecorum Antiquissimorum Fragmenta. Ed. Creuzer. 8vo. Heidelbergae. 1806.

History, Universal, from the earliest account of time. Compiled from original Authors, and illustrated with Maps, &c. 20 vols. 8vo. Dublin. 1745.

Hitchcock, Edward. See Geology of Mass.

Hoare, R. C. Classical Tour through Italy and Sicily. 2 vols. 8vo. Lond. 1819.

Hobart, J. H. Posthumous Works. 3 vols. 8vo. New York. 1833.

Hobart, J. H. Professional years of, by Dr. McVicar. 12mo. New York. 1836.

Hobbes, Thomas. Moral and Political Works. Fol. London. 1750.

Hobbes, Thomas. Translation of Thucydides. 2 vols. 8vo. London. 1812.

Hoffman, David. Legal Outlines. 3 vols. 8vo. Baltimore. 1829.

Hoffman, S. F. G. Lexicon Bibliographicum. 3 vols. 8vo. (Incomplete.) Lipsiae. 1832–1836.

Hogarth, George. Musical History, Biography, and Criticism. 8vo. London. 1835.

Holbrook, John E. North American Herpetology. 5 vols. 4to. Phila. 1825.

Hollis, Thomas. Memoirs. 2 vols. Fol. London. 1780.

Holmes, A. Annals of America from 1492–1826. 2 vols. 8vo. Cambridge. 1829.

Holmes, J. Greek Grammar. (Defective.) 12mo. 1733.

Hölty, L. H. C. Gedichte. 8vo. Carlsruhe. 1814.

Holyoke, Edward A. Memoir. 8vo. Boston. 1829.

Home, Henry, Lord Kames. Elements of Criticism. Vol. ii. 8vo. Edinburgh. 1763.

HOME, JOHN. Works, by Henry Mackenzie. 3 vols. 8vo. Edinburgh. 1822.

HOMER. Inquiry into the Life and Writings of, by Blackwall. 8vo. London. 1736.

HOMERUS. Ilias, Graece et Latine. Ed. Clarke. 2 vols. 8vo. London. 1768.

HOMERUS. Hymni et Epigrammatica. Ed. Hermann. 8vo. Lipsiae. 1806.

HOMERUS. Carmina. Ed. Heyne. 9 vols. 8vo. Lipsiae. 1811.

HOMERUS. Opera omnia. Ed. Ernesti. 5 vols. 8vo. Glasguae. 1814.

HOMERUS. Ilias, cum Comment. Eustathii. Ed. Müller. 2 vols. 8vo. Misenae. 1829.

HOMERUS. Odyssea. Ed. Baumgarten-Crusius. 3 vols. 8vo. Lips. 1832.

HOMERUS. Odyssea. 2 vols. in one. 18mo. Lipsiae. 1839.

HOOGEVEEN, HENRICUS. Doctrina Particularum Linguae Graecae. 8vo. Lipsiae. 1836.

HOOKER, RICHARD. Laws of Ecclesiastical Polity. Fol. London. s. a.

HOOPER, ROBT. Examinations in Anatomy and Physiology. 18mo. New York. 1811.

HOORNEBECK, JOHN. Theologia practica. 2 vols. 4to. Ultrajecti. 1666.

HOOSACK AND FRANCIS. American Medical and Philosophical Register. 4 vols. 8vo. New York. 1814.

HOPKINS, EZEKIEL. Works. 4 vols. 8vo. London. 1809.

HOPKINS, SAMUEL. Nature of true Holiness. 8vo. Newport. 1773.

HOPKINS, SAMUEL. System of Doctrine. 2 vols. 8vo. Boston. 1793.

HOPKINS, SAMUEL. The same. 2 vols. 8vo. Boston. 1811.

HORATIUS, Q. FLACCUS. Opera. Ed. Döring. 8vo. Oxoniae. 1831.

HORATIUS. Poemata. Ed. Min-Ellius. 18mo. Londini. 1726.

HORATIUS. Opera. Ed. Weise. 18mo. Lipsiae. 1843.

HORATIUS. Satiren. Ed. Heindorf. 8vo. Breslau. 1815.

HORN, FRANZ. Poesie und Beredsamkeit der Deutschen. 4 vols. 8vo. Berlin. 1822–1829.

HORNE, GEORGE. Commentary on the Psalms. 8vo. Phila. 1822.

HORNE, THOMAS. A Foreigner's Opinion of England. 8vo. Boston. 1832.

HORNECK, ANTHONY. The Crucified Jesus. 8vo. Edinburgh. s. a.

HORSELEY, BISHOP S. Sermons. 8vo. London. 1824.

HORTICULTURE, Annales de. Vols. XVIII–XLI. 8vo. Paris. 1836–1850.

HOSKINS, NATHAN. History of Vermont from its Discovery to the year 1830. 12mo. Vergennes. 1831.

HOUEL, EPHREM. Traité du Cheval en Bretagne. 8vo. Avrenches. 1842.

HOWARD, JOHN. Memoirs, compiled from his own Diary. 4to. London. 1818.

HOWE, JOHN. Works. 8 vols. 8vo. London. 1822.

HOYT, E. Practical Instruction for Military Officers. 8vo. Greenfield, Mass. 1811.

HOYT, E. Antiquarian Researches, or History of Indian Wars about the Connecticut River, to 1760. 8vo. Greenfield. 1824.

HUBBARD, WM. Indian Wars in New England from 1607 to 1677. 12mo. Brattleboro. 1814.

HUET, PETER. On the Weakness of the Human Understanding. 8vo. London. 1725.

HUG, J. L. Die Erfindung der Buchstabenschrift. 4to. Ulm. 1801.

HUG, J. L. Introduction to the writing of the New Testament. Transl. by Wait. 2 vols. 8vo. London. 1827.

HUG, J. L. The same translated by Fosdick. 8vo. Andover. 1836.

HUGENIUS, CHRISTIANUS. Opera Varia. 2 vols. in one. 4to. Amstelodami. 1724.

HUGENIUS, CHRISTIANUS. Opera Reliqua. 2 vols. in one. 4to. Amstelodami. 1728.

HUGHES, REV. T. S. Travels in Greece and Albania. 2 vols. 8vo. London. 1830.

HULL, GEN. WM. Revolutionary Services, and Civil Life, by his Daughter, Mrs. Campbell; and the Campaign of 1812, by J. F. Clarke. 8vo. New York. 1848.

HUMBOLDT, A. Essai Politique sur le Royaume de la Nouvelle Espagne. 2 copies of Vol. I. Fol. Paris. 1811.

HUMBOLDT, A. The same translated. 2 vols. 8vo. New York. 1811.
Atlas Géographique et Physique du R. de la N. E. Fol. Paris. 1812.

HUMBOLDT, A. Researches concerning the Monuments of the Ancient Inhabitants of America. 2 vols. 8vo. London. 1814.

HUMBOLDT, A. Personal Narrative of Travels to the Equinoctial Regions of the New Continent. 7 vols. 8vo. London. 1822.

HUME, DAVID. History of England. 8 vols. 8vo. London. 1789.

HUMPHREY, HEMAN. Miscellananeous Discourses and Reviews. 12mo. Amherst. 1834.

HUMPHREYS, COLONEL. Miscellaneous Works. 12mo. New York. 1790.

HUNS. Histoire générale des. See De Guignes.

HUNT, LEIGH. Feast of the Poets. 18mo. London. 1814.

HUNT'S MERCHANTS' MAGAZINE. See Pamphlet Cases 106–108.

HURD, RICHARD. Works, containing:

Sermons and Charges, Moral and Political Dialogues, Introduction to the Study of the Prophecies, Letters on Chivalry and Romance, and Critical Works and Dissertations. 8 vols. 8vo. London. 1811.

HURD, RICHARD. Ars Poetica of Horace, with Notes. 2 vols. 12mo. Cambridge, Eng. 1757.

HUSKISSON, WM. Speeches. 3 vols. 8vo. London. 1831.

HUTCHESON, FRANCIS. Inquiry into our Ideas of Beauty and Virtue. 8vo. London. 1826.

HUTCHESON, FRANCIS. Introduction to Moral Philosophy. 16mo. Glasgow. 1747.

HUTCHINSON, J. Works. 12 vols. 8vo. London. 1748.

HUTIN, P. Manual of the Physiology of Man, from the French. 12mo. Phila. 1828.

HUTTON, CHARLES. Mathematical and Philosophical Dictionary. 2 vols. with plates. 4to. London. 1795.

HUTTON, CHARLES. Mathematical Tables. 8vo. London. 1804.

HUTTON, CHARLES. Course of Mathematics. 2 vols. 8vo. London. 1810.

HYMNS, Watts' and Select. Worcester's ed. 6 copies. 16mo. Boston. 1849.

The same. 6 copies. 32mo. Boston. 1849.

*ICONOGRAPHIE ANCIENNE, ou Recueil des Portraits Authentiques des Empereurs, Rois, et Hommes illustres de l'antiquité, par E. Q. Visconti:

Iconographie Grecque. 3 Tomes. 4to. Paris. 1811.

Iconographie Romaine. 4 Tomes. 4to. Paris. 1817.

*Planches de l'Iconographie Grecque. Fol. Paris. 1811.

*Planches de l'Iconographie Romaine. Fol. Paris. 1817.

ILGEN, C. D. Scholia, hoc est, Carmina Convivalia Graecorum. 12mo. Jenae. 1798.

INDIAN BIOGRAPHY, by Thatcher. 2 vols. 16mo. New York. 1832.

INFANTRY Exercise of the United States Army, abridged. 12mo. Montpelier. 1820.

INFERNAL CONFERENCE, or Dialogues of Devils, by a Listener. 8vo. Worcester. 1795.

INGERSOLL, G. G. Sermons and Discourses. 8vo. Burlington. 1830–1844.

INNES, JOHN. Short Description of the Human Muscles. 8vo. New York. 1818.

INQUIRY into the Nature of the Human Soul. (Imputed to A. Baxter.) 3 vols. with the Appendix. 8vo. London. 1745.

IRISH REBELLION. History of. (Title page wanting.)

IRVING, EDWARD. Orations for Missionaries. 8vo. New York. 1825.

IRVING, EDWARD. Four Orations on the Oracles of God. 12mo. Phila. 1824.

ISCANUS, JOSEPHUS. De Bello Trojano Libri sex. Bound with Dictys Cretensis.

ISLANDE. Voyage en, par ordre de S. M. Danoise. 5 vols. 8vo. Paris. 1802.

Atlas à cela. 4to. Paris. 1802.

ISOCRATES. Orationes et Epistolae cum Scholiis antiquis, Graece. 8vo. Parisiis. 1807.

ISOCRATES. Orationes cum Versione Latina. 12mo. s. l. et a.

ITALIAN POETS. Lives, by Henry Stebbings. 3 vols. 12mo. London. 1832.

ITALY. Journal of a Tour in, by an American, in 1821. 8vo. New York. 1824.

JABLONSKIUS, P. E. Opuscula, de Lingua et Antiquitate Ægyptiorum. 4 vols. 8vo. Lugd. Bat. 1804–1813.

JACKSON, JOHN. The Existence and Unity of God; a Vindication of Dr. Clarke's Demonstration. 8vo. London. 1734.

JACKSON, ROBERT. Treatise on the Fevers of Jamaica. 12mo. Phila. 1795.

JACKSON, WM. Book-Keeping, by Double Entry. 8vo. New York. 1804.

JACOBI, F. H. Werke. 6 vols. 8vo. Leipzig. 1812.

JACOBI, F. H. Vermischte Schriften. 12mo. Breslau. 1781.

JACOBI, F. H. Von den Göttlichen Dingen. 12mo. Leipzig. 1811.

JACOBINISM. Memoirs of, from the French of Barruel. 4 vols. 8vo. Lond. 1797–1798.

JACOBS, F. Anthologia Graeca. 3 vols. 8vo. Lipsiae. 1813.

JACOBS, F. Greek Reader. 8vo. Boston. 1823.

JACOBS, F. The same. Ed. Patterson. 8vo. New York. 1827.

JACOBS, F. The same. Ed. Patterson. 8vo. New York. 1829.

JAHN, J. G. Hebrew Commonwealth, by C. E. Stowe. 8vo. Andover. 1828.

JAHN, J. G. Biblical Archaeology, by Upham. 8vo. Andover. 1833.

JAHRBUECHER der Wissenschafttiche Kritik. 4to. Berlin. 1835.

JAMBLICHUS CHALCIDENSIS. Adhortatio ad Philosophiam. Ed. Kiessling. 8vo. Lipsiae. 1813.

JAMBLICHUS CHALCIDENSIS. De Vita Pythagorica Liber, Graece et Latine. Ed. Kiessling. 2 vols. 8vo. Lipsiae. 1825.

JAMBLICHUS CHALCIDENSIS. See Taylor.

JAMES, COL. THOS. History of the Herculean Straits, now called Straits of Gibraltar, with copper plates. 2 vols. 4to. London. 1771.

JAMESON, MRS. Rome in the Nineteenth Century. 2 vols. 12mo. New York. 1827.

JAMIESON, JOHN. Hermes Scythicus, or the radical Affinities of the Greek and Latin Languages to the Gothic. 8vo. Edinburgh. 1814.

JAMIESON AND WEBER. Northern Antiquities from the earliest Teutonic and Scandinavian Romances. 4to. Edinburgh. 1814.

JAPAN. History of, by Kaempfer. 2 vols. Fol. London. 1728.

JARDINE, G. Outlines of Philosophical Education. 8vo. Glasgow. 1825.

JAY, JOHN. Life and Writings, by his son. 8vo. New York. 1833.

JAY, WILLIAM. Review of the Causes and Consequences of the Mexican War. 12mo. Boston. 1849.

JEFFERSON, THOMAS. Works and Life, by Thos. J. Randolph. 4 vols. 8vo. Boston. 1830.

JEFFREYS, JUDGE. Memoirs, by Woolrych. 8vo. London. 1827.

JENISCH, D. Vorlesungen über die Meisterwerke der Griechischen Poesie. 2 vols. 8vo. Berlin. 1803.

JENKYN, WM. Exposition of the Epistle of Jude. 4to. London. 1652.

JENNER. See Ogilvie.

JERMENT, GEORGE. Parental Duty. 12mo. Phila. 1794.

JEWETT, J. A. Passages in Foreign Travel. 2 vols. 8vo. Boston. 1838.

JOANNES SALISBERIENSIS. Polycraticus. 4to. Paris. 1513.

JOHANNES GRAMMATICUS PHILOPONUS. Commentarii in priora Analytica Aristotelis. Ed. Wineavelius. Fol. Venetiis. 1536.

JOHNSON, A. B. Treatise on Language. 8vo. New York. 1836.

JOHNSON, LAURA. Botanical Teacher for N. America. 12mo. Albany. 1834.

JOHNSON, SAMUEL. Works. 11 vols. 8vo. Oxford and London. 1825.

JOHNSON, REV. SAMUEL. Works. Fol. London. 1710.

JOHNSON, STEPHEN. Everlasting Punishment of the Ungodly. 8vo. New London. 1786.

JOLI, GUY. Mémoires de, et Mémoires de la Duchesse de Nemours. 2 vols. 12mo. Genève. 1777.

JOMINI, BARON DE. Histoire Critique et Militaire des Guerres de la Revolution. 14 vols. 8vo. Paris. 1820–1824.

*Atlas à cela. Fol. Paris.

JOMSVIKINGA Saga. 8vo. Kiobenhavn. 1829.

JONES, JOHN PAUL. Life and Correspondence, by Miss Janette Taylor. 8vo. New York. 1830.

JONES, SIR WILLIAM. Poeseos Asiaticae Commentariorum Libri sex. 8vo. Londini. 1784.

JONES, SIR WILLIAM. Works, with Life by Lord Teignmouth. 13 vols. 8vo. London. 1807.

JONES, WILLIAM. History of the Waldenses. 8vo. London. 1812.

JONSON, BEN. Dramatic Works. 4 vols. including the Dramatic Works of Beaumont and Fletcher. 8vo. London. 1811.

JOPLING, JOSEPH. Practice of Isometrical Perspective. 8vo. Lond. 1834.

JORTIN, JOHN. Works, viz: Sermons, Ecclesiastical History, Dissertations, Discourses, Life of Erasmus, and Tracts. 11 vols. 8vo. London. 1810.

JOSEPHUS, FLAVIUS. Opera, Graece et Latine. Ed. Oberthür. 3 vols. 8vo. Lipsiae. 1782.

JOSEPHUS JUDAEUS. Opera. 4to. Parrhisiis. 1514.

JOURNAL, Boston, of Natural History, from 1834. Vols. I–VI. 8vo. Boston. 1838–1850.

JOURNAL of the Academy of Natural Sciences of Philadelphia. Vols. I–VIII. 9 vols. 8vo. Phila. 1817–1839.

JOURNAL of the Society of Arts at London. Nos. 1–31. 8vo. London. 1852–1853. See Pamphlet Case 53.

JOURNAL of the Franklin Institute. See Pamphlet Case 101.

JOURNAL. See Congressional Documents, and the several States.

JULIANUS IMPERATOR. Opera quae supersunt omnia, et Cyrilli Animadversiones contra Julianum. Graece et Latine. Ed. Spanhemius. 2 vols. Fol. Lipsiae. 1696.

JURISPRUDENCE. Elémens de, par M. R. 12mo. Paris. 1762.

JUSTINIANUS. See Gaius.

JUSTINUS, M. JUNIANUS. Historiae Philippicae. 8vo. Argentorati. 1802.

JUSTINUS, PHILOSOPHUS ET MARTYR. Opera. Accedunt: Athenagorae Apologia pro Christianis, Ejusdem de Resurrectione Mortuorum, Theophili contra Christianae Religionis Calumniatores, Tatiani Oratio ad Graecos, et Hermiae Gentilium Philosophorum Irrisio. Fol. Paris. 1615.

JUVENALIS, DECIMUS JUNIUS. Satirae. Ed. Achaintre. 2 vols. 8vo. Parisiis. 1810.

KANE, ROBERT. Elements of Chemistry. Ed. by J. Draper. 8vo. New York. 1843.

KANNGIESSER, P. F. Die alte Komische Bühne in Athen. 8vo. Breslau. 1817.

KANT, IMMANUEL. Vermischte Schriften. 4 vols. 8vo. Halle. 1799.

KANT, IMMANUEL. Kritik der Urtheilskraft. 8vo. Berlin. 1799.

KANT, IMMANUEL. Kritik der practischen Vernunft. 8vo. Leipzig. 1827.

KANT, IMMANUEL. Ein Denkmal von Bouterwek. 18mo. Hamburg. 1808.

KEILL, JOHN. Introduction to the True Astronomy. 8vo. London. 1760.

KEILL, JOHN. The same. 6th Edition. 8vo. London. 1768.

KEITH, ISAAC S. Sermons, Addresses, and Letters. 8vo. Charlestown. 1816.

KELLY, MICHAEL. Reminiscences of the King's Theatre and Drury Lane. 8vo. New York. 1826.

KELSALL, CHARLES. Classical Excursion from Rome to Arpino. 8vo. Geneva. 1820.

KEMBLE, J. P. Memoirs of, with a History of the Stage from the time of Garrick to the present, by Boaden. 2 vols. in one. 8vo. Phila. 1825.

KENDALL, E. A. Travels through the Northern parts of the U. S. A. 3 vols. 8vo. New York. 1809.

KENDALL, GEO. WILKINS. The War between the United States and Mexico illustrated. Fol. Phila. 1851.

KENRICK, WM. Rhetorical Grammar of the English Language. 8vo. London. 1784.

KENT, JAMES. Commentaries on American Law. 4 vols. 8vo. New York. 1832.

Questions and Answers on the same, by A. Kinne. 8vo. New York. 1840.

KEPPEL, GEORGE. Personal Narrative of a Journey from India to England. 2 vols. 8vo. London. 1827.

KEPPLERUS, JOHANNES. Harmonices Mundi. Fol. Lincii Austriae. 1619.

KEPPLERUS, JOHANNES. Epistolae suae aliorumque. Fol. Lipsiae. 1717.

KEPPLERUS, JOHANNES. Dioptrice. 4to. Augustae Vindel. 1611.

KEPPLERUS, JOHANNES. De Cometis Libelli tres. 4to. Augustae Vindel. 1619.

KEPLER. Account of his Astronomical Discoveries, by Small. 4to. Lond. 1804.

KETTS, HENRY. Elements of General Knowledge. 2 vols. in one. 2 copies. 8vo. Baltimore. 1812.

KEYSLER, J. G. Travels through Germany, Bohemia, Hungary, Switzerland, Italy, and Lorraine. 4 vols. 4to. London. 1756.

KINGSBURY, HARMON. The Sabbath. 8vo. New York. 1840.

KIRBY, WILLIAM. Power, Wisdom, and Goodness of God as manifested in the creation of Animals, and in their History, Habits, and Instincts. 2 vols. 8vo. London. 1835.

KIRBY AND SPENCE. Introduction to Entomology. 2 vols. 8vo. Lond. 1818.

KIRCHER, ATHANASIUS. Mundus subterraneus. 2 vols. in one. Fol. Amstelodami. 1778.

KIRWAN, RICHARD. Logick. 2 vols. 8vo. London. 1807.

KIRWAN, RICHARD. On Manures. 12mo. London. 1808.

KLAPROTH, J. Lettre sur la Découverte des Hieroglyphes. 8vo. Paris. 1827.

KLEIN, G. M. Beiträge zum Studium der Philosophie als Wissenschaft des All. 8vo. Würtzburg. s. a.

KLEIN, J. T. Naturalis Dispositio Echinodermatum. 4to. Lipsiae. 1788.

KLOPSTOCK, J. Werke. 12 vols. 8vo. Leipzig. 1798–1817.

KNIGHT, R. P. Principles of Taste. 8vo. London. 1805.

KNIGHT, R. P. Prolegomena ad Homerum. 8vo. Lipsiae. 1816.

KNOOP, J. H. Pomologie, avec Planches. Fol. Amsterdam. 1771.

KNOX, JOHN. History of the Reformation in the Church of Scotland. 2 vols. 8vo. Paisly. 1791.

KNOX, JOHN. Life, by Thomas M'Crie. 2 vols. 8vo. Edinburgh. 1818.

KONG Olaf Tryggveson. Oldnordiske Saga. 3 vols. 8vo. Kiobenhavn. 1836.

KORAN, with a Preliminary Discourse by Sales. 2 vols. 8vo. London. 1801.

KÖSTER, HERMANN. De Cantilenis popularibus veterum Graecorum. 8vo. Berolini. 1831.

KOTZEBUE, AUGUSTUS. Herinneringen uit Lijfland, Rome en Napels. 3 vols. 8vo. Amsterdam. 1805.

KOTZEBUE, OTTO VON. Voyage of Discovery into the South Seas and Beerings Straits. 3 vols. 8vo. London. 1821.

KRUG, W. T. System der Practischen Philosophie. 3 vols. 8vo. Königsberg. 1830.

KRUG, W. T. System der Theoretischen Philosophie. 3 vols. 8vo. Königsberg. 1833.

KRUSENSTERN, A. J. VON. Voyage round the World. 2 vols. in one. 4to. London. 1813.

KUSTERUS, L. De vero usu Verborum Mediorum apud Graecos. Ed. Wolle. 12mo. Lipsiae. 1752.

LACHMANN, F. De Fontibus Historiarum T. Livii. 4to. Gottingae. 1822.

LACROIX, I. AMELOT DE. Field Exercise of the French Infantry. Vol. I. 12mo. Boston. 1810.

LACROIX, P. See St. Domingo.

LACROIX, S. F. Traité du Calcul Différentiel et Intégral. 3 vols. 4to. Paris. 1810–1819.

LACROIX. Traité Elémentaire du Calcul des Probabilités. 8vo. Paris. 1822.

LACROIX. Elémens d'Algèbre. 8vo. Paris. 1825.

LACROIX. Complément des Elémens d'Algèbre. 8vo. Paris. 1825.

LACROIX. Elémens de Géométrie. 8vo. Paris. 1825.

LACROIX. Complément des Elémens de Géométrie. 8vo. Paris. 1822.

LACROIX. Traité Elémentaire d'Arithmetique. 8vo. Paris. 1826.

LACROIX. Traité Elémentaire de Trigonométrie et d'Application de l'Algèbre a la Géométrie. 8vo. Paris. 1827.

LACROIX. Traité Elémentaire de Calcul Différentiel et Intégral. 8vo. Paris. 1828.

LACROIX. Essais sur l'Enseignement. 8vo. Paris. 1828.

LACROIX. Arithmetic, transl. from the French. 8vo. Cambridge. 1821.

LAENNEC, R. T. H. On Diseases of the Chest. 8vo. Phila. 1823.

LA FONTAINE. Fables. 2 vols. 8vo. Paris. 1813.

LA GRAND Nef des Folz du Monde. 4to. Lyon. 1530.

LA GRANGE, J. L. Méchanique Analytique. 2 vols. 4to. Paris. 1811–1815.

LA GRANGE, J. L. Théorie des Fonctions Analytiques. 4to. Paris. 1813.

LA HARPE, J. F. Lycèe, ou Cours de Literature Ancienne et Moderne. 2 vols. 8vo. Paris. 1834.

LAING, MALCOM. History of Scotland from the Union of the Crowns to the Union of the Kingdoms, with a Dissertation on Mary's share in the Murder of Darnley. 4 vols. 8vo. London. 1804.

LAMARCK. Histoire Naturelle des Animaux sans Vertèbres. 7 vols. 8vo. Paris. 1815.

LAMARCK. Le même. 11 vols. 8vo. Paris. 1835.

LAMARTINE, ALPHONSE DE. Souvenirs d'un Voyage en Orient. 4 vols. 8vo. Paris. 1835.

LAMBALLE, PRINCESS. Secret Memoirs of the Royal Family of France during the Revolution. 8vo. Phila. 1826.

LAMBERT, CESAR. Traité d'Arithmetique. 8vo. Paris. 1836.

LANE, B. J. Mysteries of Tobacco. 12mo. New York. 1845.

LANGLOIS, E. H. Essai sur la Peinture sur Verre. 8vo. Rouen. 1832.

LANGTOFT, PETER. Chronicle, by Hearne. 2 vols. 8vo. Oxford. 1725.

LANZI, ABATE LUIGI. History of Painting in Italy, transl. by Roscoe. 6 vols. 8vo. London. 1828.

LA PLACE. Exposition du Système du Monde. 4to. Paris. 1813.

LA PLACE. Mécanique Céleste, transl. with a Commentary by N. Bowditch. 2 copies. 4 vols. 4to. Boston. 1829–1839.

LARD, REBECCA. Miscellaneous Poems. 18mo. Woodstock. 1820.

LARDNER, NATHANIEL. Works. 10 vols. 8vo. London. 1835.

L'ART de verefier les Dates. Fol. Paris. 1770.

LAS CASAS. Oeuvres, et sa vie par Llorente. 2 vols. 8vo. Paris. 1822.

LAS CASAS. Account of the First Spanish Voyages and Discoveries in America. 12mo. London. 1699.

LAS CASES. Journal of the Private Life and Correspondence of Napoleon at St. Helena. 2 vols. 12mo. New York. 1823.

LATHAM, JOHN. General Synopsis of Birds. 6 vols. 4to. London. 1781–1785.

LATHAM, JOHN. Supplement to the above. 4to. London. 1787.

*LATHAM, JOHN. Index Ornithologicus. 2 vols. 4to. London. 1790.

LATHROP, JOSEPH. Sermons. 8vo. Worcester. 1793.

LATIMER, HUGH. Sermons. 2 vols. 8vo. London. 1758.

LAURENTIUS VALLA. Opera. Fol. Basileae. s. a.

LAVOISIER. Elements of Chemistry, transl. by R. Kerr. 8vo. Edinburgh. 1793.

LAW TRACTS, Historical. 8vo. Edinburgh. 1761.

LAW, WILLIAM. Works. 9 vols. 8vo. London. 1762.

LAWRENCE, W. Lectures on Physiology, Zoology, and Natural History of Man. 8vo. Salem. 1828.

LAWSON, J. New Voyage to Carolina. 4to. London. 1709.

LAWSON, THOMAS. Meteorological Register for twelve years, from 1831 to 1842 inclusive. 4to. Washington. 1851.

LAYS of the Minnesingers. 12mo. London. 1825.

LEAKE, W. M. Journal of a Tour in Asia Minor, with Map. 8vo. Lond. 1824.

LEÇONS de la Sagesse sur les defauts des Hommes. 3 vols. 12mo. Paris. 1747.

LEDYARD, JOHN. Life, by J. Sparks. 8vo. Cambridge. 1828.

LEE, CHARLES. Memoirs. 12mo. New York. 1792.

LEE, EDWARD. Critica Sacra. 4to. London. 1650.

LEE, HENRY. Memoirs of the War in the Southern Department of the U. S. A. 2 vols. 8vo. Phila. 1812.

LEE, HENRY. Campaign of 1781 in the Carolinas. 8vo. Phila. 1824.

LEE, R. H. Life, by his Grandson. 2 vols. 8vo. Phila. 1825.

LEE, T. J. Tables and Formulae useful in Surveying, &c. 8vo. Washington. 1853.

LEGENDRE, A. M. Dissertation sur la Question de Balistique. 4to. Berlin. 1782.

LEGENDRE, A. M. Analyse des Triangles tracés sur la surface d'un Sphéroide. 4to. Paris. 1806.

LEGENDRE, A. M. Recherches sur divers sortes d'Intégrales définies. 4to. Paris. 1809.

LEGENDRE, A. M. Memoires sur la Méthode des moindres Quarrés. 4to. Paris. 1811.

LEGENDRE, A. M. Exercises de Calcul Intégral sur divers ordres de Transcendants et sur les Quadratures. 3 vols. 4to. Paris. 1811–1816.

LEGENDRE, A. M. Traité des Fonctions Elliptiques, et des Intégrales Eulériennes avec des Tables. 3 vols. 4to. Paris. 1825–1828.

LEGENDRE, A. M. Théorie des Nombres. 2 vols. 4to. Paris. 1830.

LEGENDRE, A. M. Memoire sur l'Equation $4(x^n-1)=(x-1)(y^2 \pm nz^2)$. 4to. Paris. 1830.

LEGH, THOS. Narrative of a Journey in Egypt and the Country beyond the Cataracts. 8vo. London. 1817.

LE GRAND. See Fabliaux.

LEIBNITZ, G. G. Opera omnia. 6 vols. 4to. Genevae. 1768.

LEIGH, EDWARD. Critica Sacra. Fol. London. 1650.

LEIGHTON, ROBERT. Works. 4 vols. 8vo. London. 1830.

LELAND, JOHN. View of Deistical Writings, with Observations and Answers. 3 vols. 8vo. London. 1755.

LELAND, JOHN. Advantage and Necessity of Christian Revelation. 2 vols. 8vo. Glasgow. 1819.

LELAND, THOS. Dissertation on the Principles of Human Eloquence. 4to. London. 1764.

LELAND, THOS. History of Philip of Macedon. 2 vols. 8vo. London. 1775.

LEMPRIERE. Classical Dictionary. Ed. by Anthon. 8vo. New York. 1825.

L'ENFANT. See Constance.

LENHART, WILLIAM. Tables relating to Cube Numbers. Bound with Gills' Mathematical Miscellany. 8vo. New York. 1838.

LEPELLETIER, ALM. Traité de Physiologie Médicale et Philosophique. 4 vols. 8vo. Paris. 1832.

LERMINIER, E. Audela du Rhin. 2 vols. Vol. I, La Politique. Vol. II, La Science. 8vo. Paris. 1835.

LESBONAX. Declamationes duo, Graece et Latine. Ed. Orellius. 8vo. Lipsiae. 1820.

LESLIE, JOHN. Experiments and Instruments relating to Heat and Moisture. 8vo. Edinburgh. 1813.

LESLIE, JOHN. Geometry and Plane Trigonometry. 8vo. Edinburgh. 1817.

LESLIE, JOHN. Geometrical Analysis. 8vo. Edinburgh. 1821.

LESSING, G. E. Sämmtliche Schriften. 27 vols. 12mo. Berlin und Stettin. 1796–1809

LETTERS on Unitarianism by Drs. Woods and Ware. 8vo. Boston. 1820–1821.

LETTRES, Négociations, et Pièces secretes. 2 vols. 18mo. London. 1744.

LEYBOURNE, THOS. Mathematical Questions proposed in the Ladies' Diary from 1704 to 1816. 4 vols. 8vo. London. 1817.

LIBANIUS SOPHISTA. Epistolae, Graece et Latine. Ed. Wolfius. Fol. Amstelodami. 1738.

LIBANIUS SOPHISTA. Orationes et Declamationes, Graece. Ed. Reiske. 4 vols. 8vo. Altenburgi. 1791.

LIBES, A. Histoire Philosophique des Progrés de la Physique. 4 vols. 8vo Paris. 1810.

LICHTENBERG, G. C. Vermischte Schriften. 9 vols. 12mo. Göttingen. 1800.

LIEBIG, JUSTUS. Organic Chemistry in its applications to Agriculture and Physiology. 12mo. Boston. 1841.

LIEDER-Sammlung der vereinigten Lutherischen Gemeinen in Pennsylvanien. 12mo. Germantaun. 1812.

LINCOLN, J. L. Selections from the first five books of Livy. 8vo. New York. 1852.

LIND, JAMES. Diseases in Hot Climates. 8vo. Phila. 1811.

LINDLEY, GEORGE. Guide to the Orchard and Kitchen Garden. 8vo. Lond. 1831.

LINDLEY, JOHN. Introduction to Natural System of Botany. 8vo. New York. 1831.

LINK, H. F. Die Urwelt und das Alterthum, erlaütert durch die Naturkunde. 2 vols. 8vo. Berlin. 1834.

LINK, H. F. Elementa Philosophiae Botanicae. 8vo. Berolini. 1824.

LINN, DR., and others. Essays on Episcopacy. 8vo. New York. 1806.

LINN, WM. Discourses on the Signs of the Times. 12mo. New York. 1794.

LINNAEUS, CAROLUS A. Philosophia Botanica. 8vo. Coloniae Allob. 1787.

LINNAEUS. Systema Naturae per Regna tria Naturae, cura Jo. Frid. Gmelin. 10 vols. 8vo. Lugduni. 1796–1799.

LINNAEUS. Lachesis Laponica, or a Tour in Lapland. 2 vols. 8vo. Lond. 1811.

LINNAEUS. Systema Vegetabilium (Vols. III and IV). 8vo. Stuttgardiae. 1818.

LINNAEUS. General View of his Writings, by Pulteny; also his Diary. 4to. London. 1805.

LIPPI, LORENZO. Il Malmantile Racquistate. 8vo. Milano. 1807.

LIPSIUS, JUSTUS. Opera omnia. 2 vols. 8vo. Vesaliae. 1675.

LITERARY WORLD, by C. F. Hoffman. Vols. I and II. 4to. New York. 1847–1848.

LIVERMORE, A. A. War with Mexico reviewed. 12mo. Boston. 1850.

LIVIUS, T. PATAVINUS. Historiarum A. U. C. libri qui supersunt omnes, cur. Drakenborch. 7 vols. 4to. Lugd. Batav. 1738.

LIVIUS, T. PATAVINUS. Libri qui supersunt. 6 vols. 18mo. Lipsiae. 1848.

LLORENTE, J. A. Histoire Critique de l'Inquisition. 4 vols. 8vo. Paris. 1828.

LOCKE, JOHN. Works. 3 vols. Fol. London. 1755.

LOCKE, JOHN. Life and Correspondence by Lord King. 2 vols. 8vo. Lond. 1830.

LOCKE, JOHN. Essay concerning the Human Understanding. 3 vols. 12mo. Boston. 1803.

LOCKE, JOHN. Reasonableness of Christianity. 12mo. Boston. 1811.

LODGE, EDMUND. Illustrations of British History, Biography, and Manners from Henry VIII to James I inclusive. 4to. London. 1791.

LODGE, THOMAS. Glaucus and Silla, with other Poems.. 18mo. Chiswick. 1819.

LONDON Dissector. 12mo. London. 1804.

LONG, S. H. Narrative of a Journey from Pittsburgh to the Rocky Mountains. 3 vols. 8vo. London. 1823.

LONG, S. H. The same. 2 vols. 8vo. Phila. 1823.

LONG, S. H. Expedition to the Source of the St. Peter's River. 2 vols. 8vo. Phila. 1824.

LONGINUS, DIONYSIUS. De Sublimitate, Graece et Latine. Ed. Tollius. 4to. Traj. ad Rhenum. 1694.

LONGINUS, DIONYSIUS. Idem. Ed. Weiske. 8vo. Lipsiae. 1809.

LONGUS. Pastoralium de Daphnide et Chloe libri IV. 8vo. Parisiis. 1778.

LOOMIS, JUSTIN R. Elements of Geology. 12mo. Boston. 1852.

LORING, JAMES SPEAR. Hundred Orators of Boston. 8vo. Boston. 1853.

LORRIS, G. See Rommant de la Rose.

LORTIE, ANDRE. Traité de la Sainte Cene. s. l. 1681.

*LOUDON, J. C.. On laying out Farms, illustrated by forty Plates. Fol. London. 1812.

LOUDON, J. C. Encyclopaedia of Gardening. 8vo. London. 1835.

LOVELACE, RICHARD. Lucasta and Postume Poems. 2 vols. 18mo. Chiswick. 1817–1818.

LOWE, JOSEPH. Present State of England. 8vo. New York. 1824.

LÖWIG, CARL. Principles of Organic and Physiological Chemistry, transl. by Breed. 8vo. Phila. 1853.

LOWNDES. Modern Greek Lexicon. 8vo. Corfu. 1827.

LOWTH, R. Isaiah, a new Translation. 4to. London. 1779.

LOWTH, R. Letter to Warburton. 8vo. London. 1766.

LOWTH, R. Praelectiones de Sacra Poesi Hebraeorum. 8vo. Lipsiae. 1815.

LOWTH, R. Short Introduction to English Grammar. 12mo. Dublin. 1786.

LUCANUS, M. ANNAEUS. Pharsalia. Ed. Weber. 3 vols. 8vo. Lipsiae. 1821.

LUCIANUS, SAMOSATENSIS. Opera, Graece et Latine. Ed. Hermsterhusius et Reitzius. 10 vols. 8vo. Biponti. 1789.

LUCRETIUS, T. CARUS. De Rerum Natura. Text, and transl. by John Mason Good. 4to. London. 1805.

LULLY, RAYMOND. Opera quae ad inventam ab ipso Artem Universalem pertinent. 8vo. Argentorati. 1597.

LUTHER, MARTIN. Colloquia mensalia. Fol. London. 1791.

LUTHER, MARTIN. Loci Communes ex ipsius Scriptis collecti a T. Fabricio. 4to. London. 1651.

LUTHER, MARTIN. Commentary on Galatians. 8vo. Phila. 1801.

LUTHER, MARTIN. Werke. 10 vols. 12mo. Hamburg. 1827.

LUTHERAN Hymns and Liturgy. 12mo. Phila. 1814.

LYCOPHRON. Cassandra. Ed. Reichard. 8vo. Lipsiae. 1788.

LYELL, CHARLES. Principles of Geology. 3 vols. London. 1830.

LYON, G. F. Travels in Northern Africa, 1818–1820. 4to. London. 1821.

LYTTLETON, GEORGE, LORD. History of Henry II and his Age. 6 vols. 8vo. London. 1773.

LYTTLETON, GEORGE, LORD. Works. 3 vols. 8vo. London. 1776.

MACAULAY, T. B. History of England from the Accession of James II. 2 vols. 8vo. Phila. 1849.

MACCOVIUS, J. Tractationes Theologicae. 4to. Amstelodami. 1659.

MACCULLOCH, JOHN. Geological Classification of Rocks. 8vo. Lond. 1821.

MACCULLOCH, J. R. Dictionary of Commerce. 2 vols. 8vo. London. 1834.

MACHIAVELLI, NICCOLO. Opere. 8 vols. 8vo. s. l. 1796–1799.

MACHIAVELLI, NICCOLO. Art of War. 8vo. Albany. 1815.

MACKENNEY, THOS. L. Tour to the Lakes and Chippeway Indians. 8vo. Baltimore. 1827.

MACKENZIE, ALEX. Voyage from Montreal to the Northern Ocean. 2 vols. 8vo. London. 1802.

MACKENZIE, HENRY. Works, viz: Man of Feeling, Man of the World, Julia de Roubigné, Papers from the Mirror and Lounger, Miscellanies, Poems, and Dramas. 8 vols. 8vo. Edinburgh. 1808.

MACKINTOSH, SIR J. Progress of Ethical Philosophy. 8vo. Phila. 1832.

MACKINTOSH, SIR J. History of the Revolution in England. 8vo. Phila. 1835.

MACKINTOSH, SIR J. Discourse on the Laws of Nature and Nations. 12mo. London. 1835.

MACLAINE, A. Letters to Soame Jenyns. 12mo. Dublin. 1777.

MAC LAURIN, COLIN. A Treatise of Fluxions. 2 vols. 8vo. Edinb. 1742.

MAC LAURIN, JOHN. Sermons and Essays. 12mo. Phila. 1811.

MACLEOD, ALEX. Lectures on the Prophecies. 2 copies. 8vo. New York. 1814.

MACLEOD, NORMAN. Dictionary of the Gaelic Language. 8vo. Lond. 1845.

MAFFEI, SCIPIONE. Verona Illustrata. 5 vols. 8vo. Milano. 1825.

MAGENDIE, F. Summary of Physiology. 8vo. Baltimore. 1822.

MAGENDIE, F. The same, 2d ed. 8vo. Baltimore. 1824.

MAGENDIE, F. Précis Elémentaire de Physiologie. 2 vols. 8vo. Paris. 1825.

MAGENDIE, F. On the Use of Prussic Acid in Pthisis Pulmonalis, by Percival. 12mo. New Haven. 1820.

MAGNETIC Observations by Lovering and Bond. 4to.

MAINE. History of, by James Sullivan. 8vo. Boston. 1795.

MAINE. History of, from 1602 to 1820, by Williamson. 2 vols. 8vo. Hallowell. 1832.

MAIRE ET BOSCOVICH. Voyage Astronomique et Géographique, dans l'Etat de l'Eglise. 4to. Paris. 1770.

MALCOM, SIR JOHN. History of Persia. 2 vols. 4to. London. 1815.

MALEBRANCHE. Treatise on the Search after Truth. Fol. London. 1700.

MALEBRANCHE. De la Recherche de la Verité. 4 vols. 12mo. Paris. 1712.

MALHERBE. See Boileau.

MALLET, P. H. Northern Antiquities, or Description of the Manners, Customs, Religion, and Laws of the Ancient Danes and other Northern Nations, with Translation of the Edda and other pieces. 2 vols. 8vo. London. 1770.

MALPIGHIUS MARCELLUS. Opera omnia. Fol. London. 1686.

MALTHUS, T. R. Essay on the Principle of Population. 2 vols. 8vo. Lond. 1806.

MALTHUS, T. R. Political Economy. 8vo. London. 1820.

MALTHUS, T. R. Definitions in Political Economy. 8vo. London. 1827.

MALUS. Traité d'Optique. 4to. Paris. 1807.

MANDEVILLE, BERNARD DE. Fable of the Bees. 12mo. Edinburgh. 1755.

MANILIUS, M. Astronomicon. Interp. Mich. Fayus. 4to. Parisiis. 1679.

MANLEY, THOMAS. Interpretation of Terms in Common and Statute Laws. Fol. London. 1672.

MANN, JAMES. Medical Sketches during the War of 1812–1814. 8vo. Dedham. 1816.

MANN, JOEL. Exposition of the Apocalypse. 12mo. New York. 1851.

MANNERT, KONRAD. Geographie. 14 vols. 8vo. Leipzig. 1829.

MANSFIELD, J. Essays Mathematical and Physical. 8vo. New Haven. s. a.

MANUAL on the Cultivation of the Sugar Cane. 8vo. Washington. 1833.

MAMUEL pour les Ecoles d'Enseignement Mutuel. 8vo. Genève. 1827.

MAP of the Upper Portion of the Mississippi and of St. Peter's River. 18mo.

MAP of London, by Edward Mogg. 18mo.

MAP, Post and Travelling, of Germany, (Post-und Reise-Karte). 8vo.

MAPS. Series of Ancient and Modern, published by the Society for the Promotion of Useful Knowledge. Fol. London.

MARIGUY, ABBE. History of the Arabians under the Caliphs. 4 vols. 8vo. London. 1758.

MARLORATUS, AUGUSTINUS. Novi Testamenti Catholica Expositio Ecclesiastica. Fol. s. l. 1620.

MARLOWE AND CHAPMAN. Hero and Leader. 18mo. Chiswick. 1821.

MARSDEN. See Sumatra.

MARSH, GEORGE P. Grammar of the Old-Northern or Icelandic Language. 12mo. Burlington. 1838.

MARSH, JAMES. Life and Remains, by Joseph Torrey. 8vo. Boston. 1843.

MARSHALL, H. History of Kentucky. 2 vols. 8vo. Frankfort. 1824.

MARSHALL, WALTER. Gospel Mystery of Sanctification. 12mo. Kilmarnock. 1778.

MARTIN, BENJ. Philosophical Grammar. 8vo. London. 1769.

MARTIN, BENJ. Young Gentlemen and Ladies' Philosophy. 3 vols. 8vo. London. 1781–1782.

MARTIN, MONTGOMERY. History of the British Colonies. 5 vols. 8vo. Lond. 1835.

MARTIN DEL RIO. Adagialia Sacra Vet. et Nov. Testamenti. 4to. Lugd. 1614.

MARTYRS, Book of; an Abridgment. 8vo. New York. 1810.

MARVEL, ANDREW. Works. 3 vols. 4to. London. 1776.

MASON, JOHN. Select Remains. Brattleboro. 1810.

MASON, JOHN M. Apology for the Apostolical Order. 8vo. New York. 1807.

MASON, WILLIAM. Works. 4 vols. 8vo. London. 1811.

MASON, WILLIAM. Spiritual Treasury. 2 vols. 12mo. Boston. 1809.

MASSACHUSETTS Astronomical and Trigonometrical Survey, Tables on, by J. G. Palfrey. Boston.

MASSACHUSETTS BAY COLONY. Acts and Laws of the General Court, from 1692 to 1735. Fol.

MASSACHUSETTS BAY. History of, from 1748 to 1765, by G. R. Minot. 2 vols. 8vo. Boston. 1798–1803.

MASSACHUSETTS BAY. History of, from 1749 to 1774, comprising the Origin and Early Stages of the American Revolution, by Gov. Hutchinson. 8vo. London. 1828.

MASSACHUSETTS. History of, from 1628 to 1750, by Gov. Hutchinson. 2 vols. 8vo. Salem. 1795.

MASSACHUSETTS. History of, from 1620 to 1820, by Alden Bradford. 8vo. Boston. 1835.

MASSACHUSETTS REPORTS.

On the Fishes and Reptiles, by D. H. Storer; and on the Birds, by W. B. O. Peabody. 8vo. Boston. 1839.

On the Herbaceous Plants, by Chester Dewey, and on the Quadrupeds by E. Emmons. 8vo. Cambridge. 1840.

On the Invertebrate Animals, by Aug. W. Gould. 8vo. Cambridge. 1841.

On the Insects injurious to Vegetation, by T. W. Harris. 8vo. Cambridge. 1841.

On the Trees and Shrubs by G. B. Emerson. 8vo. Boston. 1846.

MASSACHUSETTS. Senate of 1838. Documents. 8vo. Boston. 1838.

MASSACHUSETTS House of Rep. of 1838. Documents. 8vo. Boston. 1838.

MASSACHUSETTS. Acts and Resolves for 1839–1842. 8vo. Boston. 1839–1842.

MASSACHUSETTS School Returns. Abstract of, for 1838–1839, 1839–1840, and 1840–1841. 8vo. Boston.

MASSACHUSETTS. Statistics of different branches of Industry for 1845. 8vo. Boston. 1846.

MASSEY, W. Origin and Progress of Letters. 8vo. London. 1763.

MASSILLON. Oeuvres. 2 vols. 8vo. Paris. 1836.

MASSINGER, PHILIP. Dramatic Works. 4 vols. 8vo. London. 1779.

MATHEMATICAL DIARY, conducted by R. Adrain. (Incomplete.) 12mo.

MATHER, COTTON. Life, by Saml. Mather. 8vo. Boston. 1729.

MATHER, COTTON. Magnalia Christi Americana. 2 vols. 8vo. Hartford. 1820.

MATTAIRE, MICHAELIS. Graecae Linguae Dialecti. 8vo. Lipsiae. 1807.

MATTHISSON, FRID. VON. Schriften mit sein Leben. 9 vols. 12mo. Zurich. 1825–1833.

MAUNDREL, HENRY. Journey from Aleppo to Jerusalaem in 1697. 18mo. Boston. 1836.

MAUPERTIUS. The Figure of the Earth determined by Observations made at the Polar Circle. From the French. 8vo. London. 1728.

MAURY, M. F. Astronomical Observations made in 1845 at the National Observatory at Washington. 4to. Washington. 1846.

MAWE, JOHN. Treatise on Diamonds. 8vo. London. 1823.

MAXIMUS, PHILOSOPHUS. De Principiis, Graece. Ed. Gerhardius. 8vo. Lipsiae. 1820.

MAXIMUS, TYRIUS. Dissertationes. Ed. Reiske. 2 vols. in one. 8vo. Lipsiae. 1774.

MAXWELL, JAMES. Version of the Psalms in Metre. 12mo. Glasgow. 1773.

MAYER, TOBIAS. Tabulae Motuum Solis et Lunae. 4to. Londini. 1770.

MAYO, ROBT. View of Ancient Geography and History. 2 vols. in one. 8vo. Phila. 1813.

MAZOIS. Le Palais de Scaurus. 8vo. Paris. 1822.

MECKEL, J. F. System der Vergleichenden Anatomie. 5 vols. 8vo. Halle. 1821.

MEIEROTTO, J. H. L. Ueber Sitten und Lebensart der Römer. 2 vols. 12mo. Berlin. 1814.

MEILLEUR, J. B. Cours abrégé de Leçons de Chymie. 8vo. Montreal. 1832.

MEILLEUR, J. B. On the Pronunciation of the French Language. 12mo. Montreal. 1841.

MELMOTH. See Cicero's Letters, Cato and Laelius.

MELVILLE, ANDREW. Life, by Thomas M'Crie. 2 vols. 8vo. Edinburgh. 1819.

MEMNON. Historiarum Heracleae Ponti Excerpta Servata a Photio, Graece. Ed. Orellius. 8vo. Lipsiae. 1816.

MEMOIRES de Litterature tirez des Registres de l'Académie Royale des Inscriptions et Belles-Lettres depuis l'année 1701 jusqu'a 1793, avec une Histoire de l'Académie depuis son Establissement en 1663 jusqu'en 1717. 50 vols. 4to. Paris. 1717–1808.

MENANDER, RHETOR. Commentarius de Encomiis. Ed. Heeren. 12mo. Gottingae. 1785.

MENDELSOHN, MOSES. Phädon oder über die Unsterblichkeit der Seele. 12mo. Berlin. 1821.

MENNAIS, L'ABBE DE. Essai sur l'Indifference en Matières de Religion. 4 vols. 8vo. Paris. 1817.

MERCATOR, GERARD. Atlas, sive Cosmographicae Meditationes. 3 vols. Fol. Amstelodami. 1619.

MERCURE de France. 12mo. Paris. 1759.

MESSINGER, R. Resignation. 12mo. Portsmouth. 1827.

METHODIST PREACHERS. Experiences of several eminent, written by themselves to John Wesley. 12mo. Barnard, Vt. 1812.

MEXICO. History of, collected from Spanish and Mexican Historians. From the Italian of Clavigero. 2 vols. 4to. London. 1787.

MEZERAY, SIEUR DE. Chronological History of the Kings of France, transl. by John Bulteel. Fol. s. l. et a.

MICHAEL ANGELO BUONARROTI. Life by R. Duppa. 8vo. London. 1816.

MICHAELIS, J. D. Commentary on the Laws of Moses. 4 vols. 8vo. Lond. 1814.

MICHAELIS. Recueil de Questions proposees à une Societe de Savants, qui font le Voyage de l'Arabie. (Bound with Niebuhr's Description de l'Arabie.)

MICHELET, M. Spiritual Direction and Auricular Confession. 12mo. Phila. 1845.

MIDDLETON, CONYERS. Miscellaneous Works. 5 vols. 8vo. Lond. 1755.

MIGNET, F. A. Histoire de la Revolution Française depuis 1789 jusqu'a 1814. 2 vols. 8vo. Paris. 1833.

MILLAR, JOHN. Historical View of the English Government. 8vo. Dublin. 1789.

MILLER, COL. J. P. Condition of Greece in 1827–1828. 8vo. New York. 1828.

MILLER, J. S. Natural History of the Crinoidea. 4to. Bristol. 1821.

MILLER, SAMUEL. Brief Retrospect of the 18th Century. 2 vols. 8vo. New York. 1803.

MILLIN, A. L. Galerie Mythologique. 2 vols. 8vo. Paris. 1811.

MILLOT, ABBE. Elements of General History. Vol. IV. 8vo. Salem. 1796.

MILLS, CHARLES. History of Chivalry. 2 vols. 8vo. London. 1820.

MILLS, CHARLES. History of the Crusades. 2 vols. 8vo. London. 1825.

MILLS, CHARLES. See Ducas.

MILLS, JAMES. History of British India. 6 vols. 8vo. London. 1826.

MILMAN, HENRY HART. Samor, a Heroic Poem. 8vo. London. 1818.

MILMAN, HENRY HART. Fazio, a Tragedy. 8vo. London. 1821.

MILMAN, HENRY HART. Belshazzar, a Dramatic Poem. 8vo. Lond. 1822.

MILMAN, HENRY HART. Fall of Jerusalem, a Dramatic Poem. 8vo. Lond. 1831.

MILMAN, HENRY HART. Nala and Damayanti, and other Poems, translated from the Sanscrit. 8vo. Oxford. 1835.

MILTON, JOHN. Paradise Lost, by Bentley. 4to. London. 1732.

MILTON, JOHN. Prose Works and Life by Charles Symmons. 7 vols. 8vo. London. 1806.

MILTON, JOHN. Treatise on Christian Doctrine. 2 vols. 8vo. Boston. 1825.

MILTON, JOHN. Poetical Works, with notes, by Todd. 6 vols. 8vo. Lond. 1826.

MILTON, JOHN. Life, by Toland. 12mo. London. 1761.

MIRABEAU. Recollections of, by Dumont. 8vo. London. 1832.

MIRANDA. History of his Attempt at a Revolution in South America, with a Life. 12mo. Boston. 1811.

MIRANDULA, J. F. P. De Rerum Praenotione Libri novem. 4to. Argentorati. 1511.

MISCELLANEOUS Observations on Authors. Vol. II. 8vo. London. 1832.

MISSIONARIES. Thoughts on a new Order. 12mo. New York. 1838.

MISSIONARY HERALD. Vols. XVII–XL. Duplicate of Vol. XXX. See also Pamphlet Cases 68 et seq.

MITCHEL, O. M. Sidereal Messenger, (Periodical). Vols. I and II. 4to. Cincinnati. 1847–1848.

MITFORD, WILLIAM. History of Greece. 8 vols. 8vo. Boston. 1823.

MOGG. See Map of London.

MOHNIKE, G. C. F. Geschichte der Litteratur der Griechen und Römer. Erster Band. 8vo. Greiswald. 1813.

MOLIERE, J. B. Oeuvres. 8vo. Paris. 1835.

MOLINA. See Chili.

*MOLLER, GEORG. Denkmäler der Deutschen Baukunst. Fol. Leipzig und London. s. a.

MOLLER, GEORG. Memorials of German-Gothic Architecture. 8vo. Lond. 1836.

MONBODDO, LORD. Ancient Metaphysics or the Science of Universals. 6 vols. 4to. Edinburgh. 1779.

MONBODDO, LORD. Origin and Progress of Language. 6 vols. 8vo. Edinburgh. 1774.

MONGE, G. Géométrie Descriptive. 4to. Paris. 1820.

MONRO, ALEXANDER. Structure and Functions of the Nervous System, with Tables. Fol. Edinburgh. 1783.

MONRO, A. System of Anatomy and Physiology. 3 vols. 8vo. Edinburgh. 1801.

MONTAIGNE, MICHEL DE. Essais. 5 vols. 8vo. Paris. 1818.

MONTEFIORE, J. Commercial Dictionary. 3 vols. 8vo. Phila. 1804.

MONTESQUIEU. Spirit of Laws. 2 copies. 2 vols. 8vo. Worcester. 1802.

MONTESQUIEU. Oeuvres complètes, avec des Notes. 8vo. Paris. 1835.

MONTFAUCON, BERN. DE. Palaeographia Graeca. Fol. Paris. 1708.

*MONTFAUCON, BERN. DE. L'Antiquité expliquée et representée en Figures. 10 vols. in 9. Fol. Paris. 1719.

MONTUCLA, J. E. Histoire des Mathématiques. 4 vols. 4to. Paris. 1799–1802.

MOORE, EDWARD. Poems. 18mo. Easton, Penn. 1811.

MOORE, J. H. The Practical Navigator. 8vo. London. 1791.

MORALISTS FRANÇAIS. Pensées de Blaise Pascal; Reflexions, Sentences, et Maximes de La Rochefoucauld; Caractères de La Bruyère; Oeuvres complètes de Vauvenargues. 8vo. Paris. 1834.

MORE, HANNAH. Practical Piety. 8vo. Burlington, N. J. 1811.

MORE, HENRY. Theological Works. Fol. London. 1707.

MORE, HENRY. Collection of Philosopical Writings. Fol. London. 1712.

MORE, SIR THOS. Utopia, with Notes and a Biographical and Literary Introduction by Dibdin. 4to. London. 1808.

MORRIS, GOUVERNEUR. Life and Writings, by J. Sparks. 3 vols. 8vo. Boston. 1832.

MORRIS, JOSEPH. Sermons. 8vo. London. 1743.

MORSE, JEDEDIAH. American Geography. 8vo. London. 1792.

MORSE, JEDEDIAH. American Universal Geography. 2 vols. 8vo. Boston. 1801–1805.

MORSE, JEDEDIAH. Report on Indian Affairs. 8vo. New Haven. 1822.

MORTON, N. See Davis, John.

MOSES CHORONENSIS. Historia Armeniaca, cum Praefatione de Litteratura et Versione Sacra Armeniaca et Epistolis duabus Armeniacis. 4to. London. 1736.

MOSES MAIMONIDES. More Nevochim a Buxtorf. 4to. Basil. 1629.

MUDGE, W. Trigonometrical Survey of England and Wales. 4to. London. 1801.

MUELLER, C. G. De Cyclo Graecorum Epico et Poetis Cyclicis. 8vo. Lips. 1829.

MUELLER, K. O. Denkmäler der Allen Kunst. Fünf Heften.

MUELLER, K. O. Geschichten Hellenischer Stämme und Städte Orchomenos und die Minyer. 8vo. Breslau. 1820.

MUELLER, K. O. Die Dorier. 2 vols. 8vo. Breslau. 1824.

MUELLER, K. O. Die Altere Geschichte des Makedonischen Volks. 8vo. Berlin. 1825.

MUELLER, K. O. Die Etrusker. 2 vols. 8vo. Breslau. 1828.

MUELLER, K. O. Handbuch der Archäologie der Kunst. 8vo. Breslau. 1835.

MUELLER, K. O. History and Antiquities of the Doric Race. 2 vols. 8vo. Oxford. 1830.

MUELLER, JOHANN VON. Geschichten Schweizerischer Eidgenossenschaft. 5 vols. 8vo. Leipzig. 1822–1826.

MUELLER, O. F. Vermium Terrestrium et Fluvialium succincta Historia. 2 vols. 4to. Lipsiae. 1773.

*MUELLER, WILLIAM. Elements of the Science of War, illustrated by Plates. 3 vols. 8vo. London. 1811.

MUENTER, FR. Antiquarischen Abhandlungen. 8vo. Kiobenhavn. 1816.

MULIERUM Graecarum, Fragmenta et Elogia, Graece et Latine. Ed. Wolfius. 4to. Hamburgi. 1735.

Muratori, L. A. Annali d'Italia, dal principio dell Era volgare sino all anno 1500. 12 vols. 4to. Milano. 1744–1749.

Murrey, Lindley. Key to the Exercises adapted to English Grammar. 12mo. New York. 1814.

Murrey, Lindley. Power of Religion on the Mind. 12mo. New York. 1808.

Musae Anglicanae. 2 vols. 12mo. Londini. 1761.

Musaeum Criticum, or Cambridge Classical Researches. 2 vols. 8vo. Cambridge, Eng. 1826.

Musaeus, Grammaticus. De Herone et Leandro Carmen. Ed. Schäffer. 8vo. Lipsiae. 1820.

Musaeus, J. A. Volksmärchen der Deutchen. 5 vols. 16mo. Gotha. 1826.

Musculus, W. Commentarium in Matthaeum. Fol. Basileae. 1543.

Museum of Foreign Literature. Vols. x–xvii. 8vo. Phila. 1840–1842.

Musee Royale. Notice de Tableaux. 12mo. Paris. 1833.

Musee Royale des Antiques. Description par Clarac. 12mo. Paris. 1830.

Nadir Shah. History of, by Frazer. 12mo. London. 1742.

Napier, Col. F. W. P. Peninsular War. 4 vols. 8vo. Lond. 1828–1834.

Nardini, Famiano. Roma Antica. 4 vols. 8vo. Roma. 1818.

National Preacher. See Pamphlet Cases 31, 32.

Nautical Almanack for the Year 1812. American impression. 8vo. New Brunswick, N. J.

Nautical Almanack published by order of the Lords Commissioners of the Admiralty, for the years 1836 to 1850. 14 vols. 8vo. London.

Nautical Almanack. Blunt's eds. for the years 1811, 1812, 1813, and 1814. 4 vols. 12mo. New York.

Naval Actions between Great Britain and the United States, by Wm. James. 8vo. Halifax, N. S. 1816.

Navigation. Internal, of the U. S. A. 8vo. Phila. 1826.

Neal, Daniel. Civil and Ecclesiastical History of New England, to 1700. 2 vols. 8vo. London. 1720.

Neander, Aug. Church History of the first three Centuries, translated by Rose. Vol. i. 8vo. London. 1831.

Neele, Henry. Literary Remains. 8vo. New York. 1829.

NECKER. Importance of Religious Opinions, from the French. 12mo. Boston. 1796.

NEFF, FELIX. Memoir, by Gilly. 12mo. Boston. 1832.

NEGRO PLOT. History of, in New York in 1741 and 1742, by Horsmanden. 8vo. New York. 1810.

NEILSON, WILLIAM. Greek Exercises. 12mo. New York. 1810.

NELSON, LORD VISCOUNT. Memoirs, by J. Charnock. 8vo. Boston. 1806.

*NERALCO. I tre Ordini d'Archetettura, Dorico, Ionico, e Corintio. Fol. Roma. 1744.

NEUMAN, HENRY. Dictionary of the Spanish and English Languages. 2 vols. 8vo. Phila. 1823.

NEVEU-DEROTRIE. Les Lois Rurales Françaises. 8vo. Paris. 1845.

NEWCOMB, WILLIAM. Harmony of the Gospels, in Greek. 8vo. Andover. 1814.

NEW ENGLAND. Compendious History of, by Drs. Morse and Parish. 12mo. Newburyport. 1809.

NEW HAMPSHIRE. History of, for one Century from the Discovery of the Piscataqua, by Belknap. 3 vols. 8vo. Dover. 1812.

NEW IPSWICH. History of, with Genealogical Notices. 8vo. Boston. 1852.

NEW JERSEY. History of the Colony of, to 1721, by S. Smith. 8vo. Burlington, N. J. 1765.

NEWMAN, S. P. Elements of Political Economy. 8vo. Andover. 1835.

NEWMAN, S. P. System of Rhetoric. 12mo. Andover. 1839.

NEWTON, ISAAC. Opticks, and two Treatises on the Species and Magnitude of Curvilinear Figures. 4to. London. 1704.

NEWTON, ISAAC. Lectiones Opticae. 4to. London. 1729.

NEWTON, ISAAC. Opera quae extant omnia. Ed. Horsley. 5 vols. 4to. London. 1785.

NEWTON, ISAAC. The Mathematical Principles of Natural Philosophy, transl. by De Motte. 3 vols. 8vo. London. 1803.

NEWTON, ISAAC. Philosophiae Naturalis Principia Mathematica. 4 vols. 8vo. Glasguae. 1822.

NEWTON, JOHN. Olney Hymns. 8vo. New York. 1810.

NEWTON, THOMAS. Dissertations on the Prophecies. 2 copies. 3 vols. 8vo. Phila. 1813.

NEWTON, THOMAS. Life. See Edward Pococke.

NEW TESTAMENT. Printed at Rhemes. 4to. 1582.

NEW TESTAMENT in an improved Version. 8vo. Boston. 1809.

New Testament by Wm. Tyndale, 1526. 12mo. Andover. 1837.

New Testament, Sandwich Islands. 12mo. Oahu. 1835.

New Testament in Chinese. 8vo.

New York. Documentary History of the State by E. B. O'Callaghan. 2 copies. 4 vols. 8vo. Albany. 1849–1851.

New York Historical Society.
Collections for 1809. Vol. i. 8vo. New York. 1811.
Collections for 1814. Vol. ii. 8vo. New York. 1814.
Collections. Second Series. Vol. i. 8vo. New York. 1841.
Constitution and By-Laws. 8vo. New York. 1844.
Proceedings for 1843. 8vo. New York. 1844.

New York. History of. 8vo. (Title Page wanting.)

New York Institution for the Instruction of the Deaf and Dumb. 32d Annual Report. 8vo. Albany. 1851.

New York. Laws, from 1691 to 1751. Fol. New York. 1752.

New York. Laws, from 1777 to 1809. 5 vols. 8vo. Albany. 1807.

*New York Natural History. 14 vols. 4to. Albany. 1842–1847.
Part I. Zoology, by James E. De Kay. 5 vols.
II. Botany, by John Torrey. 2 vols.
III. Mineralogy, by Lewis C. Beck.
IV. Geology, by James Hill, E. Emmons, Wm. M. Mather, and Lardner Vanuxem. 4 vols.
V. Agriculture, by E. Emmons.
VI. Paleontology, by James Hall.

New York Spectator, from 1840 to 1853. 13 vols. Fol.

New York University. Regents' Reports, for 1833, 1835, 1843, 1847, 1848, 1849, 1850, 1851, and 1853. 9 vols. 8vo. New York.

Nicander, Colophron. Theriaca, Graece. Ed. Schneider. 8vo. Lipsiae. 1816.

Nicephorus Callistus. Ecclesiasticae Historiae Libri xviii. Fol. Basileae. 1553.

Nicholson, W. First Principles of Chemistry. 8vo. London. 1792.

Nicodemus Agioreitus. Synaxaristes. 3 vols. in 2. 2 copies. Fol. Benetiae. 1819.

Nicolaus Damascenus. Supplementum Editionis Lipsiensis. 8vo. Lipsiae. 1811.

Nicole. Essais de Morale. 8 vols. 12mo. Paris. 1782.

Nicolle, Abbe. Géographie Moderne. 2 vols. 18mo. Paris. 1753.

NIEBUHR, B. G. Römische Geschichte. Vols. I and III. 8vo. Berlin. 1823.

NIEBUHR, B. G. Kleine Historische und Philologische Schriften erste Sammlung. 8vo. Bonn. 1828.

NIEBUHR, B. G. Epitome of his History of Rome, by Twiss. 8vo. Oxford. 1836.

NIEBUHR, C. Description de l'Arabie. 4to. Amsterdam. 1774.

NIEBUHR, C. Voyage en Arabie, avec Planches. 2 vols. 4to. Amsterdam. 1780.

NILES, SAMUEL. Scripture Doctrine of Original Sin. 12mo. Boston. 1757.

NILES' Weekly Register. 50 vols. 1811–1836. By H. Niles. 8vo. Baltimore.

NILES' Weekly Register from 1836 to 1844, by W. O. Niles and Hughes. 15 vols. 4to.

NILES' Weekly Register from 1844 to 1849. 7 vols. (Vols. XVIII and XIX wanting.) 4to. Baltimore.

Index to the first 12 vols. 8vo. Baltimore.

NITZSCH, C. L. De Discrimine Revelationis. 2 vols. 8vo. Wittebergae. 1830.

NOBLE, S. Plenary Inspiration of the Scriptures. 8vo. Boston. 1828.

NOEL, M. Nouvelle Grammaire Française. 12mo. Paris. 1834.

NÖHDEN, G. H. Grammar of the German Language. 8vo. London. 1830.

NONNUS PANOPOLITANUS. Dionysiacorum Libri XLVIII. Ed. Gräfe. 2 vols. 8vo. Lipsiae. 1819.

NORRIS, JOHN. Miscellanies. 8vo. Oxford. 1687.

NORRIS, JOHN. Ideal or Intelligible World. 2 vols. 8vo. London. 1701–1704.

NORTH. See Guilford.

NORTHCOTE, JAMES. Conversations of, by Wm. Hazlitt. 8vo. Lond. 1830.

NORTHERN LIGHT. 3 vols. in one. Fol. Albany. 1841–1843.

NORTON, JACOB. Sermons on various Occasions. 8vo. Boston. 1810–1816.

NOVALIS. Schriften. 2 vols. 8vo. Berlin. 1826.

NOVUM TESTAMENTUM, Graece. Ed. J. J. Griesbach. 8vo. Cambridge. 1809.

NOVUM TESTAMENTUM, Graece. Ed. Bloomfield. 2 vols. 8vo. Lond. 1836.

Idem. 12mo. Wigorniae, Massachusettensi. 1800.

Idem. 12mo. London. 1827.

NOVUM TESTAMENTUM, Syriace. 4to. Cothenis. 1622.

NOYES, GEO. R. New Translation of the Hebrew Prophets. 3 vols. 8vo. Boston. 1833.

NOYES, GEO. R. New Translation of the Book of Job. 12mo. Boston. 1838.

NOYES, GEO. R. New Translation of Proverbs, Ecclesiastes, and the Canticles. 12mo. Boston. 1846.

NUGENT, LORD. See Hampden.

NUTTAL, THOMAS. Journal of Travels into Arkansas Territory. 8vo. Phila. 1820.

NUTTAL, THOMAS. Genera of North American Plants. 2 vols. 12mo. Phila. 1818.

NUTTAL, THOMAS. Manual of the Ornithology of the U. S. A. and Canada:
On Land Birds. 12mo. Boston. 1832.
On Water Birds. 12mo. Boston. 1834.

OBSERVATIONS Physiques sur l'Agriculture, &c. 12mo. A la Haye. 1765.

OCKLEY, S. History of the Saracens. 2 vols. 12mo. London. 1708–1718.

ODIORNE, J. C. Opinions on Speculative Masonry. 8vo. Boston. 1830.

OEHLENSCHLAEGER, ADAM. Nordiske Dighte. 12mo. Kiobenhavn. 1807.

OERSTED, H. C. Recherches sur l'identité des Forces Chemiques et Electriques. 8vo. Paris. 1813.

OGDEN, SAMUEL. Sermons. 8vo. London. 1805.

OGILVIE, JOHN. Poems. Also, Jenner's Poems bound with do. 4to. Lond. 1764.

OLD ENGLISH DRAMA. 2 vols. 12mo. London. 1825.

OLDHAM, JOHN. Works and Remains. 12mo. London. 1703.

OLD PLAYS. Select Collection, by Dodsley. 12 vols. 12mo. London. 1825–1827.

OLD WHIG, or the Consistent Protestant. 2 vols. 8vo. London. 1739.

OLIVER, B. First Lines of Physiology. 8vo. Phila. 1840.

OLIVER, B. L. Rights of an American Citizen. 8vo. Boston. 1832.

*OLIVI, G. Zoologia Adriatica Ossia. 4to. Bassanae. 1792.

OLMSTED, DENISON. Natural Philosophy. 2 vols. 8vo. New Haven. 1832.

OLSHAUSEN, D. J. W. Prolegomene zu einer Kritik aller sogenannten Beweise für und wider Offenbarungen. 12mo. Kiobenhavn. 1791.

OLSHAUSEN, D. J. W. Lehrbuch der Moral und Religion. 12mo. Schleswig. 1799.

OLSHAUSEN, D. J. W. Genuineness of the Writings of the New Testament. 12mo. Andover. 1838.

OPPIANUS. Cynegetica et Halientica. Ed. Schneider. 8vo. Lipsiae. 1813.

ORATIONS Commemorative of the 5th of March, 1770. 8vo. Boston. 1807.

ORATORES GRAECI. Ed. Reiske. 9 vols. 8vo. Lipsiae. 1770.

Vols. I, II. Demosthenes.
III. Aeschines.
IV. Dinarchus, Lycurgus, Demades, Andocides.
V, VI. Lysias.
VII. Isaeus, Antiphron.
VIII. Lesbonax, Herodus, Antisthenes, Alcidamas, Gorgias.
IX. Indices.

ORIGENES. Hexaplorum quae supersunt, Graece et Latine. Ed. Bahrdt. 2 vols. 8vo. Lipsiae. 1769.

ORME, ROBT. Military Transactions of the British in Indostan. 3 vols. 4to. London. 1780–1788.

ORME, ROBT. Historical Fragments of the Mogul Empire. 4to. London. 1805.

OROSIUS. Anglo-Saxon Version by Alfred the Great, with an English Translation. 8vo. London. 1773.

ORPHICA. Rec. G. Hermann. 8vo. Lipsiae. 1805.

ORTON, JOB. Exposition of the Old Testament. 6 vols. 8vo. Charlestown. 1805.

OSBORN, MRS. SARAH. Memoirs of, by Dr. Saml. Hopkins. 12mo. Catskill. 1814.

OSBORNE, B. Truth Displayed. 8vo. Rutland. 1816.

OSGOOD, DAVID. Sermons. 8vo. Boston. 1824.

OSSIAN. Poems, transl. by James Macpherson, Esq. 8vo. Phila. 1790.

OSSIAN. The same, ed. by Malcom Laing. 2 vols. 8vo. Edinburgh. 1805.

OSTERWALD, J. F. Compendium of Christian Theology. 8vo. Hartford. 1788.

OTTLEY, W. T. History of Engraving on Copper and Wood, with an Account of Engravers and their Works. 2 vols. 4to. London. 1816.

OTWAY, THOMAS. Plays, Poems, and Letters. 2 vols. 8vo. Lond. 1812.

OUSELEY, W. G. Remarks on the Statistics and Political Institutions of the U. S. 8vo. Phila. 1832.

OVID. Tristia, transl. by N. Bailey. 12mo. London. 1740.

OVIDIUS, PUBLIUS, NASO. Opera e Textu Burmanni. 5 vols. 8vo. Oxoniae. 1825.

OWEN, JOHN. Exposition of the Epistle to the Hebrews. 4 vols. 8vo. Boston. 1811.

OWEN, JOHN. Works, ed. by Russel. 21 vols. 8vo. London. 1826.

OWEN, ROBERT. New View of Society. 12mo. New York. 1825.

PAINE, MARTYN. Letters on Cholera Asphyxia. 8vo. New York. 1832.

PAINE, MARTYN. Medical and Physiological Commentaries. 3 vols. 8vo. New York. 1840.

PAINE, MARTYN. Institutes of Medicine. 8vo. New York. 1847.

PAINE, MARTYN. Materia Medica and Therapeutics. 12mo. New York. 1848.

PAINE, MARTYN. Discourse on the Soul and Instinct. 12mo. New York. 1849.

PAINE, ROBERT TROUPE. Memoir of, by his Parents. 4to. New York. 1852.

PAINE, THOMAS. Life, by Cheatham. 8vo. New York. 1809.

PALAEPHATUS. De Incredibilibus. Ed. Fischer. 8vo. Lipsiae. 1786.

PALEY, WILLIAM. Horae Paulinae. 8vo. Dublin. 1790.

PALEY, WILLIAM. Moral and Political Philosophy. 8vo. Phila. 1794.

PALEY, WILLIAM. The same. 8vo. Boston. 1810.

PALEY, WILLIAM. The same. 8vo. Cambridge. 1830.

PALEY, WILLIAM. Evidences of Christianity. 8vo. Phila. 1795.

PALFREY, JOHN G. Chaldaic, Syriac, Samaritan, and Rabbinical Grammar. 8vo. Boston. 1835.

*PALLAS, P. S. Travels through the Southern Provinces of the Russian Empire. 2 vols. 4to. London. 1802.

PAMPHLETS BOUND IN VOLUMES. 67 vols. 8vo.

Theological and Controversial Pamphlets, containing papers by Dexter, Allyn, Eddy, Feltus, Sewall, Lowell, Norton, Upham, Jarvis, Holmes, Ballou, Stetson, Little, Bailey, Hogan, Gray, Pierpont, Cuming, Deane, Spring, Murdock, Richardson, Ware, Pearson, Stuart, Worcester, Channing, Parkman, Belsham, Perkins, Brockway, Ely, Spooney, Worral, Haven, Wood, Cornelius, Beecher, Kimball, Bartlett. 8 vols.

Pamphlets Bound in Volumes—Continued.

Ordination Sermons, by Withington, Ripley, Ware, Brainerd, Backus, Beecher, Worcester, Colman, Woods, Humphrey, Williams, Hosmer, Young, Pierce, Willard, Flint, Osgood, Porter, Bancroft, Harris, Holmes, Thurston, Thayer, Braman, Sprague, Tuckerman, Chauncey, Furness, Lowell, Brazer, Greenwood, Walker, Channing. 3 vols.

Election Sermons, (Mass.) by Gay, Prince, Eaton, Thayer, Dewey, Sharp, Stuart, Walker, Channing, Withington, Harris, Baldwin, Gray, Frothingham, Greenwood, Pierpont, Upham.

Occasional Discourses, by Pierce, Greenwood, Ware, Frothingham, Wainwright, Putnam, Channing, Stone, Pierpont, Dana, Emerson, Lincoln, Storrs, Barry, Colman, Everett, Deane, Rogers, Bancroft, Noah, Upham, Farley, Palfrey, Furness, Mason, Willard, Damon, Chauncey. 2 vols.

Occasional Addresses, by Frisbie, Story, Everett, Norton, Ware, Sprague, (Poem), Quincy, Oliver, White, Philip, Eames, Lord, Humphrey, Palfrey, Channing, Bartol, Gray, Hopkins, Dewey, Pierce, Francis, Leland, Hawley, Green, Boyd, Field, Colman. 2 vols.

Doctrinal and Practical Discourses, by Channing, Pierce, Murdock, Furness, Pierpont, Palfrey, Lowell, Bigelow, Sprague, Emerson, Cornelius, Bancroft, Waterman, Bartlett, Gay, Wood, Worcester, Kippis, Norton, Chandler, Lamson, Tuckerman, Eaton, Deane, Ware, Howe, Perry, Harris, Dewey. 3 vols.

Funeral Discourses, by Upham, Palfrey, Sprague, Colman, Putnam, Greenwood, Frothingham, Brooks, Channing, Young, Kirkland, Webster, Everett, Ware, Whitney, Pierpont, Story, Cary, Brazer. 2 vols.

Anniversary Addresses, by Woodbridge, Ware, Flint, Sprague, Story, Ripley, Quincy, Upham, Pierce.

Fast and Thanksgiving Discourses, by Prince, Mayhew, Willard, Osgood, Freeman, Thayer, Harris, Morse, Porter, Turner, Thurston, Bancroft, Colman.

Occasional Sermons, by Wayland, Porter, Lowell, Tuckerman, Harris, Beecher, Pearson, Sprague, Fisk, Dwight, Keep, Strong, Kimball, Brazer, Forbes, Ware, Holmes, Bancroft, Thacher, Sharp, Gray, Allen, Flint, Hawes, Wheelock, Kendall, Eddy, Richardson, Wisner, Bentley, Barton, Willard, Whitney, Gay. 2 vols.

Seven Sermons, by Moses Hemmenway.

Locke on Government, The Ass or the Serpent by Thos. Bradbury, Hart's Dialogue, Tracts by Smalley, Pemberton, Cleaveland, View of Wesley's Conference at Bristol.

Pamphlets Bound in Volumes—Continued.

Milton's Old Looking Glass, Tracts by Dr. Bellamy, Pike's Thoughts on the Assembly's Catechism.

Tracts by Dr. Chauncey, Farmer's Letters, Armstrong's Poem on Health.

Wigglesworths's Discourse on Eternal Punishment, Wheelock's Narrative of the Ind. Charity School, Hart's Letter to Dr. Whittaker, Tracts by Hart, Fish, Cleveland, Dickinson.

Tracts by Elliot, Wigglesworth, Hopkins, Mayhew, Barnard, Mather, Foxcroft.

Tracts on Future Punishment.

Tracts by Dickinson, Emlyn, &c.

Anti-Slavery Papers, containing Reports, Addresses, Periodicals, Memorials, Resolutions, &c. 4 vols.

African Colonization Papers. Reports and Periodicals.

Peace Papers, containing Addresses, Reports, &c., and Friend of Peace.

Temperance Tracts, containing Reports, Periodicals and Addresses. 3 vols.

Missionary and Bible Society Pamphlets, containing Reports, Addresses, &c.

Fourth of July Orations, by J. Q. Adams, G. W. Adams, Bassett, Codman, Quincy, Lincoln, Everett, Colman, Gleason, Wright, Phillips, Bodman, Webster, Whitcomb, King.

Political Speeches and Discourses, by Webster, Appleton, Choate, Seward, Cushing, Binney, J. Q. Adams, Holmes, Frelinghuysen, Sprague, Everett, Barton, Vinton, Johnson. 2 vols.

Political Tracts, containing Addresses, Speeches, Journals of Conventions, Memorials, Reports. 2 vols.

Papers on Internal Improvements, containing Lectures, Speeches, Reports, Bills, Surveys, Memorials, &c. 2 vols.

Papers on Steam Carriages and Steamboats. Washington. 1832.

Papers on Rail Roads.

Public Documents; Reports, Petitions, Opinions, &c.

Papers on Banks and Banking.

Papers on Prison Discipline, Pauperism, and Crime. 3 vols.

Miscellaneous Tracts. 8 vols.

Pamphlets in Cases:

1–10. Laws of Vermont. See Vermont State Papers.

11–20. Journals of Vermont Legislature. See Vermont State Papers.

PAMPHLETS IN CASES—Continued.

21. Addresses pronounced at the University of Vermont.
22. Literary Addresses.
23. Inaugural Addresses.
24. Fourth of July Orations.
25, 26. Medical Documents.
27. Monthly Journal of Medicine. Vols. v and vi. Hartford. 1825.
28. Literary and Theological Review. Nos. 10, 11, 17, 18. New York. 1836–1838.
29. The same. Nos. 19, 20, 21. New York. 1838–1839.
30. Antiquarian Papers.
31. National Preacher. Vols. i–iv.
32. The same. Parts of Vols. viii, xi, xvi.
33. Christian Sentinel. Vol. i. The Sabbath.
34. Brownson's Quarterly Review. Vol. i. Brande's Encyclopaedia. (Defective.)
36. New York Review. No. 40. Southern Quar. Review. No. 27. Lit. and Theol. Review. Nos. 8 and 9.
37. American Missionary. Vols. ii, iii, iv, v, vii.
38. Religious Tracts. Marsh's Theological Lectures.
39. Westminster Review. Nos. 201–203. North British Review. Nos. 11–13. Boston. 1844.
40. Lit. and Phil. Repertory. Nos. 1, 2, 3. Middlebury. 1814–1815. American Review. No. 1. Protestant Review. Nos. 2, 3. New Eng. Mag. Nos. 42, 43.
41. American Biblical Repository. Nos. 1, 4, 16, 22.
42. Peace Documents. Advocate of Peace. Jay.
43. Masonic Papers. Trials. U. S. Law Mag. Vol. iii. No. 1. 1851.
44. Reports of American Tract Soc. Nos. 2, 10, 13, 15, 16, 20.
45. Papers on Political Economy, Banks, Roads, &c.
46. Bibliotheca Sacra, Vol. i. Nos. 1, 2, 4.
47. The same. Vol. ii.
48. The same. Vol. iii.
49, 50, Eulogies.
51. College Documents. U. Vt. System of Instruction. Dartmouth, Union, West Point, Harvard Pamphlets.
52. Record Commission. Vattemare's Exchange.
53. Journal of the Soc. of Arts. Nos. 1–31. London. 1852–1853.
54. Education. Vt. State Supt. Reports.
56. Socialism. Raymond and Greely, &c.
57. Christian Examiner. Nos. 24, 27. For. Quar. Review. Nos. 27, 31. Blackwood. No. 6.

PAMPHLETS IN CASES—Continued.

58. Maps. Univ. of Vt. Mss.
59. Common School Documents.
60. Vt. State Docs. Reports on Geology of Mass.
61. Education. Art Union. Answer to "Six Months in a Convent."
62. Slavery.
63. Walton's Vt. Register. 1831–1846. (1842 wanting.)
64. Missionary Papers.
65, 66, 67. Miscellaneous.
68–72. Missionary Herald. Vols. XL–XLIX. (Vol. XLI wanting.)
73. Quarterly Review. Nos. 150, 154.
74. French Tracts.
75. Asylum Reports. Galt's Essays.
76. Proceedings of Brit. Soc. of Nat. Hist.
77. Lumley's Biographical Advertiser.
78. Baptist Documents.
79. Educational Reports.
80. Religious. Andover Course of Study.
81. Christian Review. No. 21. Lamartine's Memoirs. Correspondence between Adams and Cunningham. The Seventh Vial.
82. Missionary and Fast Sermons.
83. Doctrinal Sermons.
84. Vermont Election Sermons.
85, 86. Sermons.
87. Papers on Hartford Convention and Indian Relations.
88. Foreign Quarterly Review. Nos. 66, 71.
89. Edinburgh Review. No. 127.
90–94. Museum of Foreign Literature. Vols. X–XV. (Vol. XIV wanting.) Phila. 1827–1829.
95. Horticultural.
96–98. American Agriculturist. Vols. III, IV, V. New York. 1844–1846.
99. Agriculture Française.
100. Agriculture. British Farmer's Magazine.
101. Journal of the Franklin Institute.
102. Literary. Phonetic Magazine.
103. New York Quarterly Review. No. 4. Education in Upper Canada.
104. American S. S. Union.
105. Reports of Vt. Benevolent Societies.
106–108. Hunt's Merchants' Magazine. Vols. X–XII. New York. 1844–1845.
109. Seaman's Friend. Colonization.

PAMPHLETS IN CASES—Continued.

110. Deaf and Dumb Papers.

111, 112. Prison Discipline Soc. Reports. Nos. 13–27.

113. Theological Pamphlets.

114. Colonization Papers.

115. Educational Tracts. Mass. Reports.

116. Tracts on Nat. History; Profs. Hitchcock, Adams, and others.

117. Coleman's European Agriculture. 2 vols.

118, 119. Temperance Pamphlets.

120. Home Missionary Tracts.

121. Episcopal Documents. Trial of Bishop Onderdonk.

122. Episcopal Papers. Diocese of Vermont.

123. Election and Funeral Sermons.

124. Papers of Bible Soc., and American Home Miss. Soc.

125. Catalogues of the Univ. of Vt.

126–128. Catalogues of different Institutions.

129. Mathematical Tracts. Steam Engine.

130. Agriculture Française.

131. Agricultural.

132. Papers of Smithsonian Institute and American Agricultural Soc.

133. Non-Resistant. Vols. 1, 2, 3, 4. Boston. 1839.

134. Reports of American Education Society.

135. Unitarian Papers.

Duplicates of Pamphlets. Prison Discipline Society's Annual Reports. Nos. 1–12, exc. 4th and 8th, also Nos. 24, 25, 27, and a triplicate of the 2d.

Hunt's Merchants' Magazine. Nos. 73, 74. 1845.

PANOPLIST. Vols. 2, 3, 9, 11, 12, 13, 14, 15. (Duplicates of Vols. 12, 13.) From 1807–1819. New Series, Vols. 1, 2, 3, 4, with Duplicates. 1809–1813.

PAPILLON, J. M. Traité Historique de la Gravure en Bois. 2 vols. 8vo. Paris. 1761.

PARECBOLAE, sive Excerpta e Corpore Statutorum Universitatis Oxoniensis. 12mo. Oxoniae. 1794.

PAREUS, DAVID. Commentarius in divin. Epistolam ad Romanos. 4to. Heidelbergae. 1620.

PAREUS, DAVID. Doctrinae Christianae. 12mo. Hanoviae. 1651.

PARIS, MATTHAEUS. Historia Anglica. Fol. Tiguri. 1589.

PARISH, E. Sacred Geography. 8vo. Boston. 1813.

PARK, MUNGO. Journal of Mission to the Interior of Africa. 2 vols. 4to. London. 1815.

Park, Mungo. Travels in the Interior of Africa. 8vo. Phila. 1800.

Parkinson, James. Organic Remains of a former World. 3 vols. 4to. London. 1820.

Parr, Samuel. Works, and Life by John Johnstone. 8 vols. 8vo. Lond. 1828.

Parris, J. A. Pharmacologia. 2 vols. 8vo. Novi Eboraci. 1824.

*Parry, Wm. E. Journal of Voyage for the Discovery of a North-west Passage, 1819–1820. 4to. London. 1821.

*Parry, Wm. E. Supplement to the Appendix to the above. 4to. Lond. 1824.

*Parry, Wm. E. Journal of Second Voyage for the Discovery of a North-west Passage, 1821–1823. 4to. London. 1824.

*Parry, Wm. E. Journal of Third Voyage for the Discovery of a North-west Passage, 1824–1825. With Plates and Charts. 4to. Lond. 1826.

Pascal, Blaise. Oeuvres. 5 vols. 8vo. La Haye. 1779.

Pascal, Blaise. See Moralists Francois.

Passow, Franz. Handwörterbuch der Griechischen Sprache. 2 vols. 8vo. Leipzig. 1831.

Pausanias. Graeciae Descriptio, Graece. Ed. Siebelis. 5 vols. 8vo. Lipsiae. 1822.

Pauw, M. de. Recherches Philosophiques sur les Grecs. 2 vols. 8vo. Berlin. 1787.

Payne, John. Universal Geography. 4 vols. 8vo. New York. 1798.

Pearce, Saml. Memoirs of, by Andrew Fuller. 12mo. Newark. 1809.

Pearce, Zachary. Life. See Edward Pococke.

Pearson, T. S. Catalogue of the Graduates of Middlebury College. 8vo. Windsor. 1853.

Pecchio, Giuseppe. Storia della Economia Publica in Italia. 8vo. Lugano. 1829.

Pellico, Sylvio. Opere complete. 2 vols. 12mo. Parigi. 1838.

Pelloutier. Histoire des Celtes. 8 vols. 12mo. Paris. 1770–1771.

Pemberton, C. R. Practical Treatise on various Diseases of the Abdominal Viscera. 8vo. Worcester. 1815.

Penn, William. Select Works. Fol. London. 1771.

Penn, William. No Cross, no Crown. 8vo. Phila. 1807.

Penn, William. Memoirs of, by Thos. Clarkson. 2 vols. 12mo. Phila. 1814.

Pennsylvania. History of, to 1742, by R. Proud. 2 vols. 8vo. Phila. 1798.

PENSEES Diverses ècrites à un Docteur de Sorbonne. 4 vols. 18mo. Rotterdam. 1781.

PEPYS, SAMUEL. Memoirs. 5 vols. 8vo. London. 1828.

PERCY, THOMAS. Reliques of Ancient English Poetry. 3 vols. Phila. 1823.

PERKINS, WILLIAM. Works. Fol. London. 1626.

PERRIN, JOHN. Exercises in French Syntax. 12mo. London. 1780.

PERRON, M. F. Voyage et Découvertes aux Terres Australes. 3 vols. 4to. Paris. 1807.

*Atlas de Planches. Fol. Paris. 1807.

*Atlas, Partie Navigation et Géographie. Fol. Paris. 1812.

PERRY, CHARLES. View of the Levant. Fol. London. 1743.

PERSEUS, AULUS FLACCUS. Satirae. Ed. Achaintre. 8vo. Parisiis. 1823.

PERSOON, C. H. Synopsis Plantarum. 2 vols. 12mo. Parisiis. 1805.

PERVIGILIUM VENERIS, cum Notis Pithoei et Justi Lipsii. 8vo. Hagae Com. 1712.

PESTALOZZI, HEINRICH. Wochenschrift für Menschenbildung. 2 vols. 8vo. Aarau. 1809–1815.

PETAVIUS, D. A. Rationarium Temporum. 8vo. Lugd. Batav. 1710.

PETRARCA. Opera. Fol. Venetiis. 1501.

PETRARCA. Opera quae extant omnia. 2 vols. Fol. Basileae. 1554.

PETRARCA. Sonnetti e Canzoni. 4to. Vinegia. 1558.

PETRARCA. Memoires par de Sade. 3 vols. 4to. Amsterdam. 1664–1667.

PETRONIUS, T. Satiricon: accedunt Veterum Poetarum Catalecta. Stud. Soc. Bipont. 8vo. Biponti. 1790.

PFEFFEL. Abrégé de l'Histoire et du Droit public d'Allemagne. 2 vols. 12mo. Paris. 1777.

PHAEDRUS, AUG. Fabulae Aesopiae. 8vo. Argentorati. 1810.

PHANODEMUS. Demonis, Clitodemi, etc., Fragmenta. Ed. Siebelis. 8vo. Lipsiae. 1812.

PHILADELPHIA ACADEMY of Natural Sciences. Act of Incorporation and Library Catalogue. 8vo. Phila. 1836.

PHILIPS, WM. Elementary Introduction to Mineralogy. 8vo. New York. 1818.

PHILO JUDAEUS. In Libros Mosis, Graece. Ex Bibliotheca Regia. Fol. Parisiis. 1552.

PHILOCHORUS ATHENIENSIS. Fragmenta. Ed. Siebelis. 8vo. Lipsiae. 1811.

PHILOSOPHICAL Transactions of the Royal Society from 1665 to 1842, with an Index from 1781–1820. 61 vols. 4to. London. 1809–1842.

PHILOSTRATORUM quae supersunt omnia. Accessere:
Appollonii Tyanensis Epistolae,
Eusebii Liber adversus Hieroclem,
Callistrati Descriptio Statuarum.
Fol. Lipsiae. 1709.

PHIPPS, JOSEPH. Original and Present State of Man. 8vo. Trenton. 1793.

PHORBOEUS, JOANNES. Nova Via docendi Graeca. 12mo. s. l. 1684.

PHOTIUS. Bibliotheca. Ed. Schotus. Fol. Genevae. 1611.

PHOTIUS. Lexicon. Ed. R. Porson. 2 vols. 8vo. Londini. 1822.

PICARD, L. B. Oeuvres Choisies. 24mo. New York. 1830.

PIKE, SAMUEL. A compendious Hebrew Lexicon. 8vo. Cambridge. 1802.

PINDARUS. Opera quae supersunt, Graece. Ed. Boeckhius. 4 vols. 4to. Lipsiae. 1811.

PINGRE, A. G. Cométographie. 2 vols. 4to. Paris. 1783.

PINKERTON, JOHN. Enquiry into the History of Scotland prior to 1056. 2 vols. 8vo. Edinburgh. 1814.

PINKERTON, JOHN. Dissertation on the Goths. Bound with Vol. II of the above.

PINKERTON, JOHN. Literary Correspondence. 2 vols. 8vo. London. 1830.

PINKERTON, JOHN. Select Scottish Ballads. 6 vols. in 3. 12mo. London. 1783–1792.

PINKERTON, ROBERT. On the Greek Church. See Platon.

PINKNEY, WM. Account of the Life, Writings, and Speeches of, by Henry Wheaton. 8vo. New York. 1826.

PISCATOR, JOHANNES. Commentarium in Vetus et Novum Testamentum. [illegible] vols. Fol. Herb. Nov. 1638.

PLACITA in Domo Capitulari Westmonasteriensi asservata: abbrev. Temp. Ric. I–Edv. II. Fol. London. 1811.

PLACITA de quo Warranto. Temp. Edv. I, II, III. Fol. London. 1818. (Omitted from British State Papers.)

PLANCK, G. F. Geschichte der Christlich-Kirchlichen Gesellschafts-Verfassung. 5 vols. in 6. 12mo. Hanover. 1803.

PLATNER, ERNST. Anthropologie. 8vo. Leipzig. s. a.

PLATO. Opera, Graece. Ed. Ficinus. 4to. Venetiis. 1577.

PLATO. Quae extant Opera. Ed. Astius. 11 vols. 8vo. Lipsiae. 1819.

PLATO. De Ideis Libellus. Ed. Richter. 8vo. Lipsiae. 1827.

PLATO. Leben und Schriften, von Ast. 8vo. Leipzig. 1816.

PLATON. Present State of the Greek Church in Russia, transl. from the Slavonian by Pinkerton. 12mo. New York. 1815.

PLAYFAIR, JOHN. Illustrations of the Huttonian Theory of the Earth. 8vo. Edinburgh. 1802.

PLAYFAIR, JOHN. Works. 6 vols. 8vo. Edinburgh. 1822.

PLINIUS, C. SEC. Historia Naturalis, cum Commentariis et Adnotationibus. 10 vols. 8vo. Lipsiae. 1788.

PLINIUS, JUNIOR. Epistolarum Libri x et Panegyricus. 8vo. Lipsiae. 1805.

PLINY'S History of the World, transl. by Holland. Fol. London. 1734.

PLOTINUS. See Thomas Taylor.

PLOWDEN, FRANCIS. History of the British Empire during the last twenty months. 1792–1793. 8vo. Phila. 1794.

PLUTARCH'S LIVES, transl. by Wrangham. 6 vols. 8vo. London. 1819.

PLUTARCH'S MORALS, translated. 5 vols. 8vo. London. 1704.

PLUTARCHUS. Quae supersunt omnia, Graece et Latine. Ed. Reiske. 12 vols. 8vo. Lipsiae. 1774.

PLYMOUTH. Memoirs of, by Bailies. 2 vols. 8vo. Boston. 1830.

POCOCKE, DR. EDWARD. Life by Dr. Twells : Lives of Z. Pearce and Thos. Newton by themselves : Life of Philip Skelton, by Mr. Burdy. 2 vols. 8vo. London. 1816.

POESIS PHILOSOPHICA. Reliq. Empedoclis, Parmenidis, Pythagorae, etc. By R. W. 1573. 12mo. s. l. 1635.

POETAE LATINI MINORES. Ed. Wernsdorf. 2 copies. 8 vols. 8vo. Altenburgi. 1780.

POETAE MINORES GRAECI. Ed. Gaisford. 4 vols. 8vo. Oxford. 1814.

POETAE MINORES GRAECI. Ed Winterton. 12mo. Oxoniae. 1635.

POETRY, Ancient Popular. 12mo. London. 1791.

POISSON, S. D. Traité de Méchanique. 2 vols. 8vo. Paris. 1811.

POISSON, S. D. Le même. 2de Ed. 2 vols. 8vo. Paris. 1833.

POLANUS, AMANDUS. De Verbo Dei Didascalia. 12mo. Basileae. 1593.

POLE, REGINALD. Life by Thomas Philips. 4to. Oxford. 1764.

POLEMON, LAOD. SOPH. Funebres Laudationes II, Graece. Ed. Orellius. 8vo. Lipsiae. 1819.

POLLUX, JULIUS. Onomasticon decem Libris constans. Ed. Siberus. 4to. Francofurti. 1608.

POLUS, MATTHAEUS. Synopsis Criticorum. 4 vols. in 5. (Dupl. of Vol. III.) Fol. London. 1669–1676.

POLYBIUS. Historiarum quicquid superest. Ed. Schweighäuser. 8 vols. 8vo. Lipsiae. 1789.

POLYBIUS. Supplementum. Ed. Id. 8vo. Lipsiae. 1818.

POLYBIUS. History, translated by Hampston. 4 vols. 8vo. London. 1773.

POLYDORUS. De Rerum Inventoribus Libri VIII. 12mo. Basileae. 1563.

POMPONATIUS, PETRUS. Tractatus de Immortalitate Animae. Fol. Bononiae. 1519.

POPES. History of, by Arch'd Bower. 3 vols. 4to. London. 1748.

POPPO. See Thucydides.

POPULATION. Nouvelles vues sur. 2 vols. 12mo. Amsterdam. 1763.

PORNEY. Syllabaire Française. 12mo. Phila. 1822.

PORNY, M. A. Elements of Heraldry. 8vo. London. 1795.

PORTA, D. G. B. Dei Miracoli e Maravigliosi Effetti dalla Natura prodotti. 12mo. Venezia. 1588.

PORTALIS, J. E. M. L'Usage et l'Abus de l' Esprit Philosophique durant le dixhuitieme Siècle. 2 vols. 8vo. Paris. 1820.

PORTER, E. The Young Preacher's Manual. 8vo. Boston. 1819.

PORTER, E. Analysis of the Principles of Rhetorical Delivery. 8vo. Andover. 1831.

PORTER, E. Rhetorical Reader. 8vo. Andover. 1833.

PORTER, E. The same. 8vo. Andover. 1841.

PORTER, E. Lectures on Eloquence and Style. 8vo. Andover. 1836.

*PORTER, SIR R. K. Travels in Georgia, Persia, Armenia, &c. 2 vols. 4to. London. 1822.

PORT FOLIO. Vols. V and VI. 8vo. Phila. 1815.

PORT ROYAL Greek Grammar, transl. by Nugent. 8vo. London. 1757.

POTHIER. Oeuvres, 11 vols. 8vo. Paris. 1827.

POTTER, R. Aeschylus translated. 16mo. New York. 1836.

POWERS, GRANT. Influence of the Imagination on the Nervous System. 12mo. Andover. 1828.

PRACTICAL REFLECTIONS for every day in the year. By a Jesuit. 18mo. New York. 1808.

PREJUGES Legitimes contre l'Encyclopédie. 5 vols. in 4. 12mo. Bruxelles. 1758.

PRESCOTT, W. H. History of the Reign of Ferdinand and Isabella. 3 vols. 8vo. Boston. 1838.

PRESCRIPTIONS of Eminent Physicians. 8vo. New York. 1818.

PRICE, RICHARD. Review of Questions and Difficulties in Morals. 8vo. London. 1769.

PRICE, RICHARD. Importance of the American Revolution. 12mo. Lond. and Boston. 1784.

PRICE, RICHARD. Sermons. 12mo. Boston. 1794.

PRICE, UVEDALE. Essays on the Picturesque. 3 vols. 8vo. London. 1810.

PRIDEAUX, HUMPHREY. Old and New Testaments connected in History. 4 vols. 8vo. Edinburgh. 1799.

PRIESTLEY, JOSEPH. Experiments and Observations on different kinds of Air. 5 vols. 8vo. London. 1781.

PRIESTLEY, JOSEPH. Lectures on History and General Policy, with an Essay on Liberal Education. 2 vols. 8vo. London. 1793.

PRIESTLEY, JOSEPH. History of the Corruptions of Christianity. 2 vols. 8vo. Birmingham. 1793.

PRISCIANUS CAESARIENSIS. Opera. Ed. Krehl. 2 vols. 8vo. Lipsiae. 1819.

PRISON DISCIPLINE. See Pamphlets.

PRITCHARD, ANDREW. Microscopic Cabinet of select animated Objects. 8vo. London. 1832.

PRIZE ESSAYS on a Congress of Nations. 8vo. Boston. 1840.

PROBLEME HISTORIQUE. Qui, des Jésuits ou de Luther et Calvin ont le plus nuit à l'Eglise Chrètienne. 2 vols. 12mo. Avignon. 1757.

PROCEEDINGS of the American Association for the Advancement of Science. 8vo. Boston. 1850.

PROCLUS. In Platonis Theologiam Libri VI, Graece et Latine. Fol. Hamburgi. 1618.

PROCLUS. See Thomas Taylor.

*PRONY. Nouvelle Architecture Hydraulique. 2 vols. 4to. Paris. 1790.

PROUT, W. On Diabetis Calculus, by Calhoun. 8vo. Phila. 1826.

PSALMORUM LIBER, Hebraice. Ed. J. Leusden. 12mo. Londini. 1758.

PSALTER, Arabic. 6 copies. s. l. et a.

PSEAUMES de David, mis en Vers François. 12mo. Amsterdam. 1729.

PTOLEMAEUS, CLAUDIUS. Geographiae Libri VIII. Fol. Basileae. 1552.

PTOLEMAEUS. Composition Mathématique, traduite du Grec en Français, par M. Halma. 2 vols. 4to. Paris. 1813–1816.

PTOLEMAEUS. Tables Chronologiques des Règnes, trad. par Halma. 4to. Paris. 1819.

PTOLEMAEUS. Hypothéses et Epoques des Planètes, trad. par Halma. 4to. Paris. 1820.

PTOLEMAEUS ET THEON. Tables Manuelles Astronomiques, seconde partie, trad. par Halma. 4to. Paris. 1823.

PUFFENDORF, BARON. Law of Nature and Nations. Fol. London. 1729.

PUISSANT, L. Méthode générale pour obtenir le resultat moyen d'une Série d'Observations Astronomiques. 4to. Paris. 1823.

PULCI, M. L. Morgante Maggiore. 3 vols. 8vo. Milano. 1806.

PURCHAS, S. His Pilgrimes. 3 vols. Fol. London. 1625.

PURSH, FREDERICK. Flora of North America. 2 vols. 8vo. London. 1814.

PURSUITS of Literature, a Satiric Poem. 8vo. Phila. 1810.

PYE, H. J. Commentary on the Poetic of Aristotle. 4to. London. 1792.

PYTHAGORAS. See Poesis Philosophica.

QUARTERLY Christian Spectator. Vol. x. 8vo. New Haven. 1838.

QUATREMERE DE QUINCY. Histoire de la vie et des Oeuvres des plus célèbres Architectes. 2 vols. 8vo. Paris. 1830.

QUATREMERE DE QUINCY. Canova et ses Ouvrages. 8vo. Paris. 1834.

QUATREMERE DE QUINCY. Histoire de la Vie et des Ouvrages de Raphael. 8vo. Paris. 1835.

QUATREMERE DE QUINCY. Essai sur l'Idéal dans les Arts du Dessin. 8vo. Paris. 1837.

QUATREMERE, ETIENNE. Recherches Critiques et Historiques sur la Langue et la Litterature de l'Egypte. 8vo. Paris. 1808.

QUINTILIANUS, M. FABIUS. Institutionum Oratoriarum Libri XII. 8vo. Venetiis. 1521.

QUINTILIANUS. De Institutione Oratoria Libri XII. Ed. Spalding. 6 vols. 8vo. Lipsiae. 1798.

QUINTILIANUS. Idem. 2 vols. in one. 18mo. Lipsiae. 1829.

QUINTILIANUS. Capita quaedam ex Libris. 12mo. Glasguae. 1796.

QUOY ET GAIMARD. Voyage d'Astrolabe. Zoologie. 6 vols. Paris. 1830–1833.

*Atlas de Planches de		Mollusques.	91	Planches.	Fol.
"	"	Mammiferes.	28	"	Fol.
"	"	Oiseaux.	29	"	Fol.
"	"	Poissons.	16	"	Fol.
"	"	Zoophytes.	19	"	Fol.
"	"	Vers Apodals.	1	"	Fol.

RABELAIS, FRANÇOIS. Oeuvres. 2 vols. 8vo. London et Paris. 1783.

RACINE, JEAN. Oeuvres. 8vo. Paris. 1835.

RAFFLES, SIR T. S. History of Java. 2 vols. 8vo. London. 1830.

RAFN, C. C. Färeyinga Saga. 4to. Kiobenhavn. 1832.

RALEIGH, SIR WALTER. Works, with Lives by Oldys and Birch. 8 vols. 8vo. Oxford. 1829.

RAMBACH, J. Meditations on the Sufferings of Christ. 2 vols. 8vo. New York. 1811.

RAMSAY, DAVID. History of the American Revolution. 2 vols. 8vo. Trenton. 1811.

RAMSAY, WILLIAM. Elegiac Extracts from Tibullus and Ovid. 8vo. Glasgow. 1840.

RAPIN DE THOYRAS. History of England to the Death of James II. 2 vols. Fol. London. 1732–1733.

RASK, R. Vejlednig til Akra-Sproget. 8vo. Kiobenhavn. 1820.

RASK, R. Singalesisk Skriftläre. 8vo. Kolombo. 1821.

RASK, R. Räsonnent Lappisk Sprogläre. 8vo. Kiobenhavn. 1822.

RAWLE, W. Constitution of the U. S. A. 8vo. Phila. 1829.

RAYNAL, G. T. Histoire Philosophique et Politique des Etablissemens et du Commerce des Européens dans les Deux Indes. 4 vols. 4to. Genève. 1780.

RAYNAL, G. T. The same translated. Vols. II, IV, V. 12mo. Edinburgh. 1782.

Atlas de l'Histoire. 4to. Genève. 1780.

RECORD COMMISSION. Report to the King on the Public Records. See Brit. State Papers, and Pamphlet Case No. 52.

REDFIELD, W. C. On Whirlwind Storms, with Replies to Dr. Hare. 8vo. New York. 1842.

REES, ABRAHAM. Cyclopaedia, or Universal Dictionary of Arts, Sciences, and Literature. 41 vols. 4to. Phila.

22 vols. of Plates to the above. 4to.

Modern Atlas to the above. 4to.

REFUTATION of the Calumnies against the Lord Chancellor in the Quarterly Review. 8vo. London. 1834.

REGNAULT, M. V. Elements of Chemistry transl. by Betton. 2 vols. 8vo. Phila. 1853.

REGULATIONS for the Field Infantry of the U. S. 8vo. Phila. 1812.

REID, DR. THOS. Essays on the Active Powers of Man. 4to. Edinburgh. 1788.

REID, DR. THOS. Inquiry into the Human Mind on the Principles of Common Sense. 8vo. London. 1785.

REID, DR. THOS. Essays on the Intellectual Powers of the Human Mind. 8vo. London. 1827.

REINHARD, F. V. Plan of the Founder of Christianity, transl. by Taylor. 8vo. New York. 1831.

REINHOLD. Aenesidemus, oder Elementar-Philosophie. 8vo. Jena. 1792.

RELAND, HADRIAN. Palaestina ex Monumentis veteribus illustrata. 2 vols. 4to. Trajecti Batav. s. a.

RELIGIOUS CONFERENCE, in four Dialogues. 12mo. New York. 1818.

RENNEL, JAMES. Topography of the Plain of Troy. 4to. London. 1814.

RENNEL, JAMES. History of the Expedition of Cyrus. 4to. London. 1816.

RENNEL, JAMES. Geographical System of Herodotus examined and explained. 2 vols. 8vo. London. 1830.

RENNEL, JAMES. Treatise on the Comparative Geography of Western Asia. 2 vols. 8vo. London. 1831.

RENSSELAER. See Geology.

RENWICK, JAMES. Treatise on the Steam Engine. 8vo. New York. 1830.

REPERTORY, Literary and Philosophical. Vol. I. 8vo. Middlebury. 1812. See also Pamphlet Case 40.

REQUIJO. Thesaurus Hispano-Latinus utriusque Linguae. (Title page wanting.)

REVIEWS.

American Quarterly. Vols. I–XXII. 8vo. Phila. 1827–1837.

Archiv für Philologie und Paedagogik. Vols. XIII–XVII. 8vo. Leipz. 1847–1850.

Boston Quarterly. Vol. I. 8vo. Boston. 1838.

Brownson's Quarterly. See Pamphlet Case 34.

Democratic. Vol. XIV. 8vo. New York. 1844.

Edinburgh. Vols. I–LXII. 8vo. Edinburgh. 1802–1835. Also Vols. LXXX–LXXXIV. Edinburgh. 1824–1826.

Index to the first 20 vols. 8vo. Edinburgh. 1813.

Index to Vols. XXI–XL. 8vo. Edinburgh. 1832.

Foreign Quarterly. Vols. XXXIV, XXXV. 8vo. London. 1845. Also Nos. 66, 71. See Pamphlet Case 88.

London Quarterly. Vols. I–LIII. 8vo. London. 1809–1835.

Vol. XX. Index to the first 19 vols. 8vo. London. 1820.

Vol. XL. Index to Vols. XXI–XXXIX. 8vo. London. 1831.

REVIEWS—Continued.

Neue Jahrbücher für Philologie und Paedagogik. Vols. L–LXVII. 8vo. Leipzig. 1847–1853.

New York. Vols. I–IV. 8vo. New York. 1837–1838. Also No. 40. See Pamphlet Case 36.

North American. Vols. XXVI–XXXIX and Vols. LVIII--LXIII. 8vo. Boston. 1827–1847.

North British. Nos. 11–13. See Pamplet Case 39.

Quarterly. Vols. LXXIV, LXXVI, LXXVIII. 8vo. London. 1844–1846. Also Nos. 150, 154. See Pamphlet Case 73.

Retrospective. 16 vols. 8vo. London. 1820–1828.

Westminster. Nos. 201--203. See Pamphlet Case 39.

Southern. Vols. I, II. 8vo. Charleston, S. C. 1828.

Southern Quarterly. Vols. VIII–XIII. 8vo. Charleston, S. C. 1845–1848.

Duplicates. N. American. Nos. 58, 70--73. Lit. and Theol. Nos. 10, 18.

REYNOLDS, EDWARD. Works. 6 vols. 8vo. London. 1826.

REYNOLDS, FREDERICK. Life and Times, by himself. 2 vols. in one. 8vo. Phila. 1826.

REYNOLDS, SIR JOSHUA. Literary Works, and Life by Malone. 3 vols. 8vo. London. 1819.

RHODE, J. G. Die heilige Sage und das gesammte Religions System des Zendvolks. 8vo. Frankfurt. 1820.

RICARDI, DAVID. Principles of Political Economy. 8vo. London. 1817.

RICCIARDETTO. From the Italian of Forteguerra, by Lord Glenverbie. 8vo. London. 1822.

RICHARD, ACHILLE. Nouveaux Elémens de Botanique et de Physiologie Végétale. 8vo. Paris. 1833.

RICHARDSON, JOHN. (Assisted by Swainson.) Fauna Boreali-Americana. 2 vols. 4to. London. 1831.

RICHTER, JEAN PAUL. Das Kampaner Thal, oder über die Unsterblichkeit der Seele. 16mo. Erfurt. 1797.

RICTER, JEAN PAUL. Titan. 4 vols. 16mo. Berlin. 1800.

RICHTER, JEAN PAUL. Vorschule der Aesthetik. 3 vols. 16mo. Stuttgart. 1813.

RICHTER, JEAN PAUL. Levana. 3 vols. 16mo. Stuttgart. 1814.

RIEDESEL, MADAME. Letters and Memoirs. 8vo. New York. 1827.

RITSON, JOSEPH. The Caledonian Muse: a Selection of Scottish Poetry. 12mo. London. 1821.

RITTER, D. Geschichte der Ionischen Philosophie. 8vo. Berlin. 1821.

RITTER, H. Abriss der Philosophischen Logik. 8vo. Berlin. 1829.

ROBERT OF GLOUCESTER. Chronicle by Hearne. 2 vols. 8vo. Oxford. 1724.

ROBERTSON, JOHN. Treatise on Mathematical Instruments. 8vo. London. 1775.

ROBERTSON, WILLIAM. History of Scotland. Vol. II. 8vo. Phila. 1811.

ROBERTSON, WILLIAM. History of Charles V. 3 vols. 8vo. Phila. 1812.

ROBERTSON, WILLIAM. Works. 8 vols. 8vo. London. 1827.

ROBINSON, EDWARD. Greek and English Lexicon of the New Testament. 8vo. Andover. 1825.

ROBINSON, SAMUEL. Catalogue of American Minerals, with their localities. 2 copies. 8vo. Boston. 1825.

ROBINSON, W. D. Memoirs of the Mexican Revolution. 8vo. Phila. 1820.

ROCHEFOUCAULD. See Moralistes Francois.

ROCHESTER, EARL OF. Correspondence and Diary. See Clarendon.

RODD, THOMAS. Ancient Spanish Ballads. 2 vols. in one. 8vo. London. 1821.

RODGERS, JOHN. Memoirs of, by Dr. Miller. 8vo. New York. 1813.

ROGET, P. M. Animal and Vegetable Physiology considered with reference to Natural Theology. 2 vols. 8vo. London. 1834.

ROHAULT'S System of Natural Philosophy. 2 vols. 8vo. London. 1723.

ROLAND, MADAME. Memoirs, par Borville et Barriere. 2 vols. 8vo. Paris. 1820.

ROLL AND BOOK sent forth by the LORD GOD OF HEAVEN. 2 vols. 8vo. Canterbury, N. H. 1843.

ROLLIN. Method of Teaching and Studying Belles-Lettres. 4 vols. 12mo. Edinburgh. 1778.

ROMANCES. Popular, with introductory Dissertations by Weber. 8vo. Edinburgh. 1812.

ROME. Histoire de, ou Histoire Romaine traduite sur le Grec par M. Cousin. 2 vols. 18mo. Paris. 1686.

ROMMANT de la Rose, par Guil. de Lorris et Jean de Meun. 18mo. Paris. 1529.

RONGE, JOHN. The Holy Coat of Treves. 12mo. New York. 1825.

ROQUEFORT, J. B. B. Glossaire de la Langue Romaine. 2 vols. 8vo. Paris. 1808.

ROSCOE, THOMAS. Memoirs of Scipio de Ricci. 2 vols. 8vo. London. 1829.

ROSCOE, WILLIAM. The same. 2 vols. 8vo. Phila. 1842.

ROSCOE, WILLIAM. Life of Lorenzo di Medici. 2 vols. 8vo. Phila. 1803.

ROSCOE, WILLIAM. Life and Pontificate of Leo X. 6 vols. 8vo. London. 1806.

ROSE, H. J. Inscriptiones Graecae Vetustissimae. 8vo. Cantab. 1825.

ROSE, HENRY. Manual of Analytical Chemistry, transl. by Griffin. 8vo. London. 1831.

ROSE, WM. S. Orlando Inamorato of F. Berni transl. 12mo. Edinb. and London. 1823.

ROSE, WM. S. The Court and Parliament of Beasts, a Poem transl. from the Italian. 18mo. London. 1823.

ROSENMUELLER, E. F. C. Institutiones ad Fundamenta Linguae Arabicae. 4to. Lipsiae. 1819.

ROSETTI, GABRIELLE. The Anti-Papal Spirit which produced the Reformation, in its Influence on the Literature of Europe. 2 vols. 8vo. London. 1834.

ROSS, JAMES. Latin Grammar. 12mo. Phila. 1814.

ROSSI, M. P. Traité du Droit Pénal. 3 vols. 8vo. Genève. 1829.

ROST, V. C. F. Kleine Grammatik des Attischen Dialects. 8vo. Göttingen. 1834.

ROTH, F. Ueber Thucydides und Tacitus. 4to. München. s. a.

ROUSSEAU, J. B. See Boileau.

ROUSSEAU, J. J. Oeuvres. 11 vols. 18mo. Paris. 1822–1825.

ROWE, ELIZABETH. Devout Exercises of the Heart. 18mo. Harrisburg. 1811.

ROWLEY. History of, by Thos. Gage, with an Anniversary Address by Bradford. 12mo. Boston. 1840.

ROWNING, J. Natural Philosophy. 2 vols. 8vo. London. 1765.

ROYER, C. E. Administration des Richesses. 8vo. Paris. 1843.

ROYER, C. E. Des Institutions de Crédit Foncier en Allemagne et en Belgique. 8vo. Paris. 1845.

RUEPPEL, EDWARD. Reisen in Nubien, Kordofan, und der peträischen Arabien. 8vo. Frankfurt a. M. 1829.

RUHNKENIUS, DAVID. Opuscula. 2 vols. 8vo. Lugd. Batav. 1823.

RULES and Articles of War, &c. 8vo. Burlington. 1813.

RUMFORD, COUNT. Essays, Political, Economical, and Philosophical. 2 vols. 8vo. Boston. 1799.

RUMOHR, C. F. Italienische Forschungen. 3 vols. 8vo. Berlin. 1827.

RUMOHR, C. F. Hans Holbein der Jüngere. 8vo. Leipzig. 1836.

RUMPHIUS, GEO. EVERHARDUS. D'Amboinsche Rariteitkamer. Fol. Amsterdam. 1705.

RUSH, BENJAMIN. Diseases of the Mind. 8vo. Phila. 1835.

RUSH, JACOB. Charges on Moral and Religious Subjects. 18mo. Lenox. 1815.

RUSH, JAMES. Philosophy of the Human Voice. 8vo. Phila. 1833.

RUSH, RICHARD. Memoranda of a Residence at the Court of London. 8vo. Phila. 1833.

RUSSEL, J. Tour in Germany. 8vo. Boston. 1825.

RUSSEL, LORD WILLIAM. Life by Lord John Russel. 2 vols. 8vo. London. 1820.

RUTHERFORD, JOHN. The Principle Orations of Cicero transl., with Notes. 4to. London. 1781.

RUTHERFORD, SAMUEL. Joshua Redivivus, or 352 Religious Letters. 8vo. New York. 1826.

SABATIER, R. B. De la Médicine Operative. 4 vols. 8vo. Paris. 1821–1824.

SACHSE, CARL. Geschichte und Beschreibung der Alten Stadt Rom. 2 vols. 12mo. Hanover. 1824.

SAGA Herrands ok Bosa. 8vo. s. l. et a.

SAGA af Hrolfi Konungi Sautrekssyni. s. l. et a.

SAGAN af Niali Porgeirssyni. 4to. Kaupmannahöfn. 1772.

SAGERET. Pomologie Physiologique. 8vo. Paris. 1830.

SAINT CROIX, G. Examen Critique des Anciens Historiens d'Alexandre le Grand. 4to. Paris. 1804.

SAINT DOMINGO. History of, by Bryan Edwards. 4to. London. 1797.

SAINT DOMINGO. Memoires de la Revolution de, par Lacroix. 2 vols. 8vo. Paris. 1819.

SAINT GEORGE, ARTHUR. Examination of Candidates for Holy Orders. 8vo. London. 1766.

SAINT PIERRE, J. H. BERNARDIN DE. Beauties of the Studies of Nature. 8vo. London. 1799.

SAINT PIERRE, J. H. BERNARDIN DE. Studies of Nature transl. by H. Hunter, and ed. by G. Barton. 3 vols. 8vo. Phila. 1808.

SAINT SIMON. Memoires sur le Règne de Louis XIV. 7 vols. Lond. 1789.

SALADIN. Vita et Res Gestae, ab Abulfeda. Fol. Lugd. Batav. 1755.

SALMASIUS. De Transubstantiatione. 12mo. Hagiopoli. 1746.

*SALT, HENRY. Voyage and Travels to Abyssinia. 4to. London. 1814.

SALUSTE. Histoire de la Republique Romaine dans le Cours du VIIme Siècle. 3 vols. 4to. Dijon. 1777.

SALUSTIUS, CAIUS CRISPUS. Quae extant. Ed. Gerlach. 2 vols. 4to. Basil. 1823.

SALUSTIUS, CAIUS CRISPUS. Idem in Usum Delph. Ed. Crispinus. 8vo. Phila. 1804.

SALUSTIUS, CAIUS CRISPUS. Idem. 2 copies. 8vo. Phila. 1814.

SALUSTIUS, PHILOSOPHUS. Libellus de Diis et Mundo, Graece et Latine. 12mo. Turici. 1821.

SALVATOR ROSA. Satire, con Notizie della sua vita. 8vo. Londra. 1823.

SALVATOR ROSA. Life and Times by Lady Morgan. 2 vols. 8vo. London. 1824.

SANDERSON, ROBERT. 34 Sermons. Fol. London. 1671.

SANDFORD, D. K. Rules and Exercises in Homeric and Attic Greek. 12mo. London. 1831.

SAUMAREZ, RICHARD. Dissertation on the Universe in General. 8vo. London. 1795.

SAUMAREZ. New System of Physiology. 2 vols. 8vo. London. 1798.

SAUMAREZ. Principles of Physiological and Physical Science. 8vo. Lond. 1812.

SAUNDERS, J. C. Anatomy of the Human Ear. 8vo. Phila. 1821.

SAURIN, J. Sermons. Vols. IV, V, VI, VII. 8vo. New York. 1805–1807.

SAURIN, J. 11 Select Sermons. 8vo. Concord. 1806.

SAUSSURE, H. B. DE. Voyages dans les Alps, précédés d'un Essai sur l'Histoire Naturelle des Environs de Genève. 4 vols. 4to. Neuchatel. 1779.

SAVIGNY, FRIED. Beruf unsrer Zeit für Gesetzgebung und Rechtswissenschaft. 8vo. Heidelberg. 1828.

SAVIGNY, FRIED. Geschichte des Römisches Recht. 6 vols. 8vo. Heidelberg. 1834.

SAWYER, F. W. Plea for Amusements. 12mo. Phila. 1847.

SAXBY, HENRY. British Customs. 8vo. London. 1757.

SAXE, MAURICE, COMTE DE. Reveries or Memoirs concerning the Art of War. 8vo. Edinburgh. 1759.

SAXE-WEIMAR, DUKE OF. Travels in North America. 2 vols. in one. 8vo. Phila. 1828.

SAXIUS, CHRISTOPHORUS. Onomasticon Litterarium. 8 vols. 8vo. Traj. ad Rhenum. 1775.

SAY, J. B. Treatise on Political Economy. 8vo. Phila. 1827.

SAY, THOMAS. American Entomology. 3 vols. with colored Plates. 8vo. Phila. 1824.

SAY, THOMAS. Explanation of terms for the above. 8vo. Phila. 1828.

SCHABALIE, J. P. Die Wandlende Seele. 12mo. Germantaun. 1805.

SCHARPIUS, JOHAN. Cursus Theologicus. 4to. Aurel. Allob. 1622.

SCHEINER, C. Oculus, hoc est, Fundamentum Opticum. 4to. Londini. 1652.

SCHELLING, F. W. J. Denkmal der Schrift von der Göttlichen Dingen. 8vo. Tübingen. 1812.

SCHELLING, F. W. J. Die Gottheiten von Samo-Thrace. 8vo. Stuttgart. 1815.

SCHELLING, F. W. J. Vorlesungen über die Methode des Academischen Studium. 12mo. Stuttgart. 1830.

SCHEPELERN, J. B. Skandinavische Bibliothek, eine Zeitschrift. 8vo. Kiobenhavn. 1835.

SCHLEGEL, AUG. W. Lectures on Dramatic Art and Literature, transl. by Black. 8vo. Phila. 1833.

SCHLEGEL, AUG. W. Shakspeare's Dramatische Werke. 9 vols. 12mo. Berlin. 1825.

SCHLEGEL, FRIEDRICH. Sämmtliche Werke. 10 vols. 12mo. Vienna. 1822–1825.

SCHILLER UND GOETHE. Briefwechsel zwischen, in den jahren 1794 bis 1805. 6 vols. 12mo. Stuttgart und Tübingen. 1829.

SCHLEIERMACHER, F. Ueber die Religion-Reden an die Gebildeten unter ihren Verachtern. 8vo. Berlin. 1831.

SCHLEIERMACHER, F. Grundlinien einer Kritik der bisherigen Sittenlehre. 8vo. Berlin. 1834.

SCHLICHTHORST, H. Geographia Africae Herodotea. 8vo. Gottingae. 1788.

SCHLIPF, J. A. Manuel populaire d'Agriculture. 8vo. Paris. 1844.

SCHLOSSER, F. C. Universal Historische Uebersicht der Geschichte der Alten Welt und ihrer Cultur. 9 vols. 8vo. Frankfurt a. M. 1826--1834.

SCHMIDT, J. A. E. Russich-Deutsches und Deutsch-Russiches Hand-Wörterbuch. 12mo. Leipzig. s. a.

SCHMIDT, SEBASTIAN. Commentarii in Librum Judicum. 4to. Argentorati. 1706.

SCHNEIDER, GULIELMUS. De Originibus Comediae Graecae. 8vo. Vratislaviae. 1817.

SCHNEIDER. De Originibus Tragoediae Graecae. 8vo. Vratislavie. 1817.

* SCHOOLCRAFT, H. R. History, Condition, and Prospects of the Indian Tribes of the United States. Parts I, II, III. 3 vols. 4to. Phila. 1850–1853.

SCHOOLCRAFT, H. R. Travels from Detroit North-west. 8vo. Albany. 1821.

SCHREIBERS, CARL VON. Beiträge zur Geschichte und Kenntniss Meteorischer Stein-und Metall-Massen. Fol. Wien. 1820.

SCHREVELIUS, CORNELIUS. Lexicon Manuale. 8vo. Phila. 1808.

SCHUBERT, G. H. Ahndungen einer Allgemeinen Geschichte des Lebens. 2 vols. in 3. 8vo. Dresden. 1807.

SCHUBERT, G. H. Altes und Neues aus dem Gebiet der Seelenkunde. 3 vols. 8vo. Leipzig. 1825.

SCHUBERT, G. H. Ansichten von der Nachtseite der Naturwissenschaft. 8vo. Dresden. 1829.

SCHULZE, G. E. Encyklopädie der Philosophischen Wissenschaften. 8vo. Göttingen. 1823.

SCHULTZ, C. F. Geschichte der Römer von der Betreibung des Tarquin bis zur Erwählung des ersten plebeischen Consuls. 12mo. Leipzig. 1809.

SCHULTZ, OTTO. Lateinische Grammatik. 8vo. Halle. 1834.

SCHWARZ, F. H. C. Erziehungslehre. 3 vols. in 4. 8vo. Leipzig. 1329.

SCHWEIGHAUSER, JOHANNES. Opuscula Academica. Argentorati. 1806.

SCIENTIA BIBLICA, a Collection of parallel passages. 3 vols. 8vo. London. 1824.

SCLATERUS, W. Explicatio utriusque Epistolae ad Corinthios. 4to. Oxoniae. 1633.

SCOLIA. See Ilgen.

SCORESBY, WILLIAM. Journal of a Voyage to the Northern Whale Fishery. 8vo. Edinburgh. 1822.

SCOTT, JOHN. Inquiry into the Effect of Baptism. 12mo. New York. 1817.

SCOTT, THOMAS. Letters and Papers. 8vo. Boston. 1825.

Scott, Sir Walter. Miscellaneous Prose Works: Containing Life of Dryden, Life of Swift, Biographical Memoirs, Paul's Letters to his Kinsfolk, Essays on Chivalry, Romance, and the Drama. 6 vols. 8vo. Edinburgh and London. 1827.

Scott, Sir Walter. Life of Napoleon Bonaparte. 2 copies. 3 vols. Phila. 1827.

Scott, Sir Walter. Poetical Works. 12 vols. 12mo. Edinburgh. 1833–1834.

Scotus, J. Erigena. De Divisione Naturae Libri v. Fol. Oxoniae. 1681.

Scotus, R. R. Commentarius in Evangelium Secundum Johannem. 12mo. Edinburgh. 1607.

Scribanus, Carolus (Jesuit). Amor Divinus. 18mo. Lugduni. 1617.

Scriptores Physiognomiae Veteres, Graece et Latine. Ed. Franzius. 8vo. Altenburgi. 1780.

Scriptores Rei Rusticae: Cato, Varro, Columella, Palladius, Vegetius, et Gargilius Martialis. Ed. Gessner. 4to. Lipsiae. 1735.

Scriptorum Veterum Nova Collectio. Ed. A. Maius. Vol. ii. 4to. Romae. 1827.

Seaman, Valentine. Dissertation on the Mineral Waters of Saratoga. 12mo. New York. 1809.

Second Advent, by an American Layman. 8vo. Trenton. 1815.

Seed, Jeremiah. Posthumous Works. 2 vols. 8vo. London. 1750.

Segur, Count. Memoir and Recollections, by himself. 8vo. Boston. 1825.

Seidler, Augustus. De Versibus Dochmiacis Tragicorum Graecorum. 8vo. Lipsiae. 1811.

Selden, John. De Jure Naturali et Gentium. 4to. Argentorati. 1665.

Semple, R. B. History of the Baptists in Virginia. 8vo. Richmond. 1810.

Seneca, L. Annaeus. Opera omnia quae supersunt. 5 vols. 8vo. Lipsiae. 1797.

Seneca. Tragoediae. Ed. Bothe. 3 vols. 8vo. Lipsiae. 1819.

Septuagint. Ed. Mills. 2 vols. 12mo. Amstelodami. 1725.

Serenus Antissensis. De Sectione Cylindri et Coni Libri duo, Graece et Latine. Bound with Apollonius Pergaeus. Fol. Oxoniae. 1710.

Seringe, N. C. Le Petit Agriculteur. 18mo. Lyon. 1841.

Sermons by a number of American Ministers. Vol. ii. 8vo. Stockbridge. 1812.

Sermons. Collection of. Glasgow. 1741.

Sermons on particular Occasions. 8vo. Boston. 1812.

SERVIUS, MAURUS. Commentarii in Virgilium. Ed. Lion. 2 vols. 8vo. Gottingae. 1826.

SEWAL, THOMAS. Examination of Phrenology. 8vo. Boston. 1839.

SEXTUS EMPIRICUS. Opera, Graece et Latine. Ed. Fabrius. Fol. Lipsiae. 1718.

SEYBERT, A. Statistical Annals of the U. S. from 1789 to 1818. 4to. Phila. 1818.

* SEYFFARTH, GUSTAVUS. De Hieroglyphica Aegyptiorum Scriptura. 4to. Lipsiae. s. a.

SHAFTSBURY, ANTHONY, EARL OF. Characteristics of Men, Manners, and Times. 3 vols. 8vo. London. 1837.

SHAKSPEARE, WILLIAM. Plays, edited by A. Chalmers. 9 vols. 8vo. Lond. 1805.

SHAKSPEARE, WILLIAM. Poems. 2 vols. 18mo. London. 1804.

SHALER, WILLIAM. Sketches of Algiers. 8vo. Boston. 1826.

* SHAW, GEORGE. General Zoology, or Systematic Natural History, with Plates. 14 vols. in 28. London. 1800–1826.

Vols. I, II. Mammalia.
III. Amphibia.
IV, V. Pisces.
VI. Insecta.
VII–XIV. Aves.

SHAW, JOHN. Manual of Anatomy. 12mo. Troy. 1828.

SHAW, THOMAS. Travels and Observations in Barbary and the Levant. Fol. Oxford. 1738.

SHAY'S REBELLION in 1786, by G. R. Minot. 8vo. Boston. 1810.

SHEE, M. A. Rhymes on Art. 18mo. London. 1805.

SHEFFIELD, JOHN, LORD. On the Commerce of the American States. Bound with Sinclair's Hints, &c. 8vo. London. 1784.

SHEPARD, THOMAS. Parable of the Ten Virgins. 2 copies. Fol. London. 1695.

SHERIDAN, RICHARD BRINSLEY. Dramatic Works. 12mo. Leipsic. 1825.

SHERIDAN, THOMAS. Lectures on the Art of Reading. 8vo. London. 1775.

SHERIDAN, THOMAS. Rhetorical Grammar of the English Language. 12mo. Phila. 1783.

SHERLOCK, BISHOP THOMAS. Works. 5 vols. 8vo. London. 1830.

SHIRLEY, JAMES. Dramatic Works and Poems, edited by Gifford. 6 vols. 8vo. London. 1833.

SHUCKFORD, SAML. Sacred and Profane History of the World connected. 4 vols. in 2. 8vo. Phila. 1824.

SICARD, ABBE. Cours d'Insruction d'un Sourd-Muet. 8vo. Paris. 1800.

SICARD, ABBE. Théorie des Signes. 2 vols. 8vo. Paris. 1808.

SIDDONS, MRS. Memoirs, by James Boaden. 8vo. Phila. 1827.

SIDNEY, ALGERNON. Discourses concerning Government. Fol. Lond. 1698.

SIDNEY, SIR PHILIP. Memoirs of the Life and Writings of, by Thos. Zouch. 4to. York. 1808.

SIDNEY and the Countess of Pembroke. Version of the Psalmes of David. 18mo. Chiswick. 1823.

SIEBELIS, C. G. Hellenica, seu Antiquissimae Graecorum Historiae Res Insigniores. 12mo. Lipsiae. 1800.

SIEBELIS, C. G. Symbolae Criticae et Exegeticae ad graviores Graecorum Scriptorum locos. 8vo. Lipsiae. 1803.

SILIUS ITALICUS. Punicorum Libri XVII. Ed. Ernesti. 2 vols. 8vo. Lipsiae. 1791.

SIMPLICIUS. Commentarius in Enchyridion Epicteti. 4to. Lugduni. 1640.

SIMPSON, JAMES. Necessity of a Popular Education. 8vo. New York. 1834.

SIMSON, ROBERT. Elements of Conic Sections. 8vo. New York. 1804.

SIMSON, ROBERT. Elements of Euclid. 8vo. Phila. 1811.

SINCLAIR, SIR JOHN. Hints on the State of Finances. 8vo. London. 1783.

SINCLAIR, SIR JOHN. Correspondence. 2 vols. 8vo. London. 1831.

SINGER, G. J. Elements of Electricity and Electro-Chemistry. 8vo. Lond. 1814.

SISMONDI, J. C. L. SIMONDE DE. Histoire des Républiques Italiennes du Moyen Age. 16 vols. 8vo. Paris. 1826.

SISMONDI. Histoire des Français. 21 vols. 8vo. Paris. 1821–1836.

SISMONDI. La Littérature du Midi de l'Europe. 4 vols. 8vo. Paris. 1829.

SISMONDI. Battles of Cressy and Poictiers, translated. 12mo. Boston. 1823.

SKELTON, PHILIP. Life. See Edward Pococke.

SLADE, WILLIAM. See Vermont.

SLAVERY. Poems on, by Montgomery, Graham, and Benger. 18mo. New York. 1810.

SMALLEY, JOHN. Sermons. 8vo. Hartford. 1803.

SMELLIE, WILLIAM. Philosophy of Natural History. 8vo. Boston. 1832.

SMIRKE, ROBERT. Review of a Battalion of Infantry. 8vo. New York. 1810.

SMITH, ADAM. Wealth of Nations. 2 vols. 8vo. Hartford. 1804.

SMITH, ADAM. Theory of Moral Sentiments. 8vo. Phila. 1817.

*SMITH, JAMES ED. English Botany; figures by James Sowerby. 8 vols. 8vo. London. 1790–1797.

*SMITH, JAMES ED. Introduction to Physiological and Systematic Botany. 8vo. Boston. 1814.

SMITH, JOHN. Select Discourses. 8vo. Cambridge. 1673.

SMITH, JOHN P. Letters to Rev. Thomas Belsham. 8vo. Boston. 1809.

SMITH, R. A Complete System of Optics. 4to. 2 vols. Cambridge, Eng. 1738.

SMITH, S. S. Essay on the Causes of the Variety in the Complexion and Figure of the Human Species. 8vo. New Brunswick, N. J. 1810.

SMITH, S. S. Lectures in the College of New Jersey. 2 vols. 8vo. Trenton. 1812.

SMITH, ELY, AND H. G. O. DWIGHT. Researches in Armenia. 2 vols. 12mo. Boston. 1833.

*SMITHSONIAN CONTRIBUTIONS TO KNOWLEDGE.

Vol. I. Ancient Monuments of the Mississippi Valley, by E. G. Squier and E. H. Davis. 4to. Washington. 1847.

Vol. II. Researches relative to the Planet Neptune, by S. C. Walker.
The Vocal Sounds of Laura Bridgeman, by Francis Lieber.
Microscopic Examination of Soundings, by S. W. Baily.
Physical Geography of the Mississippi Valley, by Charles Ellet, Jr.
Memoir on Mosaurus, &c., by Robt. W. Gibbs.
Classification of Insects, by Louis Agassiz.
Memoir on the Explosiveness of Nitre, by Robert Hare.
Microscopical Observations made in S. C., Ga., and Fla., by J. W. Bailey.
Aboriginal Monuments of the State of New York, by E. G. Squier. 4to. Washington. 1851.

Vol. III. Observations on Terrestrial Magnetism, by John Locke, M. D.
Researches on Electrical Rheometry, by A. Secchi.
Nat. Hist. of the Fresh Water Fishes of N. A., by Charles Girard. Part I: Monograph of the Cottoids.
Nereis Boreali-Americana, by W. H. Harvey. Part I: Melanospermeae.
Plantae Wrightianae Texano-Neo-Mexicanae, by Asa Young. Part I.

* SMITHSONIAN CONTRIBUTIONS TO KNOWLEDGE—Continued.

Law of Deposit of the Flood Tide, by C. H. Davis.

Descriptions of Ancient Works in Ohio, by C. Whittlesey.

Occultations in 1852, by John Downey. 4to. Washington. 1851.

Vol. IV. Grammar and Dictionary of the Dakota Language, by S. R. Riggs. 4to. Washington. 1851.

Vol. V. Flora and Fauna within living Animals, by J. Leidy.

Memoir on the Extinct Species of American Ox, by J. Leidy.

Anatomy of the Nervous System of the Rana Pipiens, by J. Wyman.

Nereis Boreali-Americana. Part II. Rhodospermeae.

Plantae Wrighteanae, &c. Part II. 4to. Washington. 1853.

SMOLLET, T. Continuation of Hume's History of England from the Revolution to the Death of George II. 5 vols. 8vo. London. 1790.

SOCRATES. See Collectio Epistolarum Graecarum.

SOLIS, ANTONIO DE. Historia de la Conquista de Mexico. Fol. Bruxelles. 1741.

* SÖMMERING, SAM. THOMAS. Icones Embryonum Humanarum. Fol. Francofurti. 1799.

* SONNINI, C. S. Voyage dans la Haute et Basse Egypte. 3 vols. 8vo. Paris. 1799.

*Atlas to the above. 4to.

* SONNINI, C. S. Voyage en Grèce et Turquie. 2 vols. 8vo. Paris. 1801.

*Atlas to the above. 4to.

SOPHOCLES. Tragoediae septem. Ed. Brunck. 4 vols. in 3. 8vo. Argentorati. 1786.

SOPHOCLES. Dramata et Fragmenta. Ed. Bothe. 2 vols. 8vo. Lipsiae. 1806.

SOPHOCLES translated by Thos. Francklin. 16mo. New York. 1836.

SOTHEBY, WM. Iliad and Odyssey translated, with Designs by Flaxman. 4 vols. 8vo. London. 1834.

SOURD-MUETS, Quatrième Circulaire de l'Institut Royal des. 8vo. Paris. 1836.

SOUTHEY, ROBERT. History of the Peninsular War. 4 of the 6 vols. 8vo. London. 1828.

SPANGENBERG, ERNESTI. De Veteris Latii Religionibus Domesticis Commentatio. 4to. Gottingae. s. a.

SPANHEMIUS. Dissertationes de Praestantia et Usu Numismatum Antiquorum. 4to. Amstelodami. 1671.

SPARKS, JARED. Diplomatic Correspondence of the American Revolution. 12 vols. 8vo. Boston. 1829.

SPARKS, JARED. Letter to Lord Mahon. 8vo. Boston. 1852.

SPARKS, JARED. Reply to Strictures of Lord Mahon and others. 8vo. Cambridge. 1852.

SPARKS, JARED. Remarks on a Reprint of the Original Letters from Washington to Jos. Reed. 8vo. Boston. 1853.

SPARKS, JARED. See Jefferson, Franklin, Gouv. Morris, Washington.

SPEECHES, CONGRESSIONAL. Webster and others. 8vo. 1838–1848.

*SPENCE, JOSEPH. Polymetis, or an Enquiry concerning the Agreement between the Works of Roman Poets and the Remains of the Ancient Artists. Fol. London. 1747.

SPENCE, JOSEPH. Anecdotes relating to Books and Men. 8vo. Lond. 1820.

SPENCE, JOSEPH. Essay on Mr. Pope's Odyssey in five Dialogues. 12mo. London. 1747.

SPENCE, JOSEPH. Observations on the Greek and Roman Classics. 12mo. London. 1753.

SPENCE, W. Logarithmic Transcendents. 4to. London. 1809.

SPINOZA, BENEDICTUS. Opera quae supersunt omnia. 2 vols. 8vo. Jena. 1802.

SPITZNER, FRANZ. De Versu Graecorum Heroico, maxime Homerico. 8vo. Lipsiae. 1816.

SPOHR, F. A. G. De Agro Trojano in Carminibus Homericis Descriptio. 8vo. Lipsiae. 1814.

SPON ET WHELER. Voyage d'Italie, de Dalmatie, de Grèce, et de Levant. 2 vols. 12mo. La Haye. 1724.

SPRENGEL, KURT. Der Bau und die Natur der Gewächse. 8vo. Halle. 1812.

SPRENGEL, KURT. Einleitung zur Kenntniss der Gewächse. 3 vols. 12mo. Halle. 1817.

SPRENGEL, KURT. Neue Entdeckungen in der Pflanzenkunde. 3 vols. 12mo. Leipzig. 1820.

SPRING, GARDINER. Dissertation on Native Depravity. 8vo. New York. 1833.

SPURZHEIM, J. G. Anatomy of the Brain. 8vo. Boston. 1826.

SPURZHEIM, J. G. Phrenology in connection with the Study of Physignomy. 8vo. Boston. 1833.

SPURZHEIM, J. G. On Insanity, with Appendix by A. Brigham. 8vo. Boston. 1836.

SPURZHEIM, J. G. Phrenology, or the Doctrine of the Mental Phenomena. 2 vols. 8vo. Boston. 1836.

SPURZHEIM, J. G. Elementary Principles of Education. 12mo. Boston. 1833.

SPURZHEIM, J. G. Examination of Objections against the Doctrines of Galt and Spurzheim. 12mo. Boston. 1833.

SPY. A Newspaper, by J. Thomas. Vols. XII–XX (vol. XVI wanting) in 6 vols. Duplicate of Vol. XVII. Fol. Worcester. 1783–1791.

STACKHOUSE, THOMAS. History of the Holy Bible. 3 vols. 4to. Lond. 1817.

STAEL, MME. LA BARONNE DE. Oeuvres complétes, publiées par son Fils. 17 vols. 8vo. Paris. 1820.

STAHL, G. E. Opusculum Chymico-Physico-Medicum, cum Tractatu de Cupri Origine et Usibus a Melchiore Vendriese. 4to. Halis. 1715.

STANDLIN, C. F. Geschichte und Geist des Scepticismus. 2 vols. 8vo. Leipzig. 1794.

STANHOPE, JOHN S. Topography of the Plain of Olympia. Fol. London. 1824.

STAPLETON. See Canning.

STATE TRIALS, ENGLISH. From Richard II to the 16th year of George III. 11 vols. Fol. London. 1776.

STATIUS, P. PAPIRIUS. Opera, stud. Soc. Bipont. 8vo. Biponti. 1785.

STEELE, MISS ANNE. Works. (Incomplete.) Vol. II. 8vo. Boston. 1808.

STEFFENS, HEINRICH. Anthropologie. 2 vols. 8vo. Breslau. 1822.

STEPHANUS BYZANT. De Urbibus et Populis, Graece et Latine. Ed. Burkelius. Fol. Lugd. Bat. 1688.

STERNE, LAWRENCE. Works. 4 vols. 8vo. London. 1808.

STEUART, JAMES. Political Economy. 2 vols. 4to. London. 1767.

STEWART, DUGALD. Elements of the Philosophy of the Human Mind. 3 vols. 8vo. Phila. 1793.

STEWART, DUGALD. The same. 3 vols. 8vo. Brattleboro. 1808.

STEWART, DUGALD. Works. 7 vols. 8vo. Cambridge. 1829–1833.

STILES, DR. EZRA. Life by Holmes. 8vo. Boston. 1798.

STILLINGFLEET, EDWARD, BP. Origines Sacrae, or a rational Account of the Grounds of Christian Faith as to the Truth and Divine Origin of the Scriptures. Fol. Cambridge, Eng. 1702.

STOBAEUS, JOANNES. Florilegium, Graece. Ed. Gaisford. 4 vols. 8vo. Lipsiae. 1823.

STOICHEIA Linguae Hellenicae. Vol. II. 12mo. Viennae. 1815

STORY, JOSEPH. Commentaries on the Constitution of the United States. 3 vols. 8vo. Boston. 1833.

STRABO. Rerum Geographicarum Libri XVII, Graece et Latine. Ed. Siebenkees. 7 vols. 8vo. Lipsiae. 1796–1818.

STRAUCHIUS, GILES. Treatise on the Terms, Periods, and Epochas used in Chronology. 12mo. London. 1704.

STRONG, CALEB. Speeches. 8vo. Newburyport. 1808.

STRUENSEE, COUNT. Conversion and Death, by Dr. Munter. 8vo. London. 1822.

STRUTT, JOSEPH. Sports and Pastimes of the People of England. 8vo. London. 1834.

STRYPE, JOHN. Annals of the Reformation in England in the time of Elizabeth. 4 vols. in 7. 8vo. Oxford. 1824.

STUART, JAMES, AND NICHOLAS REVETT. Antiquities of Athens. 3 vols. Fol. London. 1762–1794.

STUART, MOSES. Grammar of the Hebrew Language. 8vo. Andover. 1828.

STUART, MOSES. Course of Hebrew Study. 2 vols. 8vo. Andover. 1829–1830.

STUART, MOSES. Commentary on the Epistle to the Hebrews. 8vo. Andover. 1833.

STUART, MOSES. Commentary on the Epistle to the Romans. 8vo. Andover. 1835.

STUART, MOSES. Letters to Channing. 12mo. Andover. 1829.

STUART, MOSES. On Greek Accent and Quantity. 18mo. Andover. 1829.

STUART, MOSES. Cicero on the Immortality of the Soul. 18mo. Andover. 1833.

STUD-BOOK Français. 2 vols. 8vo. Paris. 1838.

STURLANGS Saga Starfsama. 12mo. s. l. et a.

STURZIUS, F. G. De Dialecto Macedonica et Alexandrina. 8vo. Lipsiae. 1808.

SUETONIUS, C. TRANQUILLUS. Opera, Stud. Soc. Bipont. 8vo. Argentorati. 1800.

SUIDAS. Lexicon. Ed. Aemilius Porta. 2 vols. Fol. Coloniae Allob. 1619.

SULLY, DUC DE. Memoirs of, transl. from the French. 3 vols. 4to. Lond. 1761.

SUMATRA. History of, by Wm. Marsden. 4to. London. 1784.

SUMNER, J. B. On the Creation, and the Moral Attributes of the Creator. 2 vols. 8vo. London. 1833.

Swainson, Wm. The Naturalist's Guide for preserving Shells. 12mo. London. 1822.

Swainson, Wm. Treatise on the Geography and Classification of Animals. 12mo. London. 1825.

Swainson, Wm. Preliminary Discourse on the Study of Natural History. 12mo. London. 1833.

Swainson, Wm. Natural History and Classification of Quadrupeds. 12mo. London. 1835.

Swedenborg, Emanuel. The Wisdom of Angels. 8vo. Boston. 1796.

Swedenborg. The True Christian Religion. 8vo. Boston. 1833.

Swedenborg. Heavenly Arcana. 12 vols. 8vo. Boston. 1837.

Swedenborg. Index to the above. 8vo. Boston. 1848.

Swedenborg. Heaven and Hell. 8vo. Boston. 1837.

Swedenborg. Posthumous Philosophical Tracts. 8vo. Boston. 1848.

Swedenborg. Worship and Love of God. 12mo. Boston. 1832.

Swedenborg. Apocalypse Revealed. 12mo. Boston. 1836.

Swedenborg. Four Leading Doctrines of the New Church. 12mo. Boston. 1838.

Swedenborg. Doctrine of the New Church. 12mo. Boston. 1839.

Swedenborg. The Earths in our Solar System. 12mo. Boston. 1839.

Swedenborg. New Jerusalem Tracts. 12mo. Boston. s. a.

Swedenborg. Doctrine of Life. 18mo. Boston. 1821.

Swedenborg. On the Lord. 18mo. Cambridge. 1821.

Swedenborg. Divine Love. 18mo. Boston. 1828.

Swedenborg. Doctrine of Faith. 18mo. Boston. 1828.

Swedenborg. On the Intercourse between the Soul and the Body. 18mo. Boston. 1828.

Swedenborg. On the Athanasian Creed. 18mo. Boston. 1828.

Swedenborg. The Sacred Scriptures. 18mo. Boston. 1829.

Swedenborg. Internal Sense of the Prophetical Books. 18mo. Boston. 1833.

Swedenborg. The New Jerusalem. 18mo. Boston. 1838.

Sweet, Robert. Hothouse and Greenhouse Manual. 8vo. London. 1831.

Sweetser, William. On Cynanche Trachealis, or Croup. 8vo. Boston. 1823.

Sweetser, William. On Consumption. 8vo. Boston. 1836.

Swieten, Gerard. Commentaries on the Aphorisms of Boerhave concerning Diseases. 17 vols. ii–xviii. 8vo. London. 1744.

SWIFT, JONATHAN. Works, by Hawkesworth. 25 vols. Lond. 1768–1776.

SWINBORNE, HENRY. Travels in the two Sicilies. 2 vols. 8vo. Dublin. 1783.

SYKES, ARTHUR A. Memoirs by Disney. 8vo. London. 1785.

SYNOPSIS METAPHYSICAE. 12mo. Glasguae. 1780.

SYNTAGMA Theologiae Christianae. (Incomplete.)

TACITI ANNALES, Commentarius in, a Rupert. 2 copies. 8vo. Londini. 1825.

TACITO, CORNELIO. Opera tradotti da Da Vanzati. 2 vols. 18mo. Paris. 1760.

TACITUS, C. CORNELIUS. Opera. Ed. Bekker. 2 vols. 8vo. Lipsiae. 1831.

TACITUS. Opera quae extant omnia. 4 vols. 12mo. Glasguae. 1743.

TACITUS. Five Books of the History of. 12mo. Hartford. 1826.

TANNER, JOHN. Narrative of Captivity and Adventures by James. 8vo. New York. 1830.

TASSO, TORQUATO. Opere. 4 vols. 8vo. Milano. 1804.

TASSO, TORQUATO. Lettere inedite. 8vo. Pisa. 1827.

TASSO, TORQUATO. Jerusalem Delivered, done into English by Edward Fairfax. 8vo. London. 1749.

TASSONI, ALESSANDRO. Secchia Rapita. 18mo. Venezia. 1788.

TAXIDERMY, or the Art of preserving Animals. 12mo. London. 1820.

TAYLOR, BROOKE. New Principles of Linear Perspective. 12mo. London. 1719.

TAYLOR, JEREMY. Works. 3 vols. 8vo. London. 1835.

TAYLOR, JOHN. Records of my Life. 8vo. New York. 1833.

TAYLOR, JOHN, of Norwich. Hebrew Concordance. 2 vols. Fol. London. 1754.

TAYLOR, O. A. Views of the Savior. 12mo. Andover. 1838.

TAYLOR, THOMAS. Philosophical and Mathematical Commentaries of Proclus on Euclid's Elements, translated, with Life by Marinus, and a Dissertation on the Platonic Doctrine of Ideas. 2 vols. 4to. London. 1788.

TAYLOR, THOMAS. Six Books of Proclus on the Theology of Plato. 2 vols. 4to. London. 1816.

TAYLOR, THOMAS. Commentaries of Proclus on the Timaeus of Plato. 2 vols. 4to. London. 1820.

TAYLOR, THOMAS. The Metaphysics of Aristotle translated. 4to. London. 1801.

TAYLOR, THOMAS. Select Works of Plotinus. 8vo. London. 1817.

TAYLOR, THOMAS. Life of Pythagoras by Jamblichus. 8vo. London. 1818.

TAYLOR, THOMAS. Jamblichus on the Mysteries of the Egyptians. 8vo. Chiswick. 1821.

TAYLOR, THOMAS. Ancient Pythagorean Fragments. 8vo. Chiswick. 1822.

TAYLOR, THOMAS. Two Treatises of Proclus. 8vo. London. 1833.

TAYLOR, THOMAS. Ocellus Lucanus on the Nature of the Universe. 8vo. London. 1834.

TAYLOR, THOMAS. Translations from the Treatises of Plotinus. 8vo. Lond. 1834.

TAYLOR, W. Historic Survey of German Poetry. Vols. I, II. 8vo. Lond. 1830.

TEGNER, ESAIAS. Smarre Dikter. 8vo. Stockholm. 1832.

TEMMINCK, C. J. Manuel d'Ornithologie. 3 vols. 8vo. Paris. 1820.

TEMPLE, SIR WM. Works. 4 vols. 8vo. Edinburgh. 1754.

TEMPLE, SIR WM. Memoirs of his Life, Works, and Correspondence, by Courtenay. 2 vols. 8vo. London. 1836.

TENNEMANN, W. G. Geschichte der Philosophie. 11 vols. in 7. 8vo. Leipzig. 1798–1819.

TERENTIUS, PUBLIUS, AFER. Comoediae. Ed. Bothe. 8vo. Berolini. 1806.

TERENTIUS. Andrea et Adelphi. Ed. Dillaway. 2 copies. Phila. 1850.

TERTULLIANUS, Q. S. F. Opera. Fol. Paris. 1641.

TESTAMENT, Het Nieuwe. (Dutch.) 18mo. Amsterdam. 1691.

TESTAMENTUM Vetus. Incomplete. 12mo. s. l. et a.

THATCHER, JAMES. Military Journal during the Revolutionary War. 8vo. Boston. 1823.

THACHER, JAMES. American Medical Biography. 2 vols. in one. 8vo. Boston. 1828.

THAYER, ELIHU. Sermons, 8vo. Exeter. 1813.

THEATRE of the Greeks. 8vo. Cambridge. 1830.

THENARD, L. J. Traité de Chymie. 5 vols. 8vo. Paris. 1827.

THEOCRITUS. Reliquiae, Graece et Latine cum Scholiis Graecis. Ed. Reiske. 4to. Viennae. 1765.

THEODORUS METOCHITA. De Politia Cyrenaeorum et Corinthiorum. 8vo. Lipsiae. 1811.

THEODORUS METOCHITA. Miscellanea Philosophica et Historica, Graece. Ed. Müller. 8vo. Lipsiae. 1821.

THEOLOGIE suppliante aux pieds du Souverain Pontife. 18mo. Cologne. 1756.

THEOPHRASTUS ERESIUS. Quae supersunt Opera, Graece et Latine. Ed. Schneider. 5 vols. 8vo. Lipsiae. 1818.

THEOPHRASTUS. Characteres Ethici, Epicteti Manuale, et Cebetis Tabula. 18mo. Lipsiae. 1826.

THEOPOMPUS CHIUS. Fragmenta, Graece. Ed. Wichers. 8vo. Lugduni. 1829.

THIBERT, FELIX. Musée d'Anatomie Pathologique. 8vo. Paris. 1844.

THIERRY, A. Histoire de la Conquête de l'Angeterre par les Normands. 4 vols. 8vo. Paris. 1826.

THIERS, M. A. Histoire de la Revolution Française. 10 vols. 8vo. Paris. 1834.

THIERSCH, D. FR. Griechische Grammatik. 8vo. Leipzig. 1818.

THIERSCH, D. FR. Greek Tables. 8vo. Andover. 1818.

THIERSCH, FR. Epochen der bildenden Kunst. 8vo. München. 1829.

THOM, DAVID. Assurance of Faith. 2 vols. 8vo. London. 1833.

THOM, R. Aesop's Fables written in Chinese. 8vo. Canton. 1840.

THOMAS, ANTOINE. Oeuvres. 2 vols. 8vo. Paris. 1819.

THOMAS A KEMPIS. Opera. Fol. s. l. 1523.

THOMAS A KEMPIS. Imitation of Christ. 12mo. London. 1769.

THOMAS AQUINAS. Super Quartum Sententiarum. Fol. Venetiis. 1481.

THOMAS AQUINAS. Summa totius Theologiae. Fol. Paris. 1615.

THOMAS, BP. OF SODOR AND MAN. Christianity made easy. 12mo. Lond. 1754.

THOMAS, ISAIAH. History of Printing in America. 2 copies. 2 vols. 8vo. Worcester. 1810.

THOMAS, R. Modern Practice of Physic. 8vo. New York. 1822.

THOME AND KIMBALL. Emancipation in the West Indies. 12mo. New York. 1838.

THOMPSON, D. P. The Shaker Lovers. See Pamphlet Case 57.

THOMPSON, ZADOCK. History of Vermont, Natural, Civil, and Statistical. 8vo. Burlington. 1842.

THOMPSON, Z. Appendix to the above. 8vo. Burlington. 1853.

THOMPSON, Z. Gazeteer of Vermont. 12mo. Montpelier. 1824.

THOMPSON, Z. History of Vermont, to 1822. 12mo. Burlington. 1833.

THOMPSON, Z. Geography and History of Lower Canada. 16mo. Stanstead, C. E. 1835.

THOMSON, A. P. Lectures on the Elements of Botany. 8vo. London. 1822.

THOMSON, JAMES. Essay on the Life and Writings of. See Fletcher of Saltoun.

THOMSON, ROBERT. Divine Authority of the Bible. 12mo. Boston. 1807.

THOMSON, THOS. History of the Royal Society. 4to. London. 1812.

THOMSON, THOS. Attempt to establish the first Principles of Christianity by Experiment. 2 vols. 4to. London. 1825.

THORBURN, GRANT. Forty Years' Residence in America, by himself. 12mo. Boston. 1834.

THORESBY, RALPH. Diary and Correspondence. 4 vols. 8vo. 1830–1832.

THREE YEARS in the Pacific by an Officer in the U. S. Navy. 8vo. Phila. 1834.

THUANUS. Life, with an Account of his Writings by Collinson. 8vo. Lond. 1807.

THUCYDIDES. De Bello Peloponesiaco Libri octo, Graece et Latine. Ed. Baverus. 2 vols. 4to. Lipsiae. 1790.

THUCYDIDES. Observationes Criticae, a Poppo. 8vo. Lipsiae. 1815.

TICKNOR, CALEB. Treatise on Medical Philosophy. 12mo. New York. 1838.

TIEDEMANN, D. Griechenlands erste Philosophen. 8vo. Lipsiae. 1780.

TIEDEMANN, D. Geist der Speculativen Philosophie von Thales bis Socrates. 6 vols. 8vo. Marburg. 1791–1797.

TIEDEMANN, D. Idealistiche Briefe. 12mo. Marburg. 1788.

TIEDEMANN, D. System der Stoischen Philosophie. 3 vols. 18mo. Leipzig. 1776.

TILENUS, D. SILESIUS. Syntagma Disputationum Theologicarum in Academia Sedanensi. 12mo. Genevae. 1618.

TILLOTSON, DR. JOHN. Works. 2 vols. Fol. London. 1735.

TIRABOSCHI, G. Storia della Letteratura Italiana. 10 vols. 4to. Modena. 1772–1782.

TITTMANN, J. A. H. Libri Symbolici Ecclesiae Evangelicae. 8vo. Misenae. 1827.

TOLAND, JOHN. History of the Druids. 8vo. Montrose. 1814.

TOLAND, JOHN. Life of Milton. See Milton.

TOPLADY, A. Doctrine of Absolute Predestination. 12mo. Phila. 1793.

TORREY, JOHN. Compendium of the Flora of the Northern and Middle States. 12mo. New York. 1826.

TORREY, JOSEPH. Neander's Church History, translated. 5 vols. 8vo. Boston. 1847–1854.

TORRICELLIUS. Opera Geometrica. 4to. Florentiae. 1644.

TOURNEFORT, PITTON DE. Voyage du Levant. 3 vols. 8vo. Lyon. 1717.

TRACTS. Scientific, by J. Holbrook and others. 2 vols. 12mo. Boston. 1830.

TRANSACTIONS of the Royal Society at Edinburgh. Vols. I, II, IV, VII, IX. 4to. Edinburgh. 1788–1821.

TRANSACTIONS of the Royal Society of London for the year 1843. Part I. 4to. London. 1843.

TRANSACTIONS of the Philosophical Society at New York. Vol. I. 8vo. New York. 1815.

TRANSACTIONS of the American Philosophical Society held at Philadelphia. New Series. Vol. I. 4to. Phila. 1818.

TRANSACTIONS of the New York State Agricultural Society from 1842–1851. 11 vols. Duplicates of Vols. IX and X. 8vo. Albany.

TRAVANET, M. LE MARQUIS. Preservatif d'Agronomie Empirique. Premiere partie. 8vo. Paris. 1845.

TREDGOLD. THOMAS. On the Steam Engine, ed. by Woolhouse. 2 vols. 4to. London. 1838.

TREDGOLD, THOMAS. Tracts on Hydraulics. 8vo. London. 1826.

TREDGOLD, THOMAS. Practical Essay on the Strength of Cast Iron and other Metals. 8vo. London. 1831.

TREDGOLD, THOMAS. On Rail Roads and Carriages. 8vo. London. 1835.

TRENT. Historia del Concilio, di Pietro Soane Polano. 4to. s. l. 1629.

TROLLOPE, MRS. Belgium and Western Germany. 8vo. Phila. 1824.

TROTTER, THOMAS. View of the Nervous Temperament. 2 copies. 12mo. Troy. 1808.

TROUBADOURS. Litteraire Histoire des. 3 vols. 18mo. Paris. 1774.

TROXLER, DR. Versuche in der Organischen Physik. 8vo. Jena. 1804.

TRUMBULL, B. Twelve discourses. 12mo. Hartford. 1795.

TUCKER, ABRAHAM. Light of Nature pursued. 2 vols. 8vo. London. 1834.

TUCKEY, J. K. Narrative of Expedition to explore the River Zaire now called Congo, in 1816. 4to. London. 1818.

TUERK, VON. Erfahrungen hinsichtlich des Deutschen Seidenbaues. 8vo. Leipzig. 1827.

TURKISH PSALTER. 6 copies. 12mo. s. l. et a.

TURKISH SPELLING BOOK. 2 copies. 12mo. s. l. et a.

TURKISH SPY. Letters of. 8 vols. 18mo. London. 1754.

TURKISH VERSION of the New Testament, incapable of Defense. 8vo. Lond. 1825.

TURKS. History of, from 1679–1699, by Rycaut. Fol. London. 1700.

TURNER, SHARON. History of the Anglo-Saxons. 8vo. London. 1820.

TURNER, SHARON. History of England during the Middle Ages. 5 vols. 8vo. London. 1825.

TURNER, SHARON. History of the Reign of Henry VIII. 2 vols. 8vo. Lond. 1827.

TURNER, SHARON. History of the Reigns of Edward VI, Mary, and Elizabeth. 2 vols. 8vo. London. 1829.

TURNBULL, CAPT. Drawings in the Construction of the Alexandria Aqueduct. 4to. Washington. 1819.

TURRETINUS, F. De Satisfactione Christi. 4to. Lugd. Batav. 1696.

TYCHSEN, T. C. Der Luxus der Atheniener. 12mo. Göttingen. 1782.

TYNDALE, WM., AND JOHN FRITH. Works. 3 vols. 8vo. London. 1831.

TYRWHITT, THOMAS. Vindication of the Appendix to Rowley's Poems. London. 1782.

UKERT, FR. AUG. Geographie der Griechen und Römer. 4 vols. 8vo. Weimar. 1816.

UNIVERSAL HISTORY. See History.

UNION COLLEGE. Report of the Majority of the Commissioners appointed to examine the Affairs of. 8vo. Albany. 1853.

UPHAM, C. W. Letters on the Logos. 8vo. Boston. 1820.

UPHAM, T. C. Manual of Peace. 12mo. Boston. 1842.

USSERIUS, JACOBUS. Annales Veteris Testamenti. Fol. London. 1650.

USTERI, LEONHARD. Entwickelung des Paulinischen Lehrbegriffes. 8vo. Zurich. 1834.

VALADE, F. X. Guide de l'Instituteur. 12mo. Montreal. 1853.

VALCKENAERIUS, L. C. Opuscula Philosophica, Critica, et Oratoria. 2 vols. 8vo. Lipsiae. 1808.

*VALENTIA, GEO. VISCOUNT. Voyages and Travels to India, Ceylon, the Red Sea, Abyssinia, and Egypt, in 1802–1806. 3 vols. 4to. Lond. 1809.

VALERIUS MAXIMUS. Dictorum Factorumque memorabilium Libri IX: accedunt J. Obsequentis Opera. 2 vols. 8vo. Argentorati. 1806.

VALPY, R. Elements of Greek Grammar. 8vo. Boston. 1814.

VAN TIL, SOLOMON. Commentaria analytica in Libros Propheticos. 3 vols. 4to. Lugd. Batav. 1744.

VARLO, C. A New System of Husbandry. 2 vols. 8vo. Phila. 1785.

VARRO, M. TERENTIUS. De Lingua Latina Librorum quae supersunt. Ed. C. O. Müller. 8vo. Lipsiae. 1833.

VATER, J. S. Practische Grammatik der Russichen Sprache. 8vo. Leipzig. 1814.

VATTEL, E. DE. Law of Nations. 8vo. New York. 1796.

VATTEL, E. DE. The same. 8vo. Northampton. 1815.

VAUBAN. De l'Attaque et de la Défense des Places. 4to. La Haye. 1737.

VAUDONCOURT. Histoire des Campagnes d'Annibal en Italie pendant la deuxième Guerre Punique, avec Cartes, par Frederic Guillaume. 4 vols. 4to. Milan. 1812.

VAUVENARGUES. See Moralistes Francois.

VEGECE. Institutions Militaires. 18mo. Paris. 1743.

VEGETIUS, FLAVIUS RENATUS. De Re Militari Libri V. Ed. Schwebelius. 8vo. Argentorati. 1806.

VELLEIUS PATERCULUS, C. Quae supersunt Historiae Romanae Libris duobus. Ed. Ruhnkenius et Krausius. 8vo. Argentorati. 1811.

VENTUROLI, GIUSEPPE. Mechanics, transl. by Creswell. 8vo. Cambridge, Eng. 1822.

*VENUTI, R. Descrizione topografica della Antichitá di Roma. 2 vols. in one. 4to. Roma. 1824.

VERDICT upon the Dissenters' Plea. 8vo. London. 1681.

VERMONT SENTINEL. Vol. VI. Fol. Burlington. 1806.

VERMONT STATE PAPERS.

Journals of the General Assembly for the years 1789, 1790, 1793–1796, 1799, 1801, 1803–1818, 1820–1835.

Journals of the Senate of General Assembly for the years 1836–1852.

Journals of the House of General Assembly for the years 1836–1851.

VERMONT STATE PAPERS—Continued.

Journals of the Council of Censors for the years 1820, 1827, 1834.

Address of the Council of Censors for 1800.

Journals of the Constitutional Convention for the years 1814, 1822, 1828, 1836, 1843, 1850.

Constitutions of 1777, 1786, 1793 (two copies), 1836. See Revised Statutes of 1839 for the last.

Charter of Cumberland County, 1768. See Pamphlet Case 2.

Acts and Laws passed in the years 1779, 1782, 1787, 1792–1846, 1850.

Laws of Vermont revised and passed in 1797. 8vo. Rutland. 1798.

Laws of Vermont digested and compiled to the year 1807. 2 vols. in one. 8vo. Randolph. 1808.

Laws of Vermont to the close of the Session of 1816. Vol. III. 8vo. Rutland. 1817.

Laws of Vermont to 1824 inclusive, compiled by William Slade. 8vo. Windsor. 1824.

Laws of Vermont to 1834 inclusive, by D. P. Thompson. 8vo. Montpelier. 1835.

Revised Statutes passed 1839. 8vo. Burlington. 1840.

Vermont State Papers. 8vo. Middlebury. 1823.

Practical forms, by Asa Aikens. 12mo. Windsor. 1836.

Duplicates of the Journals of Gen. Assembly for 1801, 1804, 1805, 1806, of the Senate of 1836, of the House of 1836, 1844, 1849, 1851, of Acts and Laws for 1787, 1801, 1804 (tripl.), 1809, 1813, 1815, 1819, 1822, 1844 (tripl.), 1845, and of the Journal of the Constitutional Convention for 1850.

VERMONT REPORTS.

Of the Supreme Court, by R. Tyler. 2 vols. 8vo. New York. 1809.

Of do. by W. Brayton. 8vo. Middlebury. 1821.

Of do. by D. Chipman. Vol. I. 8vo. Middlebury. 1824.

Digest of all Cases decided in the Supreme Court, by P. T. Washburn. 8vo. Woodstock. 1845.

Of Cases argued before the Supreme Court. 21 vols. 8vo. 1829–1850.

VERPLIGTINGEN van eenen braaven Huisvader. 12mo. Amstelodami. 1795.

VESPUCCI, AMERIGO. Vita e Lettere. 8vo. Firenze. 1745.

VIAL, ANDRE. Traité du St. Sacrement de l'Euchariste. 18mo. Grenoble. 1676.

VICO, G. Principi d'una Scienza nuova. Vol. I. 8vo. Napoli. 1744.

VIEWS IN THEOLOGY, (by D. N. Lord). 8vo. New York. 1824.

VIGERUS, F. De praecipuis Graecae Dictionis Idiotismis. 8vo. London. 1824.

VIGERUS, F. De praecipuis Graecae Dictionis Idiotismis. Ed. Hermann. Lipsiae. 1834.

VILLEMAIN. Lascaris, ou les Grecs du 15ème Siècle, suivi d'un Essai Historique sur l'état des Grecs depuis la Conquête Musulmane. 8vo. Paris. 1825.

VINCE, S. Complete System of Astronomy. 3 vols. 4to. London. 1823.

VINCE, S. Elements of Astronomy. 8vo. Phila. 1811.

VINCE, S. Principles of Fluxions. 8vo. Phila. 1823.

VINCENT, THOMAS. Explicatory Catechism. 12mo. Northampton. 1805.

VINCENT, DR. WM. Voyage of Nearchus, and Periplus of the Erythrean Sea. 4 vols. 4to. London. 1797–1800.

VINCENTIUS BURGUNDUS. Speculum quadruplex, Naturale, Doctrinale, Morale, Historiale. 4 vols. Fol. Duaci. 1624.

VIRGILIUS MARO, PUBLIUS. Opera. Ed. Heyne. 4 vols. 8vo. Lipsiae. 1788.

VIRGILIUS. Opera. Ed. Staughton. 8vo. Phila. 1825.

VIRGILIUS. Opera, in usum Delphini. 8vo. Phila. 1827.

VISCONTI, E. Q. See Iconographie.

VISCONTI, E. Q. Opere. 7 vols. 8vo. Milano. 1818.

*VITRUVIUS, MARCUS. De Architectura Libri Decem. 4to. Berolini. 1800.

*VITRUVIUS, MARCUS. Formae ad explicandos Vitruvii decem Libros, cura Rode. Fol. Berolini. 1801.

*VITRUVIUS, MARCUS. Civil Architecture, with an Introduction on the Architecture of the Greeks, by Wm. Wilkins. 8vo. London. 1812.

VOLTAIRE. Beccaria on Crimes and Punishment, with a Commentary attributed to Voltaire. 12mo. Edinburgh. 1778.

VOSSIUS, G. J. Latina Grammatica. 12mo. Amstelodami. 1644.

VOYAGE en Suisse Occidentale, Historique et Litteraire. 2 vols. 12mo. s. l. 1787.

VOYAGES of the Disciples of Linnaeus. 11 vols. 8vo. viz:

Voyages and Travels in the Levant by Hasselquist. London. 1766.

Travels in Louisiana by Bossu. 2 vols. London. 1771.

Voyage to China and the East Indies by Osbeck. 2 vols. Lond. 1772.

VOYAGES of the Disciples of Linnaeus—Continued.

Travels into N. America, by Kalm. 2 vols. London. 1772.

Travels in Europe, Africa, and Asia, by Thunberg. 4 vols. London. 1795.

WADDINGTON, G. History of the Church. 8vo. New York. 1834.

WALDEGRAVE, JAMES, EARL. Memoirs from 1754 to 1758. 4to. London. 1821.

WALES. History of, from the old British of Caradoc, by Dr. Powell. 8vo. London. 1774.

WALKER, JOHN. Elements of Elocution. 8vo. Boston. 1810.

WALKER, JOHN. Rhetorical Grammar. 8vo. Boston. 1822.

WALKER, TIMOTHY. Introduction to American Law. 8vo. Phila. 1837.

WALLACE, J. New Treatise on the Globes and Practical Astronomy. 8vo. New York. 1812.

WALLENSTEIN, HERTZOG VON FRIEDLAND. Briefe. 3 vols. 8vo. Berlin. 1828.

WALLER AND ST. EVREMOND. Letters, and a Biographical Sketch. 18mo. Baltimore. 1809.

WALLIS, JOHN. Mechanica, sive de Motu. 4to. Londini. 1670.

WALPOLE, HORATIO, EARL OF ORFORD. Works. 5 vols. 4to. London. 1798.

WALPOLE, HORACE. Private Correspondence. 4 vols. 8vo. London. 1820.

WALPOLE, HORACE. Letters to Sir Horace Mann. 3 vols. 8vo. Lond. 1834.

WALSH, ROBERT. Appeal from the Judgments of Great Britain as to the U. S. A. 2 copies. 8vo. Phila. 1819.

WALTON, BRIAN. Memoir of the Life and Writings of, by H. J. Todd. 2 vols. 8vo. London. 1820.

WALTON, IZAAC. Complete Angler. 12mo. London. 1775.

WANG KEAOU SWAN, a Chinese Tale by R. Thom, Esq. 4to. Canton. 1839.

WAR OF 1812, Sketches of. 2 vols. in one. 8vo. Rutland. 1815.

WARBURTON, WM. Works. 12 vols. 8vo. London. 1811.

WARBURTON, and a Warburtonian. Tracts. 8vo. London. 1789.

WARD, H. D. Antimasonic Review and Magazine. 8vo. New York. 1828.

WARD, JOHN. Introduction to Latin Grammar. 12mo. London. 1793.

WARD, NATHANIEL. Simple Cobler of Aggawam in America. 12mo. Boston. 1843.

WARD, ROBERT. Law of Nations in Europe. 2 vols. 8vo. London. 1795.

WARDLAW, RALPH. Discourses on the Socinian Controversy. 8vo. Andover. 1815.

WARDLAW, RALPH. Christian Ethics. 8vo. New York. 1835.

WARE, HENRY. Letters to Trinitarians and Calvinists. 8vo. Cambridge. 1820.

WARE, HENRY. Inquiry into the Foundation, Evidences, and Truth of Religion. 2 vols. 8vo. Boston. 1842.

WARREN, J. C. The Mastodon Giganteus. 4to. Boston. 1852.

WARREN, J. C. Physical Education. 2 copies. 12mo. Boston. 1846.

WARTON, JOSEPH. Essay on the Genius and Writings of Pope. 2 vols. 8vo. London. 1806.

WARTON, THOMAS. Observations on Spenser's Faerie Queene. 8vo. Lond. 1754.

WARVILLE, J. P. B. DE. New Travels in the U. S. A. in 1788. 12mo. Boston. 1797.

WASHBURN, EMORY. Judicial History of Massachusetts. 8vo. Boston. 1840.

WASHINGTON, GEORGE. Life, by Ramsay. 8vo. New York. 1807.

WASHINGTON, GEORGE. Life, in Latin Prose, by Francis Glass. 8vo. New York. 1835.

WASHINGTON, GEORGE. Life, by John Marshall. 2 vols. 8vo. Phila. 1836.
Atlas to the above. 8vo. Phila.

WASHINGTON, GEORGE. Life and Writings, by Jared Sparks. 12 vols. 8vo. Boston. 1837.

WATERLAND, DAVID. Sermons. 8vo. Cambridge, Eng. 1720.

WATSON, RICHARD. Anecdotes of his Life, by himself. 2 vols. 8vo. Lond. 1818.

WATSON, RICHARD. Apology for the Bible. 12mo. New York. 1796.

WATTS, ISAAC. Works. 6 vols. 4to. London. 1810.

WATTS, ISAAC. Logick. 12mo. London. 1745.

WAYLAND, FRANCIS. Elements of Moral Science. 8vo. Boston. 1837.

WEBB, DANIEL. Inquiry into the Beauties of Painting. 12mo. London. 1760.

WEBB, E. Philosophy of Medicine. 8vo. Phila. 1833.

WEBBER, SAMUEL. Mathematics. 2 vols. 8vo. Boston. 1801.

WEBSTER, DANIEL. Works, by Everett. 6 vols. 8vo. Boston. 1853.

WEBSTER, J. W. Description of the Island of St. Michael. 8vo. Boston. 1821.

WEBSTER, NOAH. Dictionary of the English Language. 2 vols. 4to. New York. 1828.

WEBSTER, NOAH. The same. 12mo. Hartford. 1806.

WEBSTER, NOAH. Dissertation on the English Language. 8vo. Boston. 1789.

WEBSTER, NOAH. History of Epidemic and Pestilential Diseases. 8vo. Hartford. 1799.

WEDEKIND, GEORG VON. Der Pythagorische Orden. 8vo. Leipzig. 1820.

WELLS, W. C. Two Essays: one on Single Vision with two eyes, the other on Dew. 8vo. London. 1818.

WELSH GRAMMAR. 12mo. London. s. a.

WENDELINUS, M. F. Contemplationes Physicae. 4to. Cantab. 1648.

WERNER, A. G. New Theory on the formation of Veins, with its application to the Art of working Mines, transl. by Anderson. 8vo. Edinburgh. 1809.

WERNER, A. G. Traité des Caractères exterieurs des Fossiles, trad. de l'Allemand. 12mo. Dijon. 1790.

WESLEY, JOHN. Life, with Rise and Progress of Methodism, by R. Southey. 2 vols. 8vo. New York. 1829.

WEST, GILBERT. Dissertation on the Olympic Games. 12mo. Lond. 1766.

WESTMAN, H. O. The Spoon. 8vo. New York. 1844.

WHATELY, R. Elements of Rhetoric. 12mo. Cambridge. 1834.

WHATELY, R. Elements of Logic. 8vo. New York. 1836.

WHEATLEY, THOS. Observations on Modern Gardening. 8vo. Lond. 1777.

WHEATON, HENRY. History of the Northmen from the Earliest Times to the Conquest of England by William. 8vo. Phila. 1831.

WHEELOCK, ELEAZER. Memoirs by Dr. McClure. 8vo. Newburyport. 1811.

WHEWELL, WILLIAM. Dynamics. 8vo. Cambridge, Eng. 1823.

WHEWELL, WILLIAM. Mechanics. 8vo. Cambridge, Eng. 1824.

WHISTON, WM. New Theory of the Earth. 8vo. London. 1755.

WHISTON, WM. Translation of Josephus. 4 vols. 8vo. Edinburgh. 1826.

WHISTON, WM. Astronomical Lectures. 12mo. London. 1715.

WHISTON, WM. Astronomical Principles of Religion. 12mo. Lond. 1717.

WHITAKER, GUL. De Sacramentis. 4to. s. l. et a.

WHITAKER, GUL. Tractatus de Peccato Originali. 12mo. Cantab. 1600.

WHITE, CHARLES. On the Management of Pregnant and Lying-in Women. 8vo. Worcester. 1793.

WHITE, GILBERT. Works in Natural History. 2 vols. 8vo. London. 1802.

WHITE, W. Memoirs of the Protestant Episcopal Church in the U. S. A. 8vo. New York. 1836.

WHITGIFT, JOHN. Life and Acts, by John Strype. 3 vols. 8vo. Oxford. 1822.

WHITMAN, SAMUEL. Key to Justification. 8vo. Boston. 1814.

WHITNEY. See Worcester County.

WICKLIFFE, JOHN. Life and Opinions, by Vaughan. 2 vols. 8vo. London. 1731.

WIELAND, C. M. Neues Attisches Museum. 8vo. 4 vols. Zurich. 1805.

WIELAND, C. M. Attisches Museum. 3 vols. 8vo. Zurich. 1806.

WIELAND, C. M. Werke. 8 vols. 12mo. Troppau. 1785.

WIGGERS, G. F. Historical Presentation of Augustinianism and Pelagianism, transl. by Emerson. 8vo. Andover. 1840.

WILBERFORCE, WILLIAM. Practical View of the prevailing Religious System of professed Christians. 12mo. Boston. 1803.

WILCKE, W. F. Geschichte des Tempelherren Ordens. 8vo. 3 vols. Leipzig. 1826.

WILKEN, F. Geschichte der Kreuzzüge. 9 vols. 8vo. Leipzig. 1807–1832.

WILKINS, JOHN. Mathematical and Philosophical Works. 12mo. London. 1708.

WILLARD, EMMA. Journal and Letters from France and Great Britain. 12mo. Troy. 1833.

WILLARD's Body of Divinity. First 16 pages wanting. Fol.

WILLIAMS, ROGER. Memoir of, by Knowles. 12mo. Boston. 1834.

WILLIAMS, SAMUEL. Natural and Civil History of Vermont. 8vo. Walpole, N. H. 1794.

WILLIAMS, SAMUEL. The same. 2 vols. 8vo. Burlington. 1809.

WILLIAMS, T. Song of Solomon, with Notes. 8vo. Phila. 1803.

WILLIAMS, T. S. English and German Dialogues. 12mo. London. 1835.

WILLIAMSON, T. Oriental Field Sports, with Plates. 4to. London. s. a.

*Wilson, Alexander. American Ornithology, or History of the Birds in the U. S. A. 9 vols. including a supplementary Vol. 4to. Phila. 1808–1825.

Wilson, H. Account of the Pelew Islands. 4to. London. 1788.

Wilson, James. Missionary Voyage to the Southern Pacific Ocean. 4to. London. 1799.

Wilson, J. French and English Dictionary. 8vo. Paris. 1834.

Wilson, John. Illustrations of Unitarianism. 8vo. London. 1846.

Winckelmann, J. Werke, von Fernow. 9 vols. 8vo. Dresden. 1808–1820.

Winthrop, John, (Gov.) History of New England from 1630 to 1649. 2 vols. 8vo. Boston. 1820.

Winthrop, John. Lectures on Comets: also, an Essay on Comets by Oliver. 12mo. Boston. 1811.

Wirt, William. Life of Patrick Henry. 8vo. Phila. 1836.

Wistar, C. Anatomy. 2 vols. 8vo. Phila. 1823.

Wither, George. Hymns and Songs of the Church. 18mo. London. 1815.

Wither, George. A Satyre. 24mo. London. 1616.

Wither, George. Brittan's Remembrancer. 24mo. London. 1638.

Withering, Wm. Botanical Arrangement of British Plants. 4 vols. 8vo. Birmingham. 1787, and London. 1801.

Witherspoon, John. Works. 4 vols. 8vo. Phila. 1802.

Wittenhall. Latin Grammar. 18mo. Phila. 1773.

Wittman, Wm. Travels in Turkey, Asia Minor, Syria, and Egypt. 8vo. Phila. 1804.

Wolf, F. A. Prolegomena ad Homerum, sive de Operum Hom. prisca et genuina Forma, Mutationibus, etc. 8vo. Halis, Sax. 1795.

Wolf, F. A. Litterarische Analekten. 2 vols. 8vo. Berlin. 1817.

Wolf, F. A., und Buttmann. Museum der Alterthums-Wissenschaft. 2 vols. 8vo. Berlin. 1807.

Wolf, F. A., et Buttmann. Museum Antiquitatis Studiorum. 2 vols. 8vo. Berolini. 1808.

Wollaston, Wm. Religion of Nature delineated. 4to. London. 1725.

Wollebius, J. Compendium Theologiae Christianae. 2 copies. 12mo. London. 1760.

Wollstonecraft, Mary. Vindication of the Rights of Women. Vol. i. 8vo. London. 1796.

Wood, Anthony. Athenae Oxonienses. 2 vols. Fol. London. 1721.

Wood, James. Mechanics. 8vo. Cambridge. Eng. 1818.

WOOD, ROBERT. Essay on the Genius and Writings of Homer. 4to. Lond. 1775.

WOODHOUSE, ROBERT. Principles of Analytical Calculation. 4to. Cambridge, Eng. 1803.

WOODHOUSE, ROBERT. Treatise on Astronomy. 3 vols. 8vo. Cambridge, Eng. 1821.

WOODS, LEONARD. Letters to Unitarians and Reply to Dr. Ware. 8vo. Andover. 1822.

WOODWARD, JOHN. Natural History of the Earth and Terrestrial Bodies. 8vo. London. 1723.

WOODWARD, JOHN. Attempt at a Natural History of the Fossils of England. 2 vols. in one. 8vo. London. 1729.

WOOLHOUSE. See Tredgold.

WOOLMAN, JOHN. Works. 18mo. Phila. 1806.

WOOLSEY, CARDINAL. Life, by Cavendish. 8vo. London. 1708.

WORCESTER COUNTY, MASS. History of, by Peter Whitney. 8vo. Worcester. 1793.

WORCESTER, J. E. Gazetteer of the U. S. 8vo. Andover. 1818.

WORKMAN, BENJAMIN. Gauging. 8vo. Phila. 1788.

WORLAKSSYNI, JONI. Paradisar Missir. 8vo. Kaufmannahöfn. 1828.

WOTTON, WM. Reflections on Ancient and Modern Learning. 12mo. Lond. 1697.

WOTTON, WM. Reliquiae Wottoniae. 24mo. London. 1657.

WRANGHAM, FRANCIS. Sermons, Dissertations, and Translations. 3 vols. 8vo. London. 1816.

WRIGHT, J. M. F. Commentary on Newton's Principia, with a supplementary volume. 2 vols. 8vo. London. 1828.

WRIGHT, J. Currencies of the British Colonies in America. 8vo. London. 1761.

WYMAN, JEFFRIES. Anatomy of the Nervous System of the Rana Pipiens. 4to. Washington. 1853.

WYTTENBACH, DANIEL. Animadversiones in Plutarchi Opera Moralia. 2 vols. 8vo. Lipsiae. 1820.

WYTTENBACH, DANIEL. Opuscula. 2 vols. 8vo. Lipsiae. 1820.

XENOPHON. Oeconomicus, cum fragmentis Oeconomicorum Ciceronis. 8vo. Oxoniae. 1693.

XENOPHON. Quae extant. Ed. Schneider. 6 vols. 8vo. Lipsiae. 1828.

XIMENES, CARDINAL. Life, by B. Barrett. 8vo. London. 1813.

YALE COLLEGE. History of, by Baldwin. 8vo. New Haven. 1841.

YATES AND MOULTON. History of New York. Vol. I. 8vo. New York. 1824.

YOUNG, EDWARD. Night Thoughts. 18mo. New York. 1796.

YOUNG, THOMAS. Lectures on Natural Philosophy and the Mechanic Arts. 2 vols. 4to. London. 1807.

YOUNG, THOMAS. Hieroglyphical Literature and Egyptian Antiquities. 8vo. London. 1823.

YOUNG, SIR WM. History of Athens, with a Commentary on Republican Government. 8vo. London. 1804.

YOUNG Minister's Companion. 8vo. Boston. 1813.

ZABARELLA, J. De rebus naturalibus Libri xxx. Fol. Coloniae. 1590.

ZIMMERMAN, J. G. Reflections on Men and Things, 8vo. London. 1799.

*ZOEGA, GEORGIUS. De Origine et Usu Obeliscorum. Fol. Romae. 1797.

ZOLLIKOFER, G. J. Sermons on the Dignity of Man. Vol. II. 8vo. Worcester. 1807.

ZOUCH, THOMAS. Works. 2 vols. 8vo. York. 1820.

ZSCHOKKE, H. Die Geschichte des Schweizerlands. 8vo. Aarau. 1834.

ZUMPT, C. G. Lateinische Grammatik. 8vo. Berlin. 1834.

ZWINGLE, ULRICH. Life, by Hess, transl. by Lucy Aiken. 8vo. London. 1812.

BOOKS OMITTED,

OR RECEIVED SINCE THE CATALOGUE WAS PUT TO PRESS.

BACHE, A. D. Maps of the Coast Survey.

BACHE, A. D. Report of Coast Survey for 1851. 8vo. Washington. 1852.

Sketches accompanying the above. 4to. Washington. 1853.

CENSUS of the U. S. for 1850. Statistics, by J. D. B. De Bow. 4to. Washington. 1853.

COLERIDGE, H. N. Introduction to the Study of the Greek Classic Poets. 12mo. Phila. 1831.

COLERIDGE, S. T. Works, by Prof. Shedd. 7 vols. 12mo. New York. 1854.

DAVIES, CHARLES. Shades, Shadows, and Linear Perspective. 8vo. New York. 1832.

EMMONS, G. T. Statistics of the U. S. Navy, from 1775 to 1853. 4to. Washington. 1853.

GROTE, GEORGE. History of Greece. 11 vols. 12mo. New York. 1850–1854.

HAMILTON, ALEX. Works. 7 vols. 8vo. New York. 1851.

LEE, T. J. Tables and Formulae for Surveying, &c. 8vo. Washington. 1853.

MAP of Massachusetts, Topographical and Geological, compiled from Astronomical, Trigonometrical, and Local Surveys. 1844.

MAP of the Town of Woodstock, Vermont.

MESSAGE and Documents for the 33d Congress, 1st Session. Part I. 2 copies. 8vo. Washington. 1853.

NORTH AMERICAN REVIEW. Vols. I–LXXVI. 8vo. Boston.

NORTON, C. B. Literary Register for 1854. New York. 1854.

POOLE, W. T. Index to Periodical Literature. 8vo. New York. 1853.

SMITH, J. C. Map of the United States. 1845.

STANSBURY, HOWARD. Valley of the Great Salt Lake of Utah. 8vo. Washington. 1853.

Sketches accompanying the above. 8vo. Washington. 1853.

SYNOPSIS

TO THE

ANALYTICAL CATALOGUE.

ANALYTICAL CATALOGUE.

THEOLOGY.

SACRED SCRIPTURES.

Acts, in Modern Greek.
Arabic Gospels.
Bloomfield's Greek Testament.
Bible, Holy.
Bible, La Sainte.
Biblia al Espagnol.
Biblia Hebraica.
Biblia Latina.
New Testament, Rhemes.
Improved Version.
Tyndale.
Sandwich Islands.
In Chinese.
Novum Testamentum, Graece.
Syriace.
Psalmorum Liber Heb.
Psalter, Arabic.
Pseaumes de David.
Septuagint.
Testament Het. Nieuwe.
Testamentum Vetus.
Turkish Psalter.

CHURCH FATHERS.

Athanasius, Augustinus, Bernardus, Clem. Alexandrinus, Chrysostomus, Cyprianus, Eusebius Pamphilus, Gregorius Nazian., Hieronymus, Justinus Martyr, Origenes, Tertullianus.

CRITICAL THEOLOGY, RESEARCHES, AND EVIDENCES.

Ainsworth, Allen, Baldvinus, Barclay, Baumgarten, Bellamy, Boudinot, Bentley, Biblical Repository, Bielby, Brown J., Browne S., Bruno, Burkitt, Burnet, Butler C., Caedmon, Calmet, Calvin, Campbell G., Caryl, Colman B., Croly, Dale, Doddridge, Faber G. L., Fagnani, Fleming R., Gale Theo., Genesis of the World, Gerard, Grotius, Hackett, Halyburton, Hammond, Harmony Newcomb's, Herder, Hierocles, Hindoostan, Horne G., Hug, Hurd, Jahn J. G., Jenkyn, Julianus Imperator, Kirby, Koran, Lardner, Leigh, Leighton, Leland, Locke J., Lowth R., Luther, McLeod, Malebranche, Mann J., Martin del Rio, Mason J. M., Moses Choronensis, Musculus, Michaelis, Newton I., Newton T., Nitzsch, Noyes Geo. R., Olshausen, Orton, Owen J., Paley, Parcus, Parr, Pensées Diverses, Philo Judaeus, Piscator, Polus, Pomponatius, Reinhard, Roget, Schleiermacher, Schmidt, Sclaterus, Scotus R. R., Second Advent, Spangenberg, Stackhouse, Staudlein C. F., Stillingfleet, Stuart Moses, Swedenborg, Taylor John, Thomson R., Tucker A., Turkish Version, Usserius, Jacobus, Van Til Commentaria, Warburton, Ware, Henry, Watson R., Whiston Wm., Williams, Song of Solomon, Wollaston.

DOGMATIC THEOLOGY.

Alesius, Ambrose Isaac, Anselmus, Appleton Jesse, Austin Samuel, Balguy, Ballou, Barclay R., Bates Wm., Bossuet, Boston, Bellamy, Belsham, Bradbury, Brown D., Brown J., Bunyan, Burgesse, Burnap G. W., Burton A., Butler J., Calvin, Catechisme, Connecticut Evang. Magazine, Cooke P., Cranmer, Cudworth, Dens P., Derham, Doctrine of Baptism and the Supper, Doddridge P., Dwight T., Edwards Jon., Edwards P., Encyclopaedia of Religious Knowledge, Fenelon, Fessenden, Flavel, Fuller Andrew, Gervase, Gray J., Gurney J. J., Hammond H., Hildeburtus, Hobart J. H., Hopkins E., Hopkins S., Horsely, Howe J., Irving, Jackson J., Johnson T., Johnson Stephen, Kingsbury H., Law Wm., Leibnitz, Letters on Unitarianism, Lortie Andre, Luther Martin, Maccovius, Marloratus, Marshall, Mason J. M., Mason W., More Henry, Milton John, Niles S., Noble, Olshausen, Osterwald, Owen John, Pamphlets, Panoplist, Pareus, Pascal, Penn, Perkins W., Phipps, Polanus, Quarterly Christian Spectator, Reynolds Ed., Ronge, Salmasius, Scharpius J., Seed, Sherlock, Smalley J., Smith John, Smith J. P., Spring Gard., Stuart Moses, Sumner J. B., Swedenborg, Syntagma, Theo-Christianae, Taylor Jeremy, Theologie suppliante &c., Thomas Aquinas, Thomson Thos., Tilenus, Tillotson Dr. J., Toplady, Turretinus F., Tyndale and Frith, Usteri L., Verdict on the Dissenter's Plea, Vial Andre, Views in Theology, Vincent Thos., Wardlaw R., Ware Henry, Waterland D., Whitaker, Whitman S., Wickliffe's Life and Opinions, Willard, Wilson J., Witherspoon, Wollebius, Woods Leonard.

PRACTICAL RELIGION.

Adviser, American Preacher, Barclay J., Baxter R., Beveridge Bishop, Blair Hugh, Behmen J., Bourdaloue, Bull Bp., Bunyan, Cecil R., Celestial Comforter, Columbian Preacher, Common Prayer, Comstock, Dana J., Deveze, Diez P., Doddridge, Du Moulin, Edwards Jon., Exhortation, Fawcett, Felltham, Fish N., Flavel, Fleming, Fletcher, Fordyce, Fuller A., Fuller T., Genlis, Gisborne, Graham J., Guthrie, Hay, Heber, Henry T. C., Hoornebeck, Horneck, Humphrey H., Hurd, Hymns Watts' and Select, Ingersoll, Irving E., Jerment, Jortin, Keith, Lathrop, Latimer, Law W., Linn W., Luther, McLaurin, Marsh J., Mason W., Massilon, Maxwell, Morris, Murray L., Methodist Preachers, Michelet, Mennais, Missionaries, More H., National Preacher, Necker, Norton J., Olney Hymns, Ogden S., Osborne, Osgood, Pamphlets, Practical Reflections, Price R., Rambach, Roll and Book, Rowe Eliz., Rush Jacob, Rutherford, Saint George, Sanderson R., Saurin J., Scott J., Scott T., Scribanus, Sermons by American Ministers, Sermons Collection of, Sermons on Particular Occasions, Shepard T., Struensee Count, Thayer E., Thom D., Thomas a Kempis, Thomas Bp., Trumbull, Upham's Letters, Watts Isaac, Wilberforce W., Wither Geo., Wrangman, Young Ed., Young Minister's Companion, Zimmerman, Zollikoffer, Zouch, Zwingle's Life by Hess.

JURISPRUDENCE.

LAW.

Akber. Laws of Hindostan.
American Jurist.
American State Papers.
Bacon. Various.
Bentham. On Legislation and Punishment.
Blackstone. Comm. on Eng. Law.
Blondeau. Roman Law.
Boulay Paty. Maritime.
Brigham. Laws of New Plymouth.
British State Papers.
Burlamaqui. Natural Law.
Burr's Trials.
Butler, C. Grecian, Roman, Feudal, and Canon Law.
California Reports.
Chancery of England.
Chardon. On Fraud.
Codes, the Six, Criminal, and Penal.
Congressional Documents.
Connecticut Laws.
Cooper. Reports in Chancery.
Corpus, &c. Civil Law.
De Lolme. Eng. Constitution.
English Law, History of.
Gaius et Justinianus. Institutes.
Gibson. English Eccl. Law.
Girard Case.
Goguet. Origin of Laws.
Grotius. Laws of War and Peace.
Guerard. Private Roman Law.
Hoffman. Legal Outlines.
Kent. Comm. on American Law.
Law Tracts.
Leibnitz. Various.
Mackintosh. Law of Nature and Nations.
Manley. Terms of Law.
Massachusetts. Laws, &c.
Montesquieu. Spirit of Laws.
New York. Laws.
Pfeffel. Public Law of Germany.
Pothier. Works.
Parecbolae. Oxford Statutes.
Puffendorf. Law of Nature and Nations.
Rossi. Penal Law.
Savigny. Roman Law.
Selden. Law of Nature and Nations.
State Trials. (English.)
Vermont. Reports and Statutes.

POLITICS, POLITICAL AND SOCIAL ECONOMY.

AMERICAN.

Adams, J. Works.
Adams, J. Q. Masonic Institution.
American State Papers.
Ames. Works.
Bank of the United States.
Beaujour. U. S. from 1800–1810.
Beckwith. On Peace.
Burgh. Political Disquisitions.
Chipman. Principles of Government.
Congressional Documents.
Coxe, T. View of the United States.
Everett. America.
Federalist.
Felt. Mass. Currency.
Franklin. Works.
Hamilton, Alex. Works.
Hancock. On Peace.
Humboldt. New Spain.
Jay. Mexican War.
Livermore. Mexican War.
Newman. Political Economy.
Oliver. American Citizen.
Ouseley. Remarks on U. S.
Owen. View of Society.
Prize Essays. Congress of Nations.
Rawle. Constitution of U. S.
Rumford. Political Essays.
Sheffield. American Commerce.
Sparks. Diplomatic Correspondence.

Story. On the Constitution.
Upham. Manual of Peace.
Vermont State Papers.
Walsh. Appeal from Great Britain.
War of 1812.
Washburn. Judicial History of Mass.
Washington. Works.
Webster. Works.

FOREIGN.

Bacon. Various Treatises.
Beaufort. Roman Republic.
Beccaria. On Crime.
Boeckh. Polit. Economy of the Athenians.
Bolingbroke. On Parties, &c.
British State Papers.
Bulwer, H. L. Politics of France.
Burke. Works.
Cartwright. English Constitution.
Chalmers, T. Political Economy.
Chateaubriand. Mélanges Politiques.
Coleridge. Friend, and Statesman's Manual.
De Tocqueville. Democracy in America.
Flower. French Constitution.
Goddard. Banks in Europe.
Godwin. Political Justice.
Hallam. Constitutional History of Eng.
Harleian Miscellany.
Harrington. Works.
Heeren. Political System of Europe.
Hobbes. Leviathan.
Lerminier. Politics beyond the Rhine.
Locke. Money and Civil Government.
Lowe. Present State of England.
Machiavelli. Prince.
Malthus. Political Economy.
Malthus. Population.
Marvell. Various.
Millar. English Government.
Milton. Political Treatises.
Neveu-Derotrie. French Rural Law.
Paley. Political Philosophy.
Parr. Political Disquisitions.
Pecchio. Public Economy of Italy.
Price. American Revolution.
Ralegh. Trade and Commerce.
Raynal. Political History of the W. Indies.
Record Commission.
Ricardo. Political Economy.
Say. Political Economy.
Sidney. Discourses on Government.
Sinclair. Finance.
Smith, A. Wealth of Nations.
Steuart. Political Economy.
Stewart. Political Philosophy.
Swift. Political Treaties.
Temple. The Netherlands, and Various.
Thome and Kimball. Emancipation.
Turkish Spy.
Tychsen. Luxuries of the Athenians.
Vattel. Laws of Nations.
Vegece. Military Institutions.
Ward. Laws of Nations.
Wright. Currencies of the Brit. Colonies.
Xenophon. Oeconomics, and Political Treatises.

SCIENCES AND ARTS.

PHILOSOPHY AND METAPHYSICS.

Ales, A. Scholastic.
Anselmus. Prosloquium. Scholastic.
Apuleius, L. On the World. On Socrates and Plato.
Aristoteles. Metaphysics and Psychology.
Augustinus. De Anima.
Bacon, F. Inductive Philosophy.
Bacon, R. Scholastic.
Bayle. Skeptical. Historical.
Beasley, F. Search of Truth.
Becke, David von der. Phil. of Nature.
Behmen, J. Mystical Philosophy.
Berkely, G. Idealism.
Boeckh, A. Platonic Ideas.
Boethius. Platonic-Aristotelian.
Bolingbroke. Skeptical.
Boscovich, R. J. Phil. of Nature.
Browne, T. Religio Medici.
Bruckerus, J. History of Philosophy.
Bruno, G. Pantheistical.
Buffier Père. Common sense. First Truths.
Burgerdicus, F. Metaphysical Outlines.
Campanella, T. Philosophy of Experience.
Carus, F. A. Psychology.
Cicero, M. T. Academical. Stoical.
Coleridge, S. T. Metaphysics & Psychology.
Cousin, V. Metaphysics and Psychology.
Cudworth, R. Philosophy of Faith.
D'Alembert. Encyclopaedist.
Daub und Creuzer. Miscellaneous.
Descartes, R. Speculative Philosophy.
Digby, Sir K. Nature of Bodies and Man's Soul.
Diogenes Laertius. Historical.
Duperron, A. Oriental Philosophy.
Edwards, Jonathan. Metaphysics.
Enfield, W. Historical.
Epicurus. Fragments on Nature.
Eschemayer, C. A. Against Hegel.
Faber, B. Scholastic Erudition.
Feder, J. G. On Space and Causality.
Fénélon. Against Spinoza.
Ficinus, M. Platonism.
Fichte. Idealism.
Fontenelle Cartesian. Historical.
Fries, J. Kantian Philosophy.
Froemmicher. Philosophia Academica.
Fülleborn, G. G. Historical.
Gabler, G. A. Hegelian Philosophy.
Gale, T. Philosophy of Faith.
Gassendus, P. Epicurean.
Glanville, J. Skeptical.
Hamann. Against Kant.
Harris, J. Aristotelian.
Hartley, D. Empirical Psychology.
Heerebord, A. Cartesian.
Hegel, G. W. F. Logic and Metaphysics.
Herbart, J. F. Logic and Metaphysics.
Herder, J. G. Psychology and Criticism.
Heydenreich, R. H. Anthropology.
Hierocles. Pythagorean.
Hobbes, T. Materialism.

Huet, P. D. Skeptical.
Hutchinson, J. Cabalistic.
Inquiry into the Nature of the Soul.
Jackson, J. Metaphysical.
Jacobi, F. H. Metaphysical.
Jahrbücher der Wissenschaftlicher Kritik.
Jamblichus, C. Pythagorean.
Joannes Salis. Dialectical. Scholastic.
Kant, I. Critical Philosophy.
Klein, G. M. Pantheism.
Krug, W. T. Synthetism.
Leibnitz, G. G. Metaphysical.
Lessing, G. E. Education of the Human Race.
Locke, J. Essay on the Understanding.
Lucretius. Epicurean.
Malebranche. Idealism.
Marsh, James. Metaphysical.
Maximus Philosophus. De Principiis.
Memoires de l'Academie. Miscellaneous.
Mendelsohn, M. Immortality of the Soul.
Monboddo, Lord. Ancient Metaphysics.
More, Henry. Modern Platonism.
Norris, J. Plat. Idealism.
Paine, Martyn. Discourse on the Soul.
Pascal, Blaise. Philosophy of Faith.
Petrarcha, F. The Six Triumphs, &c.
Platner, E. Anthropology.
Plato. Works.
Plotinus. New Platonism.
Poesis Philosophica. Miscellaneous.
Pomponatius, P. Immortality of the Soul.
Portalis, J. E. M. Critical.
Proclus. New Platonism.
Pythagoras. Fragment.
Reid, T. Scotch Philosophy.
Reinhold. Skeptical Elementary.
Ritter, D. History of Ionian Philosophy.
Salustius, Philosophus. De Diis et Mundo.
Schelling, F. W. J. Metaphysics.
Schubert, G. H. Mystical Philosophy.
Schulze, G. E. Philosophical Outlines.
Scotus, J. Erig. Scholastic.
Sextus Empiricus. Skeptical Philosophy.
Simplicius. Peripatetic Philosophy.
Socrates. Letters ascribed to him.
Stäudlin, C. F. History of Skepticism.
Steffens, H. Anthropology.
Stewart, D. Works.
Synopsis Metaphysica.
Taylor, T. Various Translations.
Tennemann. History of Philosophy.
Tiedemann. History of Philosophy.
Tucker, T. Light of Nature pursued.
Vico, G. Principles of New Science.
Wedekin, G. Pythagorean Orders.

LOGIC.

Aldrich. Compendium of Logic.
Aristoteles. Organon.
Baumgarten, A. G. Acroasis Logica.
Fries, J. System of Logic.
Hegel, G. W. F. Objective and Subjective Logic.
Johannes Grammaticus. On Aristotle.
Kirwan, R. System of Logick.
Lully, R. Universal Art.
Milton, J. Logic of Ramus.
Ritter, H. Philosophical Logic.
Watts, I. Logic.
Whateley, R. Elements of Logic.

MORAL PHILOSOPHY AND ETHICS.

Abbt, T. Ueber die Verdienste.
Antonius, M. Meditations.
Aristoteles. Nicomachean Ethics, &c.
Bayle. Miscellaneous.
Bentham. Introduction to Morals.
Bockshammer. On the Will.
Burton, A. Principles of Ethics.
Burton, R. Anatomy of Melancholy.
Channing. Miscellaneous.
Claudius, M. Miscellaneous.
Cogan, T. On the Passions.
Coleridge, S. T. Aids to Reflection. Friend.
Combe, G. Lectures on Moral Philosophy.
Comstock, C. Duty of Parents and Children.
Edwards, J. On the Will.
Epictetus. Stoic Morality.
Essais de Morale. Miscellaneous.
Felltham. Aphoristic.
Ferguson, A. Institutes of Moral Phil.
Franklin, B. Miscellaneous.
Frisbie, Prof. Lectures on Morals.
Fuller, T. On Prudence.
Gellert, C. F. Essays on Morals.
Hurd, R. Moral Dialogues.
Jacobi, F. H. Letters of Allwill.
Johnson, S. Essays.
Lichtenberg, G. C. Miscellaneous.
Mackintosh, Sir J. History of Ethics.
Mandeville, B. Fable of the Bees.
Montaigne, M. de. Essays.
Moralistes Français.
Moses Maimonides. Jewish.
Nicole. Essays.
Olshausen. Manual of Morals.
Paley. Moral Philosophy.
Pascal, B. Miscellaneous.
Plutarch. Essays.
Price, R. Questions & Difficulties in Morals.
Schleiermacher. Criticism on moral Theories.
Seneca. Essays.
Shaftsbury. Characteristics.
Smith, A. Moral Sentiments.
Wardlaw, R. Christian Ethics.
Wayland, F. Elements of Moral Science.

PHILOLOGY.

LEXICOGRAPHY.

Ainsworth. Latin Dictionary.
Apollonius Sophista. Lexicon Homericum.
Bailey, M. Universal English Dictionary.
Barclay, James. Eng ish Dictionary.
Benson. Vocabularium Anglo-Saxon.
Bötticher. Lexicon Taciteum.
Bosworth, James. Anglo-Saxon Dictionary.
Boyer. French Dictionary.
Buttmann. Lexilogus, for Homer and Hes.
Buxtorfius. Hebrew and Chaldaic Dict.
Calepinus. Dictionary Octolingue.
Davenport. Eng., Italian and French Dict.
Dawson. Lexicon Nov. Testamenti.
Dictionaire Universel.
Dictionarium Hebraicum.
Dictionary, English.
Dictionary, English-German.
Dufief. French Dictionary.

Dumesnil. Synonymes Latins.
Entick. Latin-English Dictionary.
Etymologicum Magnum. Gr.
Etymologicum Gudianum. Gr.
Etymologicon Orionis. Gr.
Etymologicon Magnum. Eng.
Forcellinus. Totius Latinitatis Lexicon.
Gibbs. Hebrew and English.
Herodoteum Lexicon.
Hindmarsh. Dictionary of Correspondences.
Lowndes. Modern Greek Lexicon.
Macleod, N. Gaelic Dictionary.
Neuman. Spanish Dictionary.
Passow. Greek Dictionary.
Photius. Greek Lexicon.
Pike. Hebrew Dictionary.
Requijo. Hispano-Latinus Dictionary.
Robinson, Edward. Greek of N. Testament.
Roquefort. Langue Romaine.
Schmidt. Russian-German.
Suidas. Greek.
Webster, Noah. English.
Wilson, J. French.

GRAMMAR AND METRE.

Andrews & Stoddard. Latin.
Apollonius Alexandrinus. Greek.
Arabic Grammar. Richardson.
Aucher, P. Armenian.
Bopp, F. Sanskrit, Zend, Greek, &c.
Bosworth, J. Anglo-Saxon.
Buchanan, J. English.
Buttmann, P. Greek.
Chambaud, L. French.
Cobbet, W. French.
Crombie, A. Latin.
Draco Straton. Metre.
Dufief, M. G. French.
Duvivier, C. P. G. French.
Foster, J. Accent and Quantity.
Galley. Accents, Greek.
Goodrich, C. A. Greek.
Gregorius Corinth. Dialects.
Hackett, H. B. Chaldee and Hebrew.
Harris. Universal Grammar.
Hebrew Grammar. Lyons and Grey.
Hephaestion. Greek Metre.
Hermann, G. Metre.
Holmes, J. Greek.
Hoogeveen, H. Greek Particles.
Kenrick, Wm. Rhetorical.
Kusterus, L. Greek Middle Voice.
Lowth, R. English.
Marsh, G. P. Icelandic.
Martin, B. Philosophical.
Maittaire, M. Greek Dialects.
Meilleur, J. B. French Pronunciation.
Neilson, W. Greek Exercises.
Noel, M. French.
Nöhden, G. H. German.
Palfrey, J. G. Chaldaic, Syriac, &c.
Perrin, J. French.
Phorboeus, J. Greek.
Port Royal. Greek.
Priscianus, C. Latin.
Rask, R. Akra. Singalese, Lapland.
Rosenmüller, E. F. C. Arabic.
Ross, J. Latin.
Rost, V. C. F. Attic Dialect.
Sandford, D. K. Homeric and Attic.
Schultz, O. Latin.
Seidler, A. Dochmiac verse.
Sheridan, T. Rhetorical.
Spitzner, F. Homeric Metre.
Stoicheia. Ling. Hellenica.
Stuart, M. Hebrew. Greek Accent.
Sturzius. Macedonian Dialect.
Valpy, R. Greek.
Varro, M. Latin.
Vater. J. S. Russian.
Vigerus, F. Greek Particles.
Vossius, G. J. Latin.
Ward, J. Latin.
Welsh Grammar.
Wittenhall. Latin.
Zumpt, C. G. Latin.

COMMENTARIES AND MISCELLANEOUS.

Adams & Smith. Latin Tutor.
Aeschylus. Müller's Eumenides.
Anecdota Graeca. Ed. Villoison.
Anecdota Graeca. Ed. Bekker.
Apollodorus Atheniensis.
Benedict, T. F. On Sophocles.
Bentley, R. On Phalaris.
Boyle, C. On Bentley's Phalaris.
Cambridge Classical Examinations.
Casaubon, I. Satiric Poetry and Satire.
Chardon de la Rochette. Melanges.
Cleveland, C. D. Latin Lessons.
Crenius, T. Philological Dissertations.
Dalzell, A. Anal. Gr. Minora.
Dawesius, R. Miscellanea Critica.
Funccius, J. N. Ages of Latin Language.
Heyne, C. G. Academical Works.
Jacobs, F, Anthologia Graeca.
Jamieson, J. Affinities of Gr. and Lat. to Gothic.
Johnson, A. B. On Language.
Köster, H. Ancient Greek Songs.
Lachmann, F. Sources of Livy's History.
Laurentius Valla. Miscellaneous.
Lessing, G. E. Miscellaneous.
Lipsius, J. Works.
Memoires de l'Academie des Inscriptions.
Museum Criticum.
Niebuhr, B. G. Philological Writings.
Pindarus. Ed. Böckh.
Quatremère, E. Egyptian Language.
Ruhnkenius, D. Works.
Saint Croix, G. Historians of Alexander.
Schneider. Greek Comedy.
Seyffarth, G. Hieroglypical Writers.
Smithsonian Contributions.
Spence, J. Essay on Pope's Odyssey.
Spohr, F. A. J. De Agro Trojano.
Turkish Version.
Webster, N. English Language.
Wieland, C. M. Miscellaneous.
Wolf, F. A. Miscellaneous.
Wyttenbach, D. Works.

MATHEMATICS.

Agnesi. Analyt. Inst.
Arbogast. Calcul des Dériv.
Arith. Universalis.
Barlow. Theory of Numbers. Math. Dict.

Barrow. Lectures.
Berkley. Works. Vol. II.
Bernoulli. Opera.
Bezout. Equations.
Bierdemann. Arithmetik.
Bossut. Math. History.
Boucharlet. Calcul, etc.
Bourdon. Arith., Alg., etc.
Bowditch. Navigator.
Brisson. Theorie des Ombres.
Callet. Logarithmes.
Cambridge Mathematics.
Carnot. Géométrie, etc.
Commercium Epistolicum.
Condorcet. D'apprendre de compter.
Davies. Shades and Perspective.
Davis. Powers.
Day. Navigation and Surveying.
De Lambre. Determ. d'un arc du Mérid.
De Moivre. Doctrine of Chances.
Diophantes. Arithmetica.
Dumas. Equations.
Euclide. Oeuvres.
Euler. Oeuv., Alg., Calc. Diff.
Fenn. Arithmetic, Algebra.
Flint. Geom., Trig., Surveying.
Furlong. Coast Pilot.
Galileo. Discourses.
Gauss. Arithmetic.
Gibson. Surveying.
Gummere. Surveying.
Hirsche. Tables of Integ. Formulae.
Hugenius. Opera.
Hutton. Math. Dic., Math. Course. Tables.
Jopling. Perspective.
Lacroix. Arith.,Alg.,Geom.,Trig.,Calc. Dif.
La Grange. Fonctions Analyt.
Lambert. Arithmetic.
Lee. Tables, &c., for Surveying.
Legendre. Cal. Int.,Fonc. Ellipt.,Nomb. etc.
Lenhart. Cube Numbers.
Leslie. Geom., Trig., &c.
Leybourne. Math. Questions.
McLaurin. Fluxions.
Massachusetts Survey.
Monge. Géom. Descript.
Montucla. Math. Hist.
Moore. Navigator.
Mudge. Survey of England.
Müller. Science of War.
Newton. Opera.
Pascal. Oeuvres.
Playfair. Works.
Ptolemaeus.
Robertson. Math. Instruments.
Serenus. De Sectione Coni.
Simson. Conic Sections. Euclid.
Spence. Log. Transcendents.
Taylor. Perspective.
Taylor. Proclus on Euclid.
Torricellius. Opera.
Vauban. La Defense des Places.
Vince. Fluxions.
Webber. Mathematics.
Wilkins. Works.
Woodhouse. Analyt. Calculations.
Workman. Gauging.

NATURAL SCIENCES.

American Academy. Memoirs of.
American Association, Proceedings of.
American Journal of Science.
American Quarterly Journal.
American Quarterly Review.
Annales des Sciences Naturelles.
Annales du Museum National.
Annals of the Lyceum of New York.
Annual of Scientific Discovery.
Aristoteles.
Becke, David von der. Principia.
Boyle, Robert. Philosophical Works.
Buck, Leopold von.
Chili. History of. Molina.
Comptes Rendus.
Davila, D. M. Catalogue Systematique.
Denham and Clapperton. Travels.
Edinburgh Encyclopaedia.
Edinburgh Review.
Good, John M. Book of Nature.
Journal, Boston, of Natural History.
Journal, Academy of Natural Sciences.
Linnaeus, C. A. Systema Naturae.
Massachusetts Reports.
New York Natural History.
Pallas, P. S. Travels in Russia.
Philosophical Transactions, Royal Society.
Plinius, C. Sec. Historia Naturalis.
Proceedings of American Association.
Rees, Abraham. Cyclopaedia.
Reviews.
Saint Pierre. Studies of Nature.
Sausure, H. B. de. Voyages dans les Alps.
Thompson, Z. History of Vermont.
Transactions of Royal Society of Edinburgh.
Transactions of Royal Society of London.
Transactions of Philosophical Soc. of N. Y.
Transactions of Philosophical Soc. of Phila.
Voyages of the Disciples of Linnaeus. Bossu, Osbeck, Thunberg, Hasselquist & Kalm.
White, Gilbert. Natural History.
Williams, Samuel. History of Vermont.
Woodward, J. Natural History of the Earth.
Zaberella, J. De Rebus Naturalibus.

GEOLOGY AND MINERALOGY.

Accum, F. Analysis of Minerals.
Aikin, A. Manual of Mineralogy.
American Journal of Science.
Bakewell, R. Introduction to Geology.
Buckland, Wm. Reliquiae Diluvianae.
Burnet, T. Sacred Theory of the Earth.
Conybeare & Philips. Geology of England.
Cuvier, Baron G. Ossemens Fossiles.
Deshayes, M. G. P. Shells characterizing Formations.
Eaton, A. Geology of the Northern States.
Geological Report. Featherstonhaugh.
Geological Survey. District of Erie Canal.
Geological Survey. Iowa, Wisc. Minnesota.
Geological Survey. New York.
Geology. Lectures by J. Van Rensalaer.
Of South Carolina, by Tuomey.
Of Connecticut, by Percival.
Of Massachusetts. by Hitchcock.
Of Maine, by Jackson.

Geology of Aroossook Co., by Holmes.
Of Maine and Mass. Lands. Jackson.
Of Wisconsin Ter. Featherstonhaugh.
Of Michigan, by Houghton.
Of New Jersey, by H. D. Rogers.
Of Vermont, by Adams.
Geology and Mineralogy of Boston and Vicinity.
Greenough, G. B. Principles of Geology.
Hauy, M. Traité de Cristallographie.
Hayden, H. H. Geological Essays.
Hitchcock, E. Geology of Massachusetts.
Loomis, J. R. Elements of Geology.
Lyell, C. Principles of Geology.
Macculloch, J. Classification of Rocks.
Mawe, J. Treatise on Diamonds.
New York Natural History.
Mineralogy, by L. C. Beck.
Geology, by Hall, Emmons, Mather, and Vanuxem.
Paleontology, by Hall.
Parkinson, J. Organic Remains.
Philips, Wm. Introduction to Mineralogy.
Robinson, S. Catalogue of Amer. Minerals.
Werner, A. G. Theory of Veins. Fossils.
Whiston, Wm. Theory of the Earth.

ZOOLOGY.

Adanson. Histoire Naturelle du Senegal.
Aelianus, C. De Natura Animalium.
Annales des Sciences Naturelles. Zoologie.
Aristoteles. De Generatione Animalium.
Arrianus. Historia Indica.
Audubon, J. J. Ornithological Biography.
Blümenbach, J. F. Elements of Nat. Hist.
Bonaparte, C. L. American Ornithology.
Brocchi, G. Conchologia Fossile.
Brogniart, A. Crustaces Fossiles.
Catesby, M. Natural History of Carolina.
Conchyliologie. Sea, River, and Land Shells.
Cuvier, Baron F. Ossemens Fossiles.
Cuvier, Baron G. Histoire Naturelle des Poissons.
Cuvier, Baron G. Regne Animal.
Cuvier, Baron G. Progres des Sciences Nat.
Da Costa, E. M. Elements of Conchology.
De Mountfort, D. Conchyl. Systematique.
Desmarest, A. G. Crustacea.
Dillwyn. Descriptions of Recent Shells.
Eaton, A. Zoological Text Book.
Edinburgh Encyclopaedia.
Edinburgh Review.
Ellis, J. Natural History of Zoophytes.
Forskael, Petrus. Descriptiones Animalium.
Franklin, John. Narratives.
Godman, J. D. American Natural History.
Guattierus, N. Index Testarum Conchyl.
Harlan, Richard. Fauna Americana.
Hearne, S. Journey to the Northern Ocean.
Holbrook, J. E. N. American Herpetology.
Kirby & Spence. Introduction to Entomol.
Klein, J. T. Echinoderms.
Lamarck. Histoire Naturelle.
Latham, J. Synopses of Birds.
Latham, J. Index Ornithologicus.
Lawrence, W. Lectures.
Long, S. H. Narratives.
Massachusetts Reports.
Fishes and Reptiles, by Storer.
Massachusetts Reports—Continued.
Invertebrates, by Gould.
Insects, by Harris.
Miller, J. S. Natural History of Crinoidea.
Müller, C. F. Historia Vermium.
New York Natural History. Part I. Quadrupeds, Birds, Reptiles, Fishes, Mollusks, and Crustacea.
Nuttall, Thos. Manual of Ornithology. Journal of Travels.
Olivi, G. Zoologia Adriatica.
Parry, Wm. E. Voyages.
Perron, M. F. Voyages.
Pritchard, A. Microscopic Cabinet.
Quoy et Gaimard. Voyage d'Astrolabe.
Mollusques 91 Planches.
Mammiferes 28 "
Oiseaux 29 "
Poissons 16 "
Zoophytes 19 "
Vers Apodals 1 "
Rees, Abraham. Cyclopaedia.
Reviews.
Say, Thos. American Entomology.
Scoresby, Wm. Whale Fishery.
Shaw, Geo. General Zoology.
Vols. I, II. Mammalia.
III. Amphibia.
IV, V. Pisces.
VI. Insecta.
VII–XIV. Aves.
Smellie, Wm. Philosophy of Natural Hist.
Smithsonian Contributions to Knowledge.
Swainson, Wm. Naturalists' Guide.
Swainson, Wm. Classification of Animals.
Swainson, Wm. Classification of Quadrupeds.
Swainson' Wm. The Study of Natural Hist. Taxidermy.
Temminck, C. J. Manuel d'Ornithologie.
Thompson, Z. History of Vermont. Part I. Quadrupeds, Birds, Reptiles, Fishes, and Mollusks.
Walton, I· Complete Angler.
Warren, J. C. Mastodon Giganteus.
Wilson, Alex. American Ornithology.

BOTANY.

Annales des Sciences Naturelles. Botanique.
Candolle, A. P. De Famille des Melastomaces.
Candolle, A. P. Prodromus Systematis Nat.
Candolle, A. P. Organographie Vegetale.
Candolle, A. P. Physiologie Vegetale.
Candolle & Sprengel. Physiology of Plants.
Descorides, P. De Materia Medica.
Du Hamel Du Monceau. Arbres et Arbustes.
Du Hamel Du Monceau. La Physique des Arbres.
Du Hamel Du Monceau. Des Semis et Plantations des Arbres.
Eaton, A. Manual of Botany.
Eaton, A. Botanical Dictionary.
Evelyn, John. Discourse on Forest Trees.
Forskael, P. Flora Aegyptiaco-Arabica.
Franklin, John. Journey and Voyage.
Hales, Stephen. Tables of Vegetables.
Johnson, Laura. Botanical Teacher.
Lindley, John. Natural System of Botany.
Link, H. F. Elem. Philosophica Botanicae.

Linnaeus, C. A. Philosophia Botanica.
Linnaeus, C. A. Systema Naturae.
Linnaeus, C. A. Tour in Lapland.
Linnaeus, C. A. Systema Vegetabilium.
Long, S. H. Narratives.
Loudon, J. C. Encyclopaedia of Gardening.
New York Natural History.
Botany, by J. Torrey.
Agriculture, by E. Emmons.
Nuttall, T. Travels in Arkansas.
Nuttall, T. Genera of N. American Plants.
Parry, Wm. E. Voyages.
Persoon, C. H. Synopsis Plantarum.
Pursh, F. Flora of North America.
Richard, A. Elemens de Botanique.
Smith, James. English Botany.
Smith, James. Introduction to Botany.
Smithsonian Contributions to Knowledge.
Sweet, R. Greenhouse Manual.
Thompson, Z. History of Vermont.
Torrey, J. Flora of the Northern and Middle States.
Voyages of the Disciples of Linnaeus, 11 vls.
Withering, Wm. British Plants.

NATURAL PHILOSOPHY & CHEMISTRY.

Adams. Astronomical Lectures, Essays, &c.
Airy. Tracts on Astronomy.
American Journal of Science.
Anderson. Motion of Solids.
Aristotle. Meteorologica.
Astronomie des Marins.
Atwood. Rectilinear Motion, &c.
Bacon. Opus Majus.
Bagay. Tables Ast., etc.
Bailly. Traité de l'Ast., etc.
Barlow. Strength of Timber. Math. Dict.
Barnwell. Physical Investigations.
Becke. Nat. Rerum Principia.
Becquerel. Physique, etc.
Bergman, T. Chemical Affinity.
Bernoulli. Hydrodynamica.
Bernoulli, Johann. Opera.
Berthollet, C. L. Essays on Chemical Studies.
Biot. Physique.
Blake. Natural Philosophy.
Bode. Uranographia.
Boscovich. Nat. Philosophy. Opera, etc.
Bossut. Hydrodynamique.
Bouvard. Tables Astronomiques.
Boyle. Works.
Brahe, Tycho. Astronomia.
Brande. Progress of Chemistry.
Brewster. Treatise on Instruments.
Burckhardt. Tables Astronomiques.
Cambridge Physics.
Carnot. Equilibre, etc.
Cavallo. Electricity.
Chladni. Accoustique.
Christian. Mecanique Indust.
Clairaut. Figure de la Terre.
Coddington. Optics.
Copernicus. Astronomia.
Cotes. Lectures on Hydrostatics.
Coulomb. Machines.
D'Alembert. Oeuvres, Dynamique.
Damoiseau. Tables de la Lune.
Daniell. Meteorological Essays.
Davy, Sir H. Chemical Philosophy.
De Lambre. Astronomie. Histoire de l'Ast.
De Luc. Météorologie, L'Atmosphère.
Des Cartes. Princip., Phil.
Digby. Bodies.
Dubuat. Hydraulique.
Dumas. Memoires de Chimie.
Eaton. Chemistry.
Edinburgh Encyclopaedia.
Elémens de Chymie.
Enfield. Natural Philosophy.
Epicurus. Physica.
Espy. Meteorology.
Euler. Mechanica, Diopt., etc.
Ewell. Chemistry.
Ewing. Astronomy.
Exley. Natural Philosophy.
Faraday. Chemistry and Electricity.
Ferguson's Astronomy.
Forster. Atmosphere.
Francoeur. Astronomy.
Fries. Natur-Philosophie.
Galileo. Opere.
Gassendus. Opera.
Gauss. Motus Corp. Celest. etc.
Gilbert. Magnet.
Gorham. Chemistry.
Graham. Magnetic Dip.
Gray. Chemistry.
Gregory. Mechanics.
Gwilt. Arches.
Halley. Astronomical Tables.
Henry. Chemistry.
Herschel. Natural Philosophy. Astronomy.
Hevelius. Selenographia.
Hugenius. Opera.
Jones, Sir W. Works. Vol. IV.
Kane. Chemistry.
Keill. Astronomy.
Kepler. Discoveries.
La Grange. Mécanique.
La Place. Système du Monde. Mec. Cel., etc.
Lavoisier. Chemistry.
Legendre. Balistique, etc.
Leslie. Heat, &c.
Libes. Histoire de la Physique.
Liebig. Organic Chemistry.
Löwig. Organic Chemistry.
Maire et Boscovich. Voyage Astronomique.
Malus. Optique.
Manilius. Astronomicon.
Mansfield. Essays.
Martin. Philosophy.
Maupertius. Figure of the Earth.
Mayer. Tabulae.
Meilleur. Chymie.
Newton. Principia.
Oersted. Forces Chem. et Elect.
Olmsted. Natural Philosophy.
Pascal. Oeuvres, Tom IV.
Pingre. Cometographie.
Poisson. Mécanique.
Priestly. Air.
Ptolemaeus. Epoques des Planetes, etc.
Puissant. D'Observations Ast. etc.
Redfield. Storms.
Regnault. Chemistry.
Renwick. Steam Engine.
Rohault. Natural Philosophy.
Rose. Chemistry.

Rowning. Natural Philosophy.
Scheiner. Oculus.
Singer. Electricity.
Smith. Optics.
Stahl, G. E. Opusculum Chem. &c.
Thenard. Traité de Chymie.
Tredgold. Steam Engine, &c.
Venturoli. Mechanics.
Vince. Astronomy.
Wallace. Globes, Astronomy.
Wallis. De Motu.
Wells. Vision, Dew.
Wendelinus. Contemplationes, etc.
Whewell. Mechanics.
Whiston. Astronomical Lectures.
Wilkins. Works.
Winthrop. Comets.
Wood. Mechanics.
Woodhouse. Astronomy.
Wright. Newton's Principia.
Young. Lectures.

ANATOMY AND PHYSIOLOGY.

Anatomy. Treatise on.
Anderson, W. Surgical Anatomy.
Aristoteles. Various Treatises.
Baillie, M. Morbid Anatomy.
Bell, C. Anat. and Phys. of Human Body.
Bichat, X. Life and Death. Membranes.
Blümenbach, J. F. Collectio Craniorum.
Candolle, De. Organographie, et Physiologie Végétale.
Cloquet, J. Anatomie de l'homme.
Combe, A. Physiology of Digestion.
Combe, G. Constitution of Man.
Curtis, J. H. Physiology of the Ear.
Cutter, C. Anatomy and Physiology.
Cuvier, Baron de. Ossemens Fossiles.
Darwin, E. Phytologia. Zoonomia.
Du Hamel. Physique des Arbres.
Haskins, R. W. Phrenology.
Hooper, R. Examinations in Anat. and Ph.
Hutin, P. Manual of Physiology.
Innes, J. Human Muscles.
Lawrence, W. Lectures on Physiology.
Lepelletier, A. Physiologie Medicale.
Magendie, F. Precis de Physiologie.
Meckel, J. F. Vergleichende Anatomie.
Monro, A. Nervous System.
Monro, A. System of Anatomy.
Oliver, B. First Lines of Physiology.
Paine, M. Physiological Commentaries.
Powers, G. Imagination on Nervous System.
Sageret. Pomologie Physiologique.
Saumarez, R. System of Physiology.
Saunders, J. C. Anatomy of the Ear.
Sewal, T. Examination of Phrenology.
Shaw, J. Manual of Anatomy.
Smith, J. Physiological Botany.
Smith, S. S. Variety of Complexion in Man.
Sömmering, S. T. Icones Embryonum.
Sprengel, K. Bau der Gewächse.
Spurzheim, J. G. Anatomy of the Brain.
Spurzheim, J. G. Phrenology.
Troxler, Dr. Organische Physik.
Warren, J. C. Mastodon Giganteus.
Wells, W. C. Single Vision with two Eyes.
Wyman, J. Anatomy of Rana Pipiens.

MEDICINE.

Andral, G. Clinique Médicale.
Andry, F. Diseases of the Heart.
Ayre, J. Treatment of Marasmus.
Baillie, E. M. Fièvres Intermittentes.
Bailly, F. P. Fièvre jaune en Espagne.
Barton, W. P. C. Vegetable Materia Medica.
Bateman, T. Cutaneous Diseases.
Bell, J. Nature and Cure of Wounds.
Blackall, J. On Dropsy.
Boyle, R. Essays on Medicine.
Brodie, D. C. Diseases of the Joints.
Broussais, F. J. V. Phys. applied to Path.
Broussais, F. J. V. Phlegmasies.
Bulwer & Forbes. On the Water Treatment.
Burnes, J. On Inflammation.
Cabanis, P. J. G. On Certainty of Medicine.
Celsus, A. C. De Medicina.
Charas, M. Pharmacopie.
Cheyne, G. Essay on Health and Long Life.
Cooper, Sir A. Modern Surgery.
Cooper, Sam. Practical Surgery.
Coxe, J. R. Philadelphia Medical Dict.
Cullen, W. Practice of Physic.
Cullen, W. Synopsis Nosologiae.
Dean, A. Medical Jurisprudence.
Denman, T. Midwifery.
Desault, X. Fractures and Diseases of Bones.
Dewees, W. Diseases of Females.
Dioscorides, P. De Materia Medica.
Dispensatory, Edinburgh. Eclectic.
Fordyce, G. On Fever.
Gallup, J. M. On Consumptions.
Gardiner, J. On Gout.
Gregory, G. Theory and Practice of Physic.
Hall, M. Principles of Diagnosis.
Hamilton, W. History of Medicine.
Hoosac & Francis. Am. Med. Register.
Jackson, R. Fevers of Jamaica.
Laennac, R. T. H. Diseases of the Chest.
Lind, J. Diseases in Hot Climates.
Magendie, F. Use of Prussic Acid.
Paine, M. Institutes of Medicine.
Paine, M. Cholera Asphyxia.
Paine, M. Materia Medica.
Parris, J. A. Pharmacologia.
Pemberton, C. R. Diseases of Viscera.
Prescriptions of Eminent Physicians.
Prout, W. On Diabetis Calculus.
Rush, B. Diseases of the Mind.
Sabatier, R. B. Médécine Operatoire.
Sweetser, W. On Consumption.
Sweetser, W. On Cynanche Trachealis.
Swieten, G. Commentaries on Boerhaave.
Thibert, F. Anatomie Pathologique.
Thomas, R. Practice of Physic.
Ticknor, T. Medical Philosophy.
Webster, N. History of Epidemics.

EDUCATION.

American Institute of Instruction.
American Journal of Education.
Ascham. The Schoolmaster.
Cousin. Public Instruction in Germany.
Fénelon. Sur l'E. des Filles.
Godwin. Essays on Education.
Green. Scholar's Companion.
Grimkè. Objects of Science and Literature.

Jardine. Philosophical Education.
La Croix. Essays on Instruction.
Locke. Thoughts concerning Education.
Manual for Schools.
Milton. Tractate on Education.
New York Institute for Deaf and Dumb.
New York Regents' Reports.
Parr. Lectures.
Phorboeus. New Method of teaching Greek.
Rousseau, J. J. Projet sur l'Education.
Schelling. Academical Studies.
Schwarz. System of Instruction.
Sicard. Instruction for Deaf-Mutes.
Simpson. Popular Education.
Valade. Guide de l'Instituteur.
Warner. Physical Education.

FINE ARTS AND THEORIES OF ART.

Alison, A. Taste.
Allston, W. Lectures on Art.
Aristotle. Poetics.
Barres, J. Works.
Bouterwek, F. Aesthetik.
Brown, J. W. Leonardo da Vinci.
Burke, E. Sublime and Beautiful.
Chambers, Sir W. Architecture.
Charactere der Vornehmsten Dichter.
Cockerell, C. R. Architecture.
Coleridge. Lectures on the Drama.
Corregio. Life of.
Cumberland, R. Spanish Painters.
Daub & Creuzer. Essays.
Da Vinci, Leonardo. Works.
Des Campes, J. B. Painting.
Dichiarazione dei Desegni. Architecture.
Du Bos. Poetry and Painting.
Duppa. Michael Angelo.
Eckhel. Ancient Gems.
Elgin, Lord. Athenian Art.
Elmes, J. Dictionary of Fine Arts.
Felibien. Painting.
Fiorillo, J. D. History of Painting.
Flaxman, J. Sculpture.
Fuseli, H. Painting.
Gilpin, W. Landscape.
Gravina. Poetry.
Herder. Hebrew Poetry.
Hirt, A. Ancient Architecture.
Hogarth, G. Music.
Hutcheson, F. On Beauty.
Knight, R. P. Taste.
Langlois, G. H. Painting on Glass.
Lanzi, L. Painting.
Leland, T. Eloquence.
Lessing. Poetry and Sculpture.
Longinus. On the Sublime.
Moller, G. German-Gothic Architecture.
Neralco. Architecture.
Northcote. Painting.
Ottley, W. T. History of Engraving.
Papillon. Engraving on Wood.
Price. U. On the Picturesque.
Quatremere de Quincy. Painting, Sculp., &c.
Rumohr, C. F. Italian Art.
Schlegel, A. Ancient Drama.
Schiller & Goethe. Letters on Poetic Art.
Thiersch. Ancient Art.
Walpole, H. Painting.
Webb, D. Painting.
Wheatley, T. Modern Gardening.
Winckelmann. Ancient Art.

USEFUL ARTS.

Agriculture. Reports, Tracts, Journals.
Barlow, Peter. Strength of Timber.
Berthollet. Art of Dyeing.
Boullenois. Silkworms.
Camus. Wheels, Pinions, &c.
Coleman. European Agriculture.
Exposition of French Industry.
Haigh. Dyer's Assistant.
Houel. On Horses.
Jackson, W. Book-keeping.
Journal of the Society of Arts.
Kirwan. Manures.
Knoop. Pomology.
Langlois. Painting on Glass.
Liebig. Org. Chem. applied to Agriculture.
Lindley, G. Orchard and Kitchen Garden.
Loudon. Laying out Farms.
Loudon. Encyclopaedia of Gardening.
Manual on the Cultivation of Sugar Cane.
Massachusetts. Statistics of Industry.
N. Y. Nat. Hist. Agriculture.
Observations on Agriculture.
Pamphlets. Horticultural.
Pamphlets. American Agriculturist.
Pamphlets. French Agriculture.
Pamphlets. British Farmer's Magazine.
Patent Office Reports. Arts & Manufactures.
Schlipf. Agriculture.
Sweet. Hothouse and Greenhouse Manual.
Tredgold. Strength of Metals.
Tredgold. Railroads.
Workman. Gauging.
Young, T. Mechanic Arts.

ENCYCLOPAEDIAS AND SCIENTIFIC JOURNALS.

American Academy. Memoirs.
American Antiquarian Society. Proceedings.
American Association. Proceedings.
American Journal of Science.
American Phil. Register.
American Quarterly Journal of Science and Agriculture.
Annales des Sciences Naturelles.
Annales d'Industrie Nationale et Etrangère.
Annals of the Lyceum of Nat. Hist. of N. Y.
Annuaires du Bureau de Longitude.
Chamber's Cyclopaedia.
Comptes Rendus.
Edinburgh Encyclopaedia.
Encyclopaedia of Religious Knowledge.
Encyclopaedia Metropolitana.
Gill's Miscellany.
Herbelot's Bibliothèque.
Horticulture, Annales.
Journals. See Journals.
Nautical Almanac.
Philadelphia Academy.
Philosophical Transactions.
Rees' Cyclopaedia.
Transactions, &c.

BELLES LETTRES.

RHETORIC AND ORATORY.

Adams. Lectures.
Ames. Speeches.
Apollonius, Alex. Structure of the Oration.
Aristarchus, or Principles of Composition.
Aristotle. Rhetoric.
Blair. Rhetoric and Belles Lettres.
Burke. Speeches.
Campbell, G. Philosophy of Rhetoric.
Cicero. Orations and Treatises on Oratory.
Demosthenes. Orations.
Dionysius Hal. Treatises on Oratory.
Eloquence of the United States.
Fenélon. Dialogues on Eloquence.
Grattan. Speeches.
Greek Orators.
Himerius. Orations.
Horn. German Eloquence.
Huskisson. Speeches.
Irving, E. Orations.
Isocrates. Orations.
Julianus. Orations.
Leland. Principles of Eloquence.
Lesbonax. Declamations.
Libanius. Orations and Declamations.
Loring. Orators of Boston.
Menander. On Encomiums.
Newman. Rhetoric.
Niles' Register.
Pascal. Thoughts on Belles Lettres.
Porter, N. On Eloquence and Style.
Polemon. Funeral Orations.
Quintilian. Institutes.
Rollin. Belles Lettres.
Speeches. Congressional.
Strong, C. Speeches.
Webster. Orations and Speeches.
Whately. Rhetoric.

POETRY.

ORIENTAL.

Carlyle's Arabian Poetry, Herder's Hebrew Poetry, Nala and Damayanti by Milman.

GREEK.

Aeschylus, Potter's Aeschylus, Analecta Vet. Poet., Anthologia Graeca, Anstice's Choric Poetry, Apollonius Rhodius, Ausonius, Aratus, Aristophanes, Bland's Collections from Greek Anthology, Elton's Specimens, Empedocles, Euripides, Gnomici Poetee Graeci, Hermelus (Modern), Homerus, Pope's and Sotheby's Homer, Chapman's Hymns of Homer, Lycophron, Nicander, Nonnus, Orphica, Pindarus, West's Pindar, Poesis Philosophica, Poetae Minores Graeci, Scolia, Sophocles, Theocritus.

LATIN.

Buchananus, Claudianus, Elton's Specimens, Ennius, Horatius, Juvenalis, Dryden's Juvenal, Lucanus, Rowe's Lucan, Longus, Ovidius, Perseus, Dryden's Perseus, Pervigilium Veneris, Poetae Minores, Priscianus, Carmina Quadrigesimalia, Ramsay's Tibullus and Ovid, Seneca, Silius Italicus, Statius, Terentius, Virgilius, Dryden's Virgil, Pitt's Aeneid, L'Enéide par Delille.

FRENCH.

Boileau, Chateaubriand, Corneille, Delille (trad. du Paradis Perdu), Fontenelle, Malherbe, Moliere, Picard, Racine, J. B. Rousseau, Rommant de la Rose.

ITALIAN.

Berni, Casti, Rowe's Translations from Berni and Casti, Bracchiolini, Chiabrera, Dante, Filicaia, Goldoni, Gozzi, Petrarca, Pellico, Pulci, Salvator Rosa, Tasso, Tassoni.

SPANISH.

De Vega, Rodd's Spanish Ballads.

GERMAN.

Arnim und Brentano, Claudius, Goethe, Klopstock, Lessing, Lays of the Minnesingers, Novalis, Schlegel.

NORTHERN.

Baggesen, Oehlenschlaeger, Paradisar Missir, Saga, &c., Tegner.

BRITISH.

Addison, Ancient Popular Poetry, Baillie, Barbauld, Beaumont & Fletcher, Bourne, British Poets, Burns, S. Butler, Byron, Campbell, Campbell's Specimens, J. Carlyle, Chalkhill, Chaucer, Clare, Cobden, Coleridge, Cowley, Dodsley's Collection, Dryden, Ellis' Specimens, Ford, Gibbons, Gifford, Graham, Hall, J. Home, Hunt, Jenner, Johnson, Jonson, Lodge, Lovelace, Lyttleton, Mackenzie, Marlowe and Chapman, Mason, Massinger, Milman, Milton, Ogilvie, Oldham, Old English Drama, Old Plays, Ossian, Otway, Percy's Reliques, Pinkerton Scottish Ballads, Pursuits of Litterature, Ralegh, Ritson's Caledonian Muse, Scott, Shakspeare, Shee, Sheridan, Shirley, Walpole, Wither, Young.

AMERICAN.

Aborigines of America, Allston, Barlow, Dana, Hillhouse, Lard, Moore.

FICTION AND ESSAYISTS.

Achilles Tatius. Clitophon and Leucippe.
Addison. Miscellaneous Essays.
Antar, a Bedoueen Romance.
Apuleius. Metamorphoses.
Bacon, Lord. Essays.
Barclaius. Argenis.
Boccaccio. Il Decamerone.
Bolingbroke. On Human Knowledge, &c.
British Essayists.
Carey. Miscellaneous Essays.
Cervantes. Don Quixote.
Channing. Miscellaneous.
Chateaubriand. Mélanges.
Coleridge, S. T. The Friend.

Dana, R. H. Tales.
De Foe. Novels.
Ellis. Specimens of Romances.
Fabliaux. Ancient Tales.
Fénelon. Telemachus, Dialogues of the Dead, and Essays.
Fielding. Novels.
Fontenelle. Dialogues of the Dead.
Gil Blas.
Godwin. Education, Manners, and Lit.
Goethe. Wilhelm Meister, &c.
Grimkè. On Science and Literature.
Hartshorne. Metrical Tales.
Johnson, Saml. Rasselas, and Misc. Essays.
Julianus. Caesares.
Lyttleton. Dialogues of the Dead.
Mackenzie. Novels.
Montaigne. Essais.
Moralistes Francois.
Nicole. Essays on Morals.
Novalis. Novels.
Rabelais. Gargantua.
Richter. Novels.
Romances, Popular.
Rousseau. Novels and Essays.
Stael, Mde. de. Novels and Essays.
Sterne. Tristram Shandy and Sent'l Journ.
Swift. Miscellaneous.
Thompson, D. P. Shaker Lovers.
Wieland. Abderites and other Tales.

CRITICISM.

Addison. Various.
Aristotle. Poetic (by Pye).
Blümner. Ueber Aeschylus.
Bowles. Genius and Writings of Pope.
Bryant. Poems of Rowley.
Campbell. English Poetry.
Casaubon. De Satira.
Chateaubriand. Mélanges.
Coleridge, S. T. Various.
Coleridge, H. N. Classic Poets.
Collier. English Poets.
Connybeare. Anglo-Saxon Poetry.
Creuzer. Historical Art of the Greeks.
Dawesius. Miscellania Critica.
Dryden. Various.
Du Bos. Sur la Poésie.
Dyce. Eds. of Shakspeare.
Faber. Thesaurus.
Franceson. Sur Homère.
Gravina. Ragion Poetica e Tragedia.
Haslewood. Essays on Poetry, &c.
Hazlitt. Comic Writers.
Heraclides. Allegoriae Homericae.
Herder. Hebrew Poetry.
Horn. Poesie der Deutschen.
Hurd. On Horace and various.
Jenisch. Master Pieces of Greek Poetry.
Johnson. Various.
Jones. Asiatic Poetry.
Lachmann. In Livium.
Lessing. Various.
Lowth. De Poesi Hebraeorum.
Miscellaneous Observations.
Machiavelli. In Livium.
Middleton. On Cicero.
Neale. English Poetry.
Schlegel. Various.
Schneider. Greek Drama.
Scott. Various.
Spence. Greek and Roman Classics.
Stael, Mde. de. Mélanges.
Walpole. Various.
Warton, Joseph. On Pope.
Warton, Thomas. On Spencer.
Wieland. Attic Museum.
Wood. On Homer.

LETTERS AND DIARIES.

John Adams, J. Q. Adams on Masonry, Alciphron, Apollonius Tyanensis, Aristenaetus, Ascham, Athenian Letters, Austin, Bacon, Bourdeille (See Brantome), Burton's Cromwellian Diary, Carter, Cartwright, Champollion, Chiabrera, Cicero, Clarendon, Coleridge, Coll. Epist. Graecarum, Collingwood, D'Alembert, Des Cartes, Dickinson, Doddridge. Elgin, Ellis, Emerson, Epist. Obscurorum Virorum, Evelyn, Fénelon, Fichte, Fitz-Osborne, Fontenelle, Franklin, Letters on Free Masonry, Funccius, Gassendus, Gellert, Goethe, Grimm et Diderot, Harleian Miscel., Hildebertus, John Home, Howard, Isocrates, Jefferson, Julianus, Keith, Keppler, Lessing, Lettres, &c., Libanius, Linnaeus, Locke, Lyttleton's Persian Letters, Marvell, Morris, Otway, Parr, Petrarcha, Pinkerton's Literary Correspondence, Rousseau, Schiller und Goethe, Thos. Scott, Sinclair, Spark's Diplomatic Correspondence, Mde. de Stael, Tasso, Temple, Thoresby, Vespucci, Waller and St. Evremond, Walpole, Washington, Mrs. Willard.

CONVERSATIONS, ANECDOTES, &c.

Athenaeus. Grecian Customs.
Bacon. Apothegms.
Coleridge, S. T. Table Talk & Conversations.
Collier. English Poetry.
Cumberland. Spanish Painters.
Dibdin. Reminiscences.
Fuller. Worthies of England.
Hesychius. Onomasticon.
Hollis Memoirs. Milton, Locke, Alg. Sidney, Marvell, Hutcheson, &c.
Johnson. Various.
Kelly. Theatres.
Luther. Table Talk.
Northcote. Conversations.
Spence. Conversations of Pope and others.
Valerius Max. Of Distinguished Men.
Walpole. Painters and Engravers.

PERIODICALS.

Adviser, Agriculturist, African Repository, American Almanac, American Annual Register, A. B. C. F. M. Annual Reports, American Journal of Education, American Jurist, American Quarterly Register, Athaeneum, Biblical Repository, Boston Recorder, Conn. Ev. Magazine, Crisis, Green Mountain Gem, Green Mountain Rep., Hunt's Merchants' Magazine, Literary World, Museum of Foreign Literature, National Preacher, N. Y. Spectator, Niles' Register, Northern Light, Panoplist, Periodicals unbound, see Pamph., Port-Folio, Quar. Chris. Spec., Lit. & Phil. Repertory, Reviews, Spy, Vermont Sent., Ward's Antimasonic Review.

HISTORY.

GEOGRAPHY AND TOPOGRAPHY.

Adams, Geo. Geographical Essays.
Atlas of Ancient and Modern History.
Atlas, A New and Universal.
Bouchette, J. Lower Canada.
Cramer, J. A. Ancient Greece.
D'Anville. Ancient Geography.
Dickinson, R. Elements of Geography.
Du Halde, J. B. China and Chinese Tartary.
Flint, T. Geography of Mississippi Valley.
Goldsmith, J. View of the World.
Gordon, P. Geographical Grammar.
Haskel, D. Gazetteer and Maps.
Heeren, A. H. L. Geography of Ptolemy.
Hennicke, J. F. Geography of Africa.
Herodotus. Geographical System.
Humboldt, A. Researches, Travels, &c.
Mannert, Konrad. Geographie.
Maps, Ancient and Modern.
Mayo, Robt. View of Ancient Geography.
Morse, J. American Geography.
Morse, J. Universal Geography.
Nicolle, Abbè. Geographie Moderne.
Parish, E. Sacred Georgraphy.
Pausanias. Graecae Descriptio.
Payne, John. Universal Geography.
Rennel, J. Expedition of Cyrus.
Rennel, J. Geography of Herodotus.
Rennel, J. Comparative Geography.
Stanhope, J. S. Topography of Olympia.
Strabo. Geography.
Thompson, Z. Gazetteer of Vermont.
Ukert, Fr. Aug. Geographie.
Valentia, Geo. Vis. Voyages and Travels.
Webster, J. W. Island of St. Michael.
Wilson, H. Pelew Islands.
Worcester, J. E. Gazetteer of U. S.

VOYAGES AND TRAVELS.

Anson. Round the World.
Barrow. China. South Africa.
Barthelemy. Grèce.
Bartram. North and South Carolina.
Batuta. Travels.
Baudin. Voyages aux Terr. Aust.
Beaumont. The Alps.
Beechy. North Africa. North Pacific.
Bell. Russia and Asia.
Belzoni. Egypt.
Benyousky. Travels.
Blainville. Europe.
Blume. Iter Italicum.
Bougainville. Round the World.
Bruce. Up the Nile.
Buck. Norwegen und Lapland.
Burckhardt. Nubia, Arabia, Palestine.
Burnes. Bokharia, Indus.
Cadell. Italy and France.
Caillie. Central Africa.
Carver. North America.
Cella. North Africa.
Champlain. Voyages to America.
Champollion. Lettres d'Egypte, etc.
Chandler. Asia Minor. Greece.
Chardin. Perse.
Chastellux. North America.
Clark. Europe, Asia, and Africa.
Cochrane. Russia and Tartary.
Columbus. Narrative of first Voyage.
Cooke, Capt. Voyages.
D'Arvieux. Memoires.
De Guignes. Voyage à Peking, etc.
De Kay. Turkey.
Delano. Voyages.
Denham and Clapperton. Africa.
Denon. Egypte.
Des Campes. Voyage Pittoresque, etc.
Dibdin. France and Germany.
Dodwell. Greece.
Drake. Collections.
Ducas. Travels.
Dupin.
Dwight. New England and New York.
Edmonstone. Upper Egypt.
Emerson. Letters from the Aegean.
Flinders. Terra Aust.
Forsyth. Remarks on Italy.
Franklin. Polar Sea.
Fraser. Himmelayas.
Gell. Itinerary of Greece.
Hakluyt. English Voyages.
Harmon. North America.
Harris. Travels, &c.
Harris, T. M. North West Territory.
Head. South America.
Hearne. Northern Ocean.
Heber. Upper India.
Hoare. Greece.
Hughes. Greece and Albania.
Humboldt. America.
Islande. Voyage en, etc.
Italy, By an American.
Jewett. Foreign Travel.
Kelsall. Italy.
Kendall. Northern States.
Keppel. India to England.
Keysler. Germany, Italy, etc.
Kotzebue. South Seas. Bherings Straits.
Krusenstern. Round the World.
Lamartine. Voyage en Orient.
Las Cases. First Spanish Voyages.
Lawson. Voyage to Carolina.
Lake. Asia Minor.
Lerminier. Audela du Rhin.
Linnaeus. Tour in Lapland.
Long. Rocky Mountains.
Lyon. North Africa.
MacKenney. Tour to the Lakes.
KacKenzie. Northern Ocean.
Maundrell. Aleppo to Jerusalem.
Niebuhr. Arabie.
Nuttall. Arkansas Territory.

Pallas. Russian Empire.
Park. Interior Africa.
Parry. Polar Sea.
Perron. Terres Aust.
Perry. The Levant.
Porter. Persia, Armenia, &c.
Purchas. His Pilgrimes.
Russel. Germany.
Salt. Abyssinia.
Saussure. Les Alps.
Saxe-Weimar. North America.
Schoolcraft. In the North-west.
Scoresby. North Whale Fishery.
Shaler. Algiers.
Shaw. Barbary and the Levant.
Smith and Dwight. Armenia.
Sonnini. Egypte, Grèce, etc.
Spon et Wheler. Italie, Grèce, etc.
Swinborne. Sicily.
Three years in the Pacific.
Tournefort. The Levant.
Trollope, Mrs. Germany.
Tuckey. Congo River.
Valentia. India, Abyssinia, etc.
Vincent. Voyage of Nearchus.
Voyage en Suisse.
Voyages of the Disciples of Linnaeus.
Warville. United States of America.
Willard, Mrs. England and France.
Wilson. Pelew Islands.
Wilson. Missionary Voyage.
Wittman. Turkey and Asia Minor.

CHRONOLOGY AND STATISTICS.

Census of U. S. A., 5th, 1830.
Census of U. S. A. Statistical View.
Census of U. S. A., 6th, 1840.
Census Compendium and Statistics.
Census of Pensions.
Congressional Documents.
Du Fresnoy, Abbe L. Chronological Tables.
Hales, S. Statistical Tables of Vegetables.
Hegewisch, D. H. Einleitung.
Mezeray, Sieur de. Kings of France.
Ouseley, W. G. Statistics of U. S. A.

ANTIQUITIES.

Adam, A. Roman.
Adam, R. Ruins at Spalatro.
Addison, J. Coins.
Antiquitates Americanae.
Archaeologia Americana.
Astle, Thomas. Origin of Writing.
Athenaeus. Various.
Athenian Letters. Greek.
Barbault, A. L. Roman Remains.
Barthelemy, J. J. Greek.
Bellorius. J. P. Ancient Rome.
Bingham, J. Ecclesiastical.
Böckh, A. Athens.
Böttiger, C. A. Roman Manners.
Brand, J. Popular English.
Calmet. Biblical.
Cambden, W. British.
Caussinus. Egyptian.
Caylus, Comte de. Greek and Roman.
Champollion. Egyptian.
Charnock, J. Marine Architecture.
Coleman, L. Ecclesiastical.
Commerce, History of, by Anderson.
Creuzer, F. Rites of Bacchus.
Dale, A. von. Oracles.
Davies, E. Celtic.
Denon, V. Egyptian.
Dibdin, T. F. Miscellaneous.
Drummond. Herculanensian.
Ellesmere. Northern.
Fontenelle. Oracles.
Forsyth, J. Divers Roman.
Gell, W. Pompeian.
Gellius, A. Latin.
Goguet. Laws, Arts and Sciences.
Greece. Antiquities of.
Guerard, A. Roman Private Law.
Heyne, C. G. Miscellaneous.
Hezel, W. F. Greek Language.
Herbelot, M. Oriental.
Jablonskius. Egyptian.
Jahn, J. Biblical.
Jamieson & Weber. Teutonic & Scandinav.
Jones, Sir W. Oriental.
Josephus, F. Jewish.
Kanngiesser, P. F. Comic Stage of Athens.
Klaproth. Hieroglyphic.
Link, H. F. Antiquity illustrated by Nat. History.
Maffei, S. Verona illustrated.
Mallet, P. H. Northern.
Massey, W. Letters.
Mazois. Roman Manners.
Meierotto, J. H. L. Roman Manners.
Monboddo, Lord. Language.
Montfauçon. Antiquity explained by figures.
Montfauçon. Palaeography.
Müller, K. O. Archaeology and Art.
Münter. Antiquarian Essays.
Musée Royale. Antiquities of the Louvre.
Nardini. Roman.
Pinkerton, J. Gothic.
Plinius, C. Greek and Roman.
Porny, M. A. Heraldry.
Rose, H. J. Greek Inscriptions.
Sachse, C. Ancient Rome.
Smithsonian Contributions. American.
Spanhemius. Numismatic.
Strutt. English Sports.
Stuart and Revett. Athenian.
Theatre of the Greeks.
Theodorus Metochita. Cyrene and Corinth.
West, G. Olympic Games.
Wolf and Buttmann. Various.
Young, T. Egyptian.

MYTHOLOGY.

Bryant, J. Ancient Mythology.
Creuzer, J. Symbolic Mythology.
Blümner. Idea of Fate in Greek Tragedy.
Gale, T. Court of the Gentiles.
Hindoostan, History of. Oriental.
Mallet. Northern.
Memoires de l'Academie des Inscriptions.
Millin, A. L. Gallery of Mythology.
Montfauçon. Antiquité Expliquée.
Schelling, F. W. J. Gottheiten von Samo Thrace.
Spangenberg. Latin Domestic Religions.

ANCIENT.

GREECE.

Athenaeus. Customs.
Athenian Letters.
Conon. Mythical Period.
Cramer. Descriptive.
Curtius. Alexander.
Dictys et Dares. Trojan War.
Gillies. General.
Grote. General.
Guischard. Military Memoirs.
Herodotus. Early.
Hezel. Mythology and Philology.
Hist. Gr. Fragmenta.
Iscanus. Trojan War.
Justinus. Macedonian.
Leland. Philip of Macedon.
Memnon. Heraclea.
Mitford. General.
Müller. Dorian, Macedonian.
Pauw. Philosophical Researches.
Siebelis. Early.
Thucydides. Peloponnesian War.
Xenophon. Expedition of Cyrus.
Young. Athens.

ROME.

Appianus. General.
Beaufort. Republic.
Böttiger. Customs.
Bridges. Empire under Constantine.
Brosse. Republic.
Caesar. Gallic War.
Dio Cassius. General.
Dionysius Halicarnassus. Early.
Ennius. Republic.
Eutropius. Epitome.
Florus. Epitome.
Gibbon. Decline and Fall of Roman Empire.
Guischard. Military Memoirs.
Herodianus. Later Roman Empire.
Historiae Augustae Scriptores.
Livius. General.
Meierotto. Customs.
Suetonius. The Caesars.
Tacitus. The Empire.
Vaudoncourt. Campaigns of Hannibal.
Velleius. General.

OTHER ANCIENT HISTORY.

Arrianus. India.
Chamich. Armenia.
Darius et Hidarne. Persia.
Davies. Celtic Researches, Druids.
Gutzlaff. China.
Josephus. Jews.
Moses Choronensis. Armenia.
Pelloutier. Celts.
Pinkerton. Goths.
Powell. Wales.
Rennel. Expedition of Cyrus.
Rhodes. The Zends.
Schlosser. Universal.

MIDDLE AGES.

Byzantine Historians. Eastern Empire.
De Guignes. Huns, Turks, and Mogols.
Gibbon. Decline and Fall of Roman Empire.
Hallam. Middle Ages.
Marigny. Arabians.
Mills. Chivalry and Crusades.
Ockley. Saracens.
Sismondi. Italian Republics.
Turner. England.
Villemain. Greece.
Wheaton. Northmen.
Wilcke. Knights Templar.
Wilken. Crusades.

MODERN.

ASIA AND AFRICA.

Asiatic Dissertations.
Cantemir. Ottoman Empire.
Chamich. Armenia.
Dow. Hindostan.
Grant. East India Company.
Gutzlaff. China.
Hamilton. Nepal.
Jones, Sir W. Persia.
Kaempfer. Japan.
Malcolm. Persia.
Marsden. Sumatra.
Mills. British India.
Orme. Indostan and Mogul Empire.
Raffles. Java.
Robertson. India.
Rycaut. Turks.
Shaler. Algiers.
Shaw. Barbary.
Smith and Dwight. Armenia.

EUROPE.

England.

Bacon. Henry VII.
Baker. Chronicle of Kings.
Bigland. General.
Bolingbroke. Remarks.
Burke. Early.
Burnet. The Revolution.
Cambden. Brittannia.
Chateaubriand. The Four Stuarts.
Clarendon. The Rebellion.
Dalrymple. Memoirs. (17th Century.)
Ellis. Letters. Miscellaneous.
Harleian Miscellany. Various.
Henry. Great Britain.
Home. The Rebellion.
Hume. General.
Hurd. Age of Elizabeth.
Langtoft. Chronicle.
Lodge. Illustrations.
Lyttleton. Henry II.
Macaulay. From James II.
Marsolier. Henry VII.
Mackintosh. The Revolution.
Milton. Early.
Paris. William I to Henry III.
Parr. James II.
Plowden. British Empire.
Rapin de Thoyras. Early.
Robert of Gloucester. Chronicle.
Smollett. Continuation of Hume.
Strutt. Sports and Pastimes.
Thierry. Norman Conquest.
Turner. Anglo-Saxons.
Waldegrave. Memoirs, 1754–1758.

France.

Barruel. Jacobinism.
Bignon. From 1799 to 1807.
Brantome. Illustrious Men.
Capefigue. Philip Augustus.
Chateaubriand. Summary.
Comines. From 1464 to 1498.
De Genlis. Eighteenth Century.
Jomini. Wars of the Revolution.
Lamballe. Revolution.
Mezeray. French Kings.
Mignet. Revolution.
St. Simon. Louis XIV.
Sismondi. General to 1598.
Stael, Madame de. Revolution.
Sully. Memoirs. Henry the Great.
Thiers. Revolution.

Other European History.

Alison. Europe.
Botta. Italy.
Bower. Popes.
Buchanan. Scotland.
Butler, C. German Empire.
Campbell. Balearic Islands.
Coote. Modern Europe.
Coxe, W. Austria and Spain.
Daru. Venice.
De Kay. Turkey.
Greece. Modern History.
Grellman. Gypsies.
Guicciardini. History and Wars of Italy.
Irish Rebellion.
Jameson, Mrs. Modern Rome.
Jesuits. General History.
Jones, Wm. Waldenses.
Laing. Scotland.
Llorente. Inquisition.
Machiavelli. Florentine Republic.
Miller, J. P. Greece.
Müller, J. Switzerland.
Muratori. Italy.
Napier. Peninsular War.
Pinkerton. Scotland.
Prescott. Spain.
Robertson. Scotland, Charles V.
Ricaut. Turks.
Southey. Peninsular War.
Trollope, Mrs. Belgium and Germany.
Zschokke. Switzerland.

AMERICA.

Allen, I. Vermont.
American Archives.
Baldwin. Yale College.
Baillie. Plymouth.
Bancroft. United States.
Belknap. New Hampshire.
Bentote. America, (in Modern Greek.)
Berkshire County.
Beverly.
Botta. War of Indedendence.
Braford. Massachusetts.
Clavigero. Mexico.
Crantz. Greenland.
Davis. New England.
Diaz. Conquest of Mexico.
Dobrizhoffer. Abipones.
Dunn. Guatimala.
Edwards, B. West Indies.
Egede. Greenland.
Flint. Mississippi Valley.
Foot. North Carolina.
Francis, Dr. Paraguay.
Gage. Rowley.
Georgia Historical Collections.
Greenhow. Oregon and California.
Hinman. Connecticut.
Holmes. Annals, 1692 to 1826.
Hoskins. Vermont.
Hubbard. New England.
Hutchinson. Massachusetts.
Kendall. Mexican War.
La Croix. St. Domingo.
Lee. Campaign and Memoirs.
Marshall, H. Kentucky.
Martin. British Colonies.
Minot. Massachusetts; Shay's Rebellion.
Maranda. South America.
Morse and Parish. New England.
Molina. Chili.
Neal. New England.
New Ipswich.
New York.
New York Hist. Society. Collections.
O'Callaghan, E. B. Documentary of N. Y.
Peirce. Harvard University.
Powers. Coos County.
Proud. Pennsylvania.
Quincy. Harvard University.
Ramsay. American Revolution.
Robinson. Mexican Revolution.
Solis. Conquest of Mexico.
Sullivan. Maine.
Thatcher. Revolutionary War.
Thompson, Z. Vermont.
Whitney. Worcester County.
Williamson. Maine.
Williams, S. Vermont.
Winthrop, J. New England.
Worcester. Gazetteer of the United States.

UNIVERSAL.

Aelianus. Ancient.
Anderson. Commerce.
Bolingbroke. Uses of History.
Chateaubriand. Historical Studies.
Diodorus. Ancient.
Du Fresnoy. Chronological Tables.
Heeren. Politics of Europe.
Hegel. Philosophy of History.
Herder. Philosophy of Man.
Hesychius. Chronicon.
Historical Collections.
History, Universal.
Hurd. Chivalry.
Miller. Retrospect of the 18th Century.
Millot. Elements of General History.
Priestley. Lectures on History.
Purchas. Pilgrimes.
Ralegh. History of the World.
Schlosser. Historical Survey.

ECCLESIASTICAL HISTORY.

American Board C. F. M. Reports.
Austin, T. View of the Church.
Backus. Church of New England.
Baxter, R. Life and Times.

Beverly. Ecclesiastical History of.
Bogue and Bennet. Dissenters.
Boston Recorder.
Bowden. Episcopacy.
Bingham, J. Antiquities.
Buchanan. Christian Researches.
Bull, G. Primitive Christianity.
Burnet, G. Reformation of the Ch. of Eng.
Clarkson. Quakerism.
Coleman. Antiquities.
Conder. Protestant Nonconformity.
Connecticut. Civil and Eccl. History of.
Constance. Council of.
Constitution of the Ref. Dutch Church.
Davis, J. New England's Memorial.
D'Aubignè. Reformation.
Eusebius. Church History.
Fagnani. Comm. on 2d Book of Decretals.
Fox, John. Book of Martyrs.
Fuller, T. Church Hist. of Great Britain.
Gibson, Ed. Eng. Ecclesiastical Law.
Greenland. Mission of the Un. Brethren.
Gregoire, H. Religious Sects.
Haweis. Church History.
Hawks. Eccl. History of the U. S.
Histoire Generale de la Compagnie de Jesus.
Hooker, R. Eccl. Polity.
Jahn. Hebrew Commonwealth.
Jahn. Biblical Archaeology.
Jones, W. The Waldenses.
Jortin. Ecclesiastical History.
Josephus. History of the Jews.
Knox. Reformation in Scotland.
Linn, Dr. Episcopacy.
Llorente. The Inquisition.
Mather, C. Magnalia Christi Americana.
Neal. Eccl. Hist. of New England.
Neander. Church Hist., transl. by Rose, and Torrey.
Missionary Herald.
Nicephorus Callistus. Eccl. History.
Panoplist. From 1807 to 1819.
Pinkerton. On the Greek Church.
Prideaux. Connection of Old and New Test.
Priestley. Corruptions of Christianity.
Probleme Historique. Jesuits and Luther.
Roscoe. Pontificate of Leo x.
Semple. Baptists in Virginia.
Shuckford, Saml. Sacred and Profane Hist. connected.
Smith and Dwight. Armenian Researches.
Strype, John. Reformation in the time of Elizabeth.
Tittman. Symbolical Books.
Trent. Historia del Concilio.
Waddington. History of the Church.
Wesley, John. Rise of Methodism.
White, W. Episcopal Church in the U. S.
Wiggins, G. T. Augustinianism and Pelagianism.

LITERARY HISTORY AND BIBLIOGRAPHY.

Asiatic Dissertations.
Astle. Origin of Writing and Printing.
Bayle. Dictionaire Historique et Critique.
Bentley. On the Epistles of Phalaris.
Berington. Lit. Hist. of the Middle Ages.
Bibliotheca Americana.
Bibliothèque Italique.
Bibliothèque Universelle.
Blackwall. Life and Writings of Homer.
Boyle. On the Epistles of Phalaris.
Brunck. Bibliographical Researches.
Bryant. Poems of Rowley.
Campbell. On Eng. Language and Poetry.
Catalogues.
Charactere der Dichter, &c.
Conybeare. Anglo-Saxon Poetry.
Diodorus Sic. Bibliotheca.
Dunlop. Roman Literature.
Eichhorn. Lit. of Modern Europe.
Ellis. Early Eng. Romances and Poetry.
Flögel. Roman Literature.
Greswell. Parisian Typography.
Harles. Litteratura Romana.
Harleian Miscellany.
Heine. Romantic School.
Heraclitus. De Incredibilibus Libellis.
Heeren. Greek and Roman Literature.
Hug. Invention of Writing.
Jones. Asiatic Poetry.
Klaproth. Hieroglyphics.
Köster. De Cantilenis Graecorum.
La Harpe. Ancient and Modern Lit.
Mémoires de Littérature.
Mohnike. Greek and Roman Literature.
Müller, C. G. Cyclic Poets.
Rosetti. Literature prior to the Ref.
Saxius. Onomasticon Literarium.
Schlegel. Various.
Sismondi. La Lit. du Midi de l'Europe.
Taylor. German Poetry.
Theatre of the Greeks.
Thomas. Hist. of Printing.
Tiraboschi. Letteratura Italiana.
Troubadours. Histoire des.
Walpole. Royal and Noble Authors.
Wotton. Ancient and Mod. Learning.

BIOGRAPHY.

Abeillard and Heloisa, by Berington.
Abercrombie, by Mackenzie.
Les Académiciens de l'Académie Royale des Sciences, par Fontenelle.
J. Adams, by C. F. Adams.
Alexander Magnus, a Curtio.
Ethan Allen's Captivity, by himself.
American Missionaries, Lives.
Apollonii Tyan. Vita, a Philostrato.
Architectes, par Q. De Quincy.
Ascham, by Dr. Johnson.
Ashmun, by Gurley.
Baber, by himself.
J. Bacon, by Cecil.
Barclay, Life.
Behmen, by Okely.
Bentley, by Monk.
Benyousky, Memoirs.
Duc de Berry, par Chateaubriand.
Biographia Britannica.
American Biographical Dictionary.
Blacklock, by Mackenzie.
Blair, by Hill.
Blake, by Johnson.
Boerhaave, by Johnson.
Bolingbroke, Life.
Bossuet, by C. Butler.

Sir T. Browne, by Johnson.
Bp. Burnet, by Thos. Burnet.
Burns, by Cunningham.
Alban Butler, by C. Butler.
S. Butler, by Johnson.
Byron, by Lake, and Scott.
Cadogan, by Cecil.
Caesarum Vitae, a Suetonio.
D. Campbell, Life.
Canning, by Stapleton.
Canova, par Q. De Quincy.
Cartwright, by his Niece.
Casiodore, la Vie.
Cecil, by Pratt.
Cellini, Vita da Carpani, and Memoirs by himself.
Chatterton, by Gregory.
Chaucer, by Godwin.
D. Chipman, by N. Chipman.
Cibber, by himself.
Cicero, by Lyttleton.
E. D. Clark, by Otter.
J. Clark, by Jay.
Coleridge's Biog. Lit.
Columbus, Memorials and Personal Narr.
Comines, par Godefroy.
Capt. Cook, by Kippis.
Corneille, par Fontenelle.
Cornelius, by Edwards.
Corregio, Memorie.
Cromwell, by T. Cromwell.
Cumberland, by himself, and by Scott.
D'Arvieux, Memoires.
Da Vinci, by Brown.
De Foe, by Wilson and Scott.
De Montgon, Memoires.
Demosthenis Vita, a Libanio.
De Rance, by C. Butler.
De Retz, Memoires.
Des Cartes, Eloge par Thomas.
De Vega, by Holland.
Dibdin, Biographical Tour.
Doddridge, by Orton.
Drake, by Johnson.
Dryden, by Malone, Johnson, Scott.
J. Edwards, Life.
Egede, Life.
Erasmus, by Jortin.
Prince Eugene, by Dumont.
Evelyn, Memoirs.
Fenélon, by C. Butler and Lady Guion.
Fichte, Leben.
Fielding, by Scott.
Fletcher of Saltoun, by D. Stuart.
Frisbie, by Norton.
Franklin, by Sparks.
Fuseli, by Knowles.
Gardiner, by Doddridge.
Geddes, by Good.
Goethe, by himself.
Graham, by Allen.
Greene, by Caldwell.
Guilford, by R. North.
Lady Guion, Life.
G. Hall, by Bardwell.
J. Hall, by W. Jones.
Hampden, by Nugent.
Heber, by his Widow.
Patrick Henry, by Wirt.
Henry VII, par Marsolier.
Hervey, by Ryland.
Hobart, by McVicar and Berrien.
Hollis, Memoirs.
John Home, by Mackenzie.
Homer, by Blackwall.
Hommes illustres, par Brantome et D'Auvigny.
Howard, from his own Diary.
Hull, by his Daughter.
Hutton, by Playfair.
Imperatorum Vitae, a Cornelio Nepote.
Indian Biography, by Thatcher.
Italian Poets, by Stebbings.
John Jay, by his Son.
Jefferson, by Randolph.
Jeffreys, by Woolrych.
Johnson, by Boswell, Black, and Scott.
Joli, Memoires.
Sir W. Jones, by Teignmouth.
Kemble, by Boaden.
Thomas a Kempis, by C. Butler.
Knox, by McCrie.
Lardner, by Kippis.
Las Casas, par Llorente.
Ledyard, by Sparks.
C. Lee, Memoirs.
R. H. Lee, by his Grandson.
Leighton, by Pearson.
Leo X, by Roscoe.
Lessing, von Schink.
L' Hopital, by C. Butler.
Locke, by King.
Lorenzo de Medici, by Roscoe.
Mansfield, by C. Butler.
Marlborough, by Dumont.
Marsh, by Torrey.
Matthison, Leben.
Melville, by McCrie.
Michael Angelo, by Duppa.
Milton, by Todd, Symmons, Toland, Johnson, and Hollis.
Mirabeau, by Dumont.
Molino, by Lady Guion.
More, by Dibdin.
Morris, by Sparks.
Nadir Shah, by W. Jones.
Napoleon, by Scott and Las Cases.
Neff, by Gilly.
Duchesse de Nemours, Memoires.
Isaac Newton, by Playfair.
John Newton, by Cecil.
Thomas Newton, by himself.
Osborne, by Hopkins.
R. T. Paine, by his Parents.
Thomas Paine, by Cheetham.
Parr, by Johnstone.
S. Pearce, by Fuller.
Z. Pearce, by himself.
Peintres, par Des Campes et Felibien.
Penn, by Clarkson.
Pepys' Memoirs.
Petrarque, par De Sade.
Philip of Macedon, by Leland.
Philippe Auguste, par Capefigue.
Philosophes Anciens, par Fénelon.
Philosophorum Vitae, a Diog. Laertio.
Pinkney, by Wheaton.
Plato, von Ast.

Playfair, Life.
Pococke, by Twells.
Poets, by Johnson.
Pole, by Philips.
Pythagoras, a Jamblicho.
Ralegh, by Oldys and Birch.
E. Reynolds, by Chalmers.
F. Reynolds, by himself.
J. Reynolds, by Malone and Farrington.
Richardson, by Scott.
Robertson, by Stuart.
Rodger, by Miller.
Lord W. Russell, by Lord J. Russell.
Mde. Roland, par Borville et Berrien.
Rousseau, Confessions.
Saladin, ab Abulfeda.
Salvator Rosa, by Lady Morgan.
Sanctorum Vitae, a Hildeberto.
Sarpi, by Johnson.
Scipio di Ricci, by Roscoe.
Count Segur, by himself.
Sir P. Sidney, by Zouch.
Smollett, by Scott.
Sophocles, von Lessing.
Sophistae, a Philostrato.
Spanish Kings, by Coxe.
Sterne, by himself, and by Scott.
Stiles, by Holmes.
Swift, by Scott and Hawkesworth.
Sykes, by Disney.
Jeremy Taylor, Life.
John Taylor, by himself.
Temple, by Courtenay.
Thompson, by D. Stuart.
Thuanus, by Collinson.
Tytler, by Mackenzie.
Vespucci, Vita.
Waldegrave, Memoirs.
Walton, by Todd.
Warburton, by Hurd.
Washington, by Glass, Marshall, Ramsay, Sparks.
Watson, by himself.
Watts, by Burder and Johnson.
Webster, by Everett.
Wesley, by Southey.
Wheelock, by McClure.
Whitgift, by Strype.
Wickliffe, by Vaughan.
Williams, by Knowles.
Wood's Athenae Oxoniensis.
Woolsey, by Cavendish.
Worthies of England, by Fuller.
Ximenes, by Barrett.
Zwingle, by Hess.

ERRATA.

Page 6. For APPOLLODORUS, read APOLLODORUS.
" 14, line 1. For BRITTANICA, read BRITANNICA.
" 15, line 11 from bottom. For *at* read *ad.*
" 21, " 4 " After *Disquisitions*, read 3 *vols.*
" 23, " 6 " After *Testamentum*, read 7 *vols.*
" 23, " 2 " For *Cambden*, read *Camden*; also, for *Brittania*, read *Britannia.*
" 27, " 3 " For *Hyeroglyphique*, read *Hieroglyphique.*
" 28. Remove the Asterisk from CHARNOCKE, to CHARNOCK.
" 31, line 14. For *Stewart*, read *Stuart.*
" 33, line 9 from bottom. For 2 *vols.*, read 2 *copies.*
" 37, " 4. For COURS DE REDACTION, read COUSIN, VICTOR.
" 47, " 18. (In a few copies,) For AMARICA, read AMERICA.
" 47, " 20. For *Animalium*, read *Annalium.*
" 53, " 10, from bottom For AULIUS, read AULUS.
" 58, " 16. For GUILFORD, BARON; Francis North, read GUILFORD, BARON (Francis North).
" 60 " 17. For *B. Pierce*, read *B. Peirce.*
" 63. For HILDEBURTUS, read HILDEBERTUS.
" 74. For LAING, MALCOM, read LAING, MALCOLM.
" 80. For MALCOM, read MALCOLM.
" 81. For MARIGUY, read MARIGNY.
" 82. For MARVEL, read MARVELL.
" 83. For MATTAIRE, read MAITTAIRE.
" 86. For MORALISTS, read MORALISTES.
" 90, line 21. For *Hill*, read *Hall.*
" 92, line 4 from bottom. After *Adriatica*, dele *ossia.*
" 93, line 5. For *Halientica*, read *Halieutica.*
" 94, line 18 from bottom. For *Cheatham*, read *Cheetham.*
" 100, " 15. For *Moralists*, read *Moralistes.*
" 101. For PERSEUS, read PERSIUS.
" 101, line 17 from bottom. For *de Sade*, read *De Sade.*
" 107. For RALEIGH, read RALEGH.
" 109, For RICARDI, read RICARDO.
" 112, line 14. For *Principle*, read *Principal.*
" 112, line 17 from bottom. For *Operative*, read *Operatoire.*
" 114, " 8 " For *Religion-Reden*, read *Religion. Reden, &c.*
" 119. For SMITH, ELY, read SMITH, ELI ;.
" 122. For STANDLIN, read STAUDLIN.
" 127, last line. For 1822, read 1832.
" 128, line 17. For *Peloponesiaco*, read *Peloponnesiaco.*
" 130, line 6. After *Saxons*, read 3 *vols.*
" 150, line 7. For *Boucharlet*, read *Boucharlat.*
" 157, line 7 from bottom. For *Buck*, read *Buch.*
" 157, " 5 " For *Kac Kenzie*, read *Mac Kenzie.*

www.ingramcontent.com/pod-product-compliance
Lightning Source LLC
LaVergne TN
LVHW021357110826
845150LV00007B/1689

* 9 7 8 1 4 2 5 5 1 2 9 2 7 *